AB 04835 25,-

CHRONICLES OF MILTON
VILLAGE LEFT BEHIND BY TIME

MILTON WOMAN'S CLUB

Printed by
Rainbow Press
Torrington, Connecticut 06790

Available from
Milton Woman's Club
P.O. Box 473, Litchfield, Connecticut 06759

ISBN 0-9657126-0-5

Library of Congress Catalog Card Number: 97-70832

Published by Milton Woman's Club

Copyright ©1997 by Milton Woman's Club

All rights in this book are reserved. No part of *Chronicles of Milton* may be reproduced in any form without written permission from Milton Woman's Club, Litchfield, Connecticut 06759, U.S.A.

DEDICATION

With much love, this history of Milton is dedicated to Ellen Margaret Doyle, who originated the idea for the *Chronicles of Milton* and over many years gathered material through extensive research. This book is the realization of her dream.

Ellen M. Doyle
(Miss Nellie Doyle)
1883 - 1974

LIST OF ILLUSTRATIONS

Jacket - Old Scene of Milton Center
Inside Front Cover - Recent Picture of Milton Center
Inside Back Cover - Old Map of Milton Center
Frontispiece - Ellen M. Doyle

Milton Center, Congregational Church	1
Milton Pond	4
Barnraising at Doyles', West Goshen Road, July 1896	7
Boundaries of Blue Swamp, Milton Society, 1795	11
Ice cutting on Milton (Mill) Pond, 1930's	13
Milton Ladies Aid Society, Summer 1940	16
View of Milton Center from Milton Hill	20
Anson Dickinson	29
Amy Duggan Archer Gilligan	40
Rev. Irving J. Enslin, pastor of Milton Congregational Church, ca. 1959	42
Beatrice M. McKechnie & John O'Neill	56
Thomas Hinchliffe/Beatrice McKechnie House	57
Rev. Hiram Stone, rector of Trinity Episcopal Church	62
Walter E. Vaill, Milton historian	65
Frances S. Walkley, pastor of Milton Congregational Church, ca. 1940	68
Ens. Jonathan Wright	74
Auction Poster, 1897	102
Barnes & Earle Store	104
Fourth of July celebration on Milton Green	110
Fourth of July picnic & ballgame, 1920	111
The Antique Horribles, ca. 1905	112
Milton Public Hall, built 1900	118

Joseph D. Coffill, R.F.D. mailman	122
Milton Woman's Club, late 1930's	123
"Cotillon" Invitation, 1848	127
Seelye/Larned/Cohen House	146
David Welch/Edward & Mary Raymond House	147
Isaac Catlin/Doyle/Stevens House	148
Jehiel Parmalee/David Welch/Reeves W. Hart House	149
Bissell/Seelye/Sheldon House	152
John Bissell/Malcolm Forbes House	153
Moore Gibbs/Parsonage	158
Joseph Birge, Jr./Edwin Dickinson/Goldring House	159
James Birge House on Maple Street	160
Isaac Baldwin/James Duggan House	160
Guild Tavern, after 1883	161
Jeremiah Griswold/Morey/Worthington House	162
Guild/Kenney/Litwin House	163
Beach/Earle/Wilson House	169
The Mansion House - Welch/Derby/Nesbitt	170
Jonathan Wright/Ackerman/Kizzia House	171
Blacksmith Shop, 1884	182
The Carriage Shop	184
Aetna Shear Shop	188
Shears from Aetna Shear Shop	189
Saw Mill, corner of Saw Mill & Blue Swamp Roads	191
Horace Seelye/Martin Kubish House	195
Nails forged at Reuben Dickinson/William Hall place	196
Old-time peddler, Mr. Squires, & Egbert Sheldon at Page/Skidmore House	206
Ellen Doyle with horse and buggy	209
Old Milton School on Cornwall Road & schoolchildren, before 1896	212
The Milton Academy	220

Milton School children, about 1900	230
Ellen Doyle - ready to start for school with racoon coat and Dodge	232
Milton School children, 1908	236
Milton School children, 1923	238
Milton School children, 1939	245
Milton Congregational Church, 1791	253
Trinity Episcopal Church, 1802	262
Methodist Church, Milton, after removal to Prospect Mt.	266
Proposed Russian Orothodox Chapel, 1958	274
Map of Milton Center	279
Map of Lower Milton	281
Headquarters Road	288
Twin Bridges on Milton-Cornwall Road	291
Milton Cemetery on Blue Swamp Road	298
Headquarters Cemetery with stone wall	307
Garage at Donald & Janet Sibley's after July 10, 1989, tornado	332
Milton Center after 1938 Hurricane	338
1955 Flood	340

TABLE OF CONTENTS

❖

Dedication	i
List of Illustrations	ii
Introduction - How We Started	1
Organization - How We Grew	7
People - Who We Were	23
Social Life - How We Lived and Played	101
(1) Dwelling Houses to 19th Century Where We Lived	129
(2) Dwelling Houses to 20th Century Where We Lived	167
Industries - How We Made a Living	181
Schools - Where We Studied	209
Churches - Where We Worshipped	253
Roads - How We Got from Here to There	279
Burying Grounds Where We Were Laid to Rest	297
Military - In Defense of Freedom Our Fighting Men and Women	313
Catastrophes - Our Times of Trouble	327
Acknowledgements	345
Appendix	351
Index	375

Milton Center, Congregational Church, old bridge railing and old barn

Chapter I

INTRODUCTION — How We Started

❖

The tall forest trees were nearly bare. A few leaves still fell silently through the night air. It was late autumn, but the evening was warm, the wind soft. Sharp white stars pricked the black sky. From a colonial homestead high on the ridge east of the village the flares of Indian signal fires on Mount Tom could be seen off to the southwest. The village was young then, as was our nation. This is the story of that village, Milton, located in the Town of Litchfield in the northwestern part of the State of Connecticut.

Often called the most beautiful and untouched section of the Town of Litchfield, Milton has about it an aura of timelessness. In the center, grouped around unspoiled Milton Green, are some of the first homes, two churches, the Milton Public Hall, one of the former schoolhouses and the Milton

Academy building. At the foot of Milton Hill the road turns sharply past Trinity Episcopal Church with its precious stained glass windows and ancient organ. Beside it, on the site of a store which burned long ago, is the Public Hall, built in the winter of 1900 and containing a rare stage curtain. The Hall has been the focal point for the community's social life since the beginning of this century. Across the bridge on a rise of ground is the Milton Congregational Church, the oldest church in the Town, moved from its original site on the Green. Children lucky enough to have grown up in Milton remember special haunts such as paths through woods and fields, caves in ledges along some of the roads, dust and mud and snow, long (or short) walks to the schoolhouse — often in bitter cold — and games played at recess on the Green. They remember neighbors who shared almost everything including arguments, and who were family in many ways.

A spirit of camaraderie has been part of Milton since its beginning. Set off as it is from nearby towns, it is an enclave of sorts, dependent upon others but integral unto itself. This closeness has been expressed throughout Milton's history, but especially so after the 1989 tornado, when neighbors pulled together as a team to restore the village. Milton is truly home, the place to come back to. Roots grow deep and sturdy here. Someone said, most aptly, "You can't get anywhere from here." It is not a short-cut to any other place. There are no hotels or motels, no souvenir shops or stores, no movie houses or restaurants. There is only peace and quiet, a place to walk or jog, with people usually ready to chat to a passerby. And you might be in time for a community pot-luck picnic or supper at the Hall, or a dance or play or carol sing and Christmas tree lighting.

INTRODUCTION

The writing of this history has been a community effort, evolving over more than sixty years from a dream Ellen M. Doyle had and which she presented to the Milton Woman's Club in June 1930. At that meeting Miss Doyle was appointed chairman of a research committee to write the *Chronicles of Milton*. The Club, and Miss Doyle in particular, gathered material over many years, but the book was never finished. In early 1991 Miss Doyle's niece, Frances Barrett, gave the Milton community all the accumulated notes and information, and work began on this story of the unique village called Milton.

Situated on the Marshepaug River, Milton in its earliest days was a lonely wilderness. It was settled around 1740 and lies in what were the "Western Lands" in the northwest part of the Town of Litchfield. Originally known as the Northwest Section, it was later called Blue Swamp for the tamarack trees and blue gentians which grew here. The name Milton was chosen in 1795, probably by one of the Welch ladies, for the English poet, John Milton. In 1768 it was set off by the Connecticut General Assembly as the Third Society in Litchfield, made up of parts of Litchfield, Cornwall, Goshen and Warren. The Milton meetinghouse building was erected on the Green, until then called the Common, in 1791. In 1795 the Milton Society was established as a full ecclesiastical society and boundaries were laid out in detail. Three years later, in 1798, the Congregational Presbyterian Church was organized.

Lying on the good waters of the Marshepaug, Milton encouraged early industry. Numerous dams supported many mills, shops and other enterprises. For years Milton was more industrialized than Litchfield. Later when the railroad bypassed the village and the carriage trade dropped off,

Milton became agrarian as it is today. Now almost all of the numerous farms have disappeared along with the shops and mills. Also gone are the two ponds, Milton (Mill) Pond, lost when the hurricane of 1955 washed out the dam, and Shear Shop (Forge) Pond, destroyed by the City of Waterbury which owns the watershed rights along the Marshepaug.

Milton Pond

Walking through the two cemeteries in Milton one might discover an ancestor or two, for gravestones date back to the late 1700's. Jeremiah Griswold, Justus Seelye and David Welch, all land brokers from New Milford, were among the first to come here, and each left his mark in homes, industries and descendants whose roots reach back to the beginning of the village.

Two churches have come and gone — the East Cornwall Baptist Church and the Methodist Church which stood south of the present schoolhouse building. There were six school districts, each with its own schoolhouse — the first erected on land west of Trinity Church and moved to the East Cornwall road, the last located on Milton Green and today a private home. From the center of Milton in any direction are the woods which stretch for miles, interspersed here and there with houses. The open areas of two and one-half centuries past have grown up, and other areas of forests have been opened up, changing the landscape seen by the first settlers. The tornado of July 10, 1989, destroyed many of the ancient trees in and around Milton, further altering the village.

We discovered when compiling this history that a place is not just dimensions and dates and names. Its essential character and particular flavor are drawn from the people who live here, labor at their jobs, think their thoughts, dream their dreams, and by so doing create a special place. This is so in Milton; each generation has brought new and vital contributions.

When he was an old man, Walter E. Vaill, who lived in Milton for nearly one-hundred years, wrote the following:

"As I look back a long way, Milton was not such a bad place to live — a boy could enjoy life as well in Milton as he could anywhere. The people might have some little jealousies and quarrels. But they were mighty good neighbors when trouble came to anyone here. I see in my mind old faces gone long ago. But I think I always loved Milton." To which we say, "Amen."

Barnraising at Doyles', West Goshen Road, July 3, 1896

Chapter II

ORGANIZATION — How We Grew

❖

From an uncharted wilderness in the early eighteenth century a village was born. It grew quickly for almost two hundred years before returning to a semblance of what it had been, a place forgotten by time. People from the early days of Milton would still recognize the village of today.

Around 1740 the proprietors of Litchfield laid out this Northwest Section, as it was called, in two north and south tiers of one-hundred-acre numbered lots running east and west and set them off to various men. One of the first was Joseph Bird, who acquired one hundred acres on what was known as East Street, the present West Goshen Road. On

October 11, 1749, he deeded to Jeremiah Griswold fifty acres. This deed is one of the earliest in the Litchfield Land Records pertaining to the Northwest Section and was probably Griswold's first deed in Milton. He was a wheelwright and built dams along the Marshepaug River as well as waterwheels and pulleys.

Along with Jeremiah Griswold, two other men contributed to Milton's early growth — Justus Seelye and David Welch. Justus Seelye's first deed in Milton was from Daniel Barnes, April 13, 1752. Before 1760 he had constructed the first dam on the Marshepaug and a saw mill at the southwest corner of the present Saw Mill and Blue Swamp Roads. The saw mill was torn down early in 1947. Seelye's dam, washed out in the August 1955 flood, formed the pond on Saw Mill Road known as Seelye's Pond, later Mill Pond and then Milton Pond. Here John Griswold tested his ironclad vessel, a precursor by almost one hundred years of the *Monitor*. The Seelyes had a trip hammer at Seelyeville off the Milton-East Cornwall Road, where some of the Martin Kubish family now live.

David Welch bought land in Milton in 1753 and lived in one of the first houses — later known as the Bissell home — in the new settlement. He started the important iron business with his puddling furnace and forge on Shear Shop Road, where he dammed the river to harness the water power. Pig iron was brought from Salisbury to be refined here, some of it purported to have been carried by Ethan Allen.

Colonial records of the State of Connecticut attest to the establishment of Milton as the Third Society in Litchfield in May 1768, enacted January 1769, "Upon the memorial of David Welch, Jehiel Parmely and others..." At this time the limits of this Third Society were spelled out, and the area became known as Blue Swamp.

The Society of Milton was incorporated as a full ecclesiastical society by resolve in May 1795. This gave the residents more complete powers as allowed the Congregational Church. The Society was supported by taxation. Boundaries of the Society were laid out in detail at this time, following closely those established for the Third Society. The name was changed to Milton at this time. The first clerk was John Welch.

On April 9, 1849, the lines and boundaries of Milton were perambulated. Involved were A.S. Lewis and P.K. Kilbourn, committee for Litchfield, and Samuel Dudley and William Bissell, committee for Milton, with William Dudley and Lorenzo Wheeler, chairmen, representing upper Maple Street and the Headquarters-Mount Tom area. A.D. Catlin of Litchfield and Truman Guild of Milton were the surveyors.

The Congregational meetinghouse was built on the Green in 1791, making the church building the oldest one in the Town of Litchfield. A group of people organized the Congregational Presbyterian Church on August 19, 1798. The building was moved across the river in November 1828 to a piece of land given by Asa Morris. Milton Green continues to be owned by the Congregational Church to this day.

Land for Trinity Episcopal Church was given by John Welch — previous to this the Episcopalians of Milton often met in the schoolhouse. The church, begun in 1802 and completed in 1827, was built by Oliver Dickinson, Jr. who designed the exterior after the second Trinity Episcopal Church in New York. The church contains unique stained glass windows and an antique organ.

The East Cornwall Baptist Church near Flat Rocks was included in Milton Society. It was organized in 1787 as the

Warren Baptist Church, later as the College Street Baptist Church of Cornwall. It was torn down around 1949.

A Methodist Church, a simple, unpainted structure built about 1824 through the efforts of Isaac Baldwin and Abraham Wadhams, stood just south of the present school-house building on Headquarters Road. The building was sold to the Connecticut Mining Company in the mid-1850's, dismantled and moved down Prospect Mountain Road, where it still stands today as a private home. In earlier days Milton Methodists gathered for services in the Guild house, where the Craig Litwin family now lives at 122 Saw Mill Road.

In addition to the Congregationalists, the Episcopalians and the Methodists, there were twenty-six Catholic families in Milton in the early 1930's, most of whom attended St. Anthony's Catholic Church in Litchfield. A priest from the church came one afternoon each week to Milton School to teach catechism to the Catholic children.

From its earliest days Milton was concerned with education. School records are well documented in the town. Before the first schoolhouse was erected prior to 1797, school was held in different homes and in the Congregational meetinghouse. A private school was conducted in the upper room of the church in 1834/35, taught by Birdsey Gibbs. It is also believed that classes were held in the house now owned by Walter C. Sheldon (557 Milton Road), and in the David Welch house on the Green, now called the Raymond Cottage (529 Milton Road). The last schoolhouse, now a private home, was built on Milton Green in 1896. Several generations attended this school before it was discontinued in 1946. It was here that Ellen M. Doyle taught for many years.

At one time, during the early and mid-1800's, there were nearly twice as many people in Milton as in Litchfield, and schoolhouses were built in strategic locations, with school being held year round. In 1797 there were schools in Milton, Gilbert corner (Maple Street and Forge Hollow Road), Headquarters, Mount Tom (then included in the Milton district), East Cornwall (also part of the district) and Newcomb in Goshen, considered part of Milton. Perhaps the best known school was the Milton Academy founded in 1856 by Rev. George A. Harrison. The small building still stands on the Green north and east of the schoolhouse.

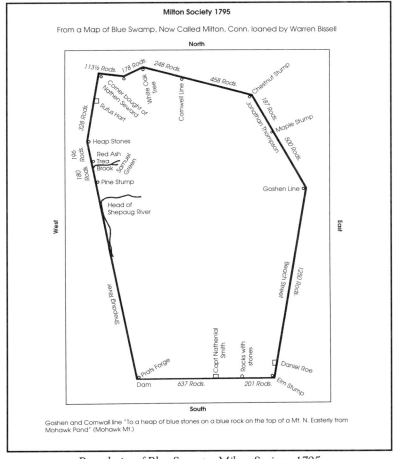

Boundaries of Blue Swamp - Milton Society, 1795

Two hundred years ago Milton was a prosperous center of industry with a number of dams on the Marshepaug River supplying power for five saw mills, two grist mills, two iron works, a trip hammer, wagon maker, carriage and sleigh shops, carding machine, a machine for the manufacture of wooden clocks, fulling and cider mills, two turners, forges, as well as two shoemakers, stores and several nailmakers. Quantities of charcoal were made here for the forges and shops and sold to iron furnaces in Cornwall. Granite was mined on the Granniss farm on Prospect Mountain and on the Hall property on Blue Swamp Road. Farming was also one of the chief industries for many years.

One of the major commercial enterprises was Thomas Hinchliffe's Aetna Shear Shop which operated from 1873 until the early 1900's. *The Milton Chronicle*, handwritten by Milton schoolchildren around 1900, reports that "...the only industry in Milton is the manufacture of shears conducted by Mr. Hinchliff (sic). The shop is situated north of the center of Milton. They make nothing but steel lined shears and scissors. ...Mr. Hinchliff has been in business for thirty six years. ... He has employed as many as thirty seven men but now he only employs seven. His shears have always ranked high and are as good as any made in the country." His shop was in the building on the site of David Welch's forge where the Bissells also manufactured sleighs. Hinchliffe built a large house on the hill across the road from Shear Shop Pond. The house was torn down in 1978.

In 1854, a charter to operate two nickel mines on Prospect Mountain was granted to the Connecticut Mining Company. Other companies also ventured into mining; good ore was found but proved too costly to mine. Some of the ore was sold to the United States government for nickel cents. In the mid-1900's further attempts to mine the nickel produced little results.

Headquarters, about a mile and one-half from the center of Milton, was chosen as a site for Revolutionary War "training days" for the military companies of Bantam (then known as Bradleyville) and Milton. Maneuvers were carried out at this location which was situated half-way between the two companies. Legend derives the name from George Washington's stay in a local house while planning military strategy for one of his campaigns.

Ice cutting on Milton (Mill) Pond, 1930's

The two ponds here, Milton Pond and Shear Shop Pond along with their dams, produced not only water power but places for the residents to swim, skate and picnic. They were also sources of the ice which was harvested each winter. Unfortunately, the ponds no longer exist. Milton Pond was lost when the Saw Mill Road dam washed out in the flood of 1955, and Shear Shop Pond was demolished by the City of Waterbury in the late 1930's. Today the Marshepaug River flows through Milton, unstopped except for the beaver dams that form natural ponds behind them.

The first store in Milton was located in the east end of the David Welch house by the year 1784. Later, Frank Barnes and Frank Earle had a store where Milton Public Hall now stands. This store, built in the mid-1800's, burned in January 1894. A store that operated in the present home of Paul Deering (541 Milton Road) was in existence for many years. When Herbert T. Register was proprietor, the first telephone in the village was installed there around 1916, with lines coming from Goshen. Poles had to be put in by the patrons. Almost all phones were on party lines until the 1950's. The stores were meeting places for the people of the community. For awhile there was a gas pump outside the store, which was run by Jacob Ackerman at that time. When the Ackermans gave up the store, many residents had groceries delivered from the Bantam Store once a week.

The Milton Public Hall was built by Jesse H. Derby in the winter of 1900 with physical and monetary assistance from the men of Milton. It has been the hub of the community's social life ever since. Milton school children put on plays and programs to raise money for the unique and beautiful stage curtain. Every Christmas the children of the school presented a program for parents and friends. There were always dances from the very beginning, and many a boy and girl learned the intricate steps of square dances in the Hall. Often the room was so crowded with stamping, hopping bodies that the floor would sway visibly up and down, but it never gave way, a tribute to the skills of the builders. There was seldom any disciplinary problem until after World War II when an unruly element from other towns began to come to the Milton dances, which had to be stopped.

Community meetings and special events have always been held in the Hall. After the July 10, 1989, tornado the whole of Milton met there to focus aid and volunteers in the clean-up process.

For years the Fourth of July picnic was held on the Milton Green with almost everyone in Milton having a part. Sometimes as many as three hundred people attended. Again, as with the dances, rowdies from other areas put a stop to the picnics.

Baseball games were played evenings and Sundays on the Green through the years. Teams from other towns came to play against the Milton team, for years managed by G. Herbert (Herb) Griffin. One of the best of Mr. Griffin's teams was that of teenagers from 1935 into the 1940's.

Milton people made their own entertainment. At home they sat around the kitchen or dining room table, under the hanging kerosene or gas lamp, and talked, sewed, read aloud, played games and told stories. They retired early, for their days began before dawn. When radio came there were programs to listen to, selectively, because the large dry-cell batteries had a limited life. Television changed family life in many ways — it discouraged reading and conversation for one thing. The nearest movie houses were ten miles away in Torrington until the Bantam Theater opened in the late 1930's. Schoolchildren traipsed one day a week to the Milton Library in the parsonage. Later, when the parsonage was sold, the Library was moved to the upper room of the Congregational Church where it continued until around 1969, when it was abandoned.

During the years when Miss Frances S. Walkley was minister of the Milton Congregational Church (1924 to

1938), she had several clubs for the village children, including Honey Bees, Camp Fire Girls, a boys' club and sewing club, as well as "cootie parties," marshmallow and wiener roasts. Under her tutelage the children put on splendid Children's Day programs.

Milton Ladies Aid Society, summer 1940

The women had social outlets in the Congregational Church Ladies' Aid, Women's Guild of Trinity Church, the Milton Woman's Club, card parties, suppers, sales and auctions. Visiting among neighbors was frequent, and community life was confined to the village for the most part.

The Milton Woman's Club, which helped lay the foundation for this history, was organized June 1927, the brainchild of Mary B. Smith, who enlisted the aid of Ellen M. Doyle, Frances S. Walkley, Edith D. Axford and Mercy I. Birge. Today, more than sixty-five years later, it is still an important part of the cultural life of Milton women.

There were tea parties and quilting parties. From Everett H. Perkins came an old Milton quilt called a "Friendship Quilt," made in the mid-1800's by thirty-eight Milton women who wrote their names on pieces of paper and sewed them onto the quilt (see Appendix for a list of names on this quilt).

Milton men had their activities, too. There were card parties, for one thing, and the men hunted, fished, helped with community events, had impromptu or organized bands. They tended large gardens and helped with harvesting and preserving. Families played together and worked together.

Milton took an active part in all the wars which her country fought, sending her men to active duty and sometimes to death. Many are buried in our cemeteries.

The Milton Civil Defense Unit of the Red Cross was set up in the mid-1950's, and soon afterwards helped during and after the disastrous fire at the Karl Thoma home on April 14, 1954.

There are two cemeteries in Milton, the older being Milton Cemetery on Blue Swamp Road, the other Headquarters Cemetery on Headquarters Road. The date and beginnings of Milton Cemetery are unclear, but there is a deed to Justus Seelye in 1791 which mentions the cemetery as a boundary.

Headquarters Cemetery, smaller and somewhat younger, is also of unknown origin, although it was established around the latter half of the eighteenth century. The oldest headstone, that of Israel Potter, is inscribed "The first in this burying ground." The date is October 12, 1785. The cemetery at the Crooked Esses, which is no longer used, and the West Goshen Cemetery, were once included in Milton.

Early roads in Milton were rough and narrow dirt roads, often not much more than trails. There are still several dirt roads here. It is believed that one of the first roads to Milton from Litchfield came up by Goodhouse Road, over the East Road just above the Catlin house on upper Maple Street (number 566), now home of the E. Seward Stevens family. This road was discontinued around 1920.

The road from Hartford to Poughkeepsie ran through Headquarters, Dug Way and over to Warren, Kent and on. A later road through Milton was called the Litchfield and Cornwall Turnpike, and was administered by the Litchfield and Cornwall Turnpike Company.

Tollhouses were located at several points on the local roads, including one near the Bunnell farm, one on the Milton-East Cornwall Road where the Misses Worthington, later the Carroll Fischers, lived. The Guild Tavern in the center of Milton was a busy place under several owners, among whom were Alban Guild and Horatio Griswold.

A rather unusual ornate wrought iron bridge in Milton center, built in 1885 by the Berlin Iron Bridge Company at a cost of $900, was replaced in 1992 by a wooden structure. On the road to East Cornwall were the twin bridges, which spanned two diverging streams of the river, set at an angle to one another. A new section of road was constructed in the 1970's to replace these bridges.

There was an attractive stone sluice, called the arch sluice, at the foot of Headquarters Cemetery, which was washed out by Hurricane Diane in 1955. Another sluice, smaller than this one, was located west of the house at 10 Headquarters Road, along an old road. This sluice, sometimes with a plank across it, was used by the schoolchildren when Headquarters Road was flooded at the end of the road nearest the schoolhouse.

Very early inhabitants of the Milton area were the Algonquin Indians, a branch of the Mohawks of New York State. While the local population was not large or particularly unfriendly, settlers stayed on the defensive. The fierce Mohawks, a tribe of the Six Nations, used to come through this area, camping at Bantam Lake. Local Indians retained Mount Tom for their hunting grounds. From the summit their signal fires could be seen for miles. They traveled on trails and narrow footpaths through this area. It is said that they used to make pottery up by the dam on the brook west of the O'Brien place on the old road (now abandoned) from Shear Shop road to upper Maple Street. This was the site of the saw mill run by Samuel Bassett in the middle of the nineteenth century. One of the most famous Indians in this area was Eli Bunker who lived, and died, above Seelyeville at the foot of Mohawk Mountain. Indian artifacts, like arrowheads, can still be found around Milton.

For many years the New York Herald Tribune Fresh Air Home at the juncture of Maple Street and Milton Road hosted groups of a hundred or so children from crowded New York City streets for two weeks at a time. The Home, started by Mrs. Shepherd Knapp in 1905 in memory of her husband, was sponsored by the Tribune's Fresh Air Fund. It gave disadvantaged youngsters (called "Shepherd Knapp kids" or "Fresh Air kids" by Miltonites) the opportunity to see the countryside, often for the first time in their lives, to live here for two weeks, to learn about nature, to swim, camp, hike, put on entertainments and attend local churches.

Foundations of buildings now long gone give evidence of former industrial activity and dwelling houses, including Pratt's forge on Saw Mill road, Justus Seelye's saw mill and mill pond, Welch's puddling forge with the remnants of the earthworks of Shear Shop dam and sluice, Hinchliffe's Shear

Shop and house, Smith's carriage shop, Hutchinson's cider mill, the largest of several nail forges west of the Reuben Dickinson house, the foundation of a small dwelling house on Shear Shop road owned by the Welchs, the site of the second schoolhouse, foundation of a house perhaps associated with the Pratts on the corner of Saw Mill and Blue Swamp roads, Dickinson's grist mill, the place where the Methodist Church stood, the foundation of the house where Anson Dickinson was born and died, numerous traces of old roadways, the remains of barns, fences, stonewalls and church sheds.

View of Milton Center from Milton Hill

From small industries at home in the eighteenth century, there was a change early in the 1900's as machines began to produce necessities which could be purchased at the village store. The hand-crafting of articles at home began to disappear, except where they were produced for marketing.

Milton industry slowed down and eventually ceased altogether, and the tempo of village life came to be similar to today. And yet, the years roll back as one enters the village, and the Milton of yesteryear can still be recognized.

Information comes from "Milton History Papers"; The Chronicle, hand-printed by Milton schoolchildren, 1903; Bantam Almanac, published by Warren McArthur Corp., 1942; Litchfield Land Records, Vol. 4, pp. 327 and 43, Vol. 13, p. 428, Vol. 2, p. 161; Recollections of Walter C. Sheldon and Everett H. Perkins.

Chapter III

PEOPLE — Who We Were

❖

We have written about people in Milton only where there is information available concerning them in the "Milton History Papers," or from memories of those who remain. Other people who were just as important have had to be omitted for lack of knowledge.

Almon James Beach

Known locally as Jim Beach, Almon James Beach, son of Anson and Pamelia Abernathy Beach, was born October 2, 1819. In October 1840 he married Antoinette Birge, and they had one son and five daughters, including Mary Pamela who married Frank Earle and was the mother of Charles A. Earle.

Jim Beach lived his early years on the family farm east of Milton and later built the present David Wilson house (552 Milton Road) on land purchased from Bradley Beach. He began the foundation in December 1885, and probably finished the house in 1886.

He was, according to Walter E. Vaill, a "tall, rather handsome (man), easy going, a fox hunter, a musician, singer, kindly, very much a gentleman. In fact I have always looked up to him and Capt. (William) Bissell as the gentlemen of Milton in my time." Fred M. Seelye, who was young then, said of Almon James Beach, "Mr. Beach was surely a great asset to the community life in those days. We all loved him." Years later Sarah Harrison, daughter of Rev. George J. Harrison, wrote to Ellen M. Doyle, speaking of Almon James, "When I was a girl I enjoyed the Singing School conducted by Mr. James A. (sic) Beach — He was an exceptional instructor — Mrs. Earle (his daughter) was his accompanist and a good one."

His Singing School was noted here for its excellence. Singers met and practiced in the winter in the Milton Academy and probably also in Trinity Episcopal Church, where he was choir leader. A concert was given in Trinity at the end of the season to which everyone came. One year, however, the bishop was alerted that the concert was planned, and he forbade it, saying that the church was to be used for religious purposes only. As a result, Jim Beach held the concert in the Milton Congregational Church, according to Fred M. Seelye, and thereafter switched his religious affiliation to that church. He also had singing schools in Goshen and Litchfield.

Beach was an accomplished singer and teacher, and was leader of an orchestra which played for public parties and dances. Members of his orchestra included, among others, Charles Blake — violin, Seelye Hart — bass viol and Lucius Carter — drums.

Besides these musical talents, Jim Beach had another "vocation" — he had a turnkey and would pull teeth for "everyone around." He was also a storekeeper in Hugh G. Welch's store, later Jacob Ackerman's, now the home of Paul and Patricia Deering (541 Milton Road).

Almon James Beach died May 8, 1897, and he and his wife Antoinette and five daughters and one son are memorialized on the Beach monument in Milton Cemetery, Blue Swamp Road.

Anson Bradley Beach

Called Bradley, Anson Bradley Beach, son of Anson and Pamelia Abernathy Beach and brother of Almon James Beach, was born May 5, 1804, and died March 19, 1885. He married Elizabeth Perkins, daughter of Daniel, in March 1826; both are buried in Milton Cemetery. Their children are probably George, Theoren, Edwin and Sarah.

Bradley was called "mean" and penurious; it was said that he and his wife lived "very closely," sparingly. A story to that effect says that when his wife's niece lived with them, they would boil two eggs for a meal: Bradley would eat one and the other was cut in half for the women. Another story, showing as well his eccentricity, goes like this: his wife was calling on her uncle on the Milton-Cornwall road when a load of furniture passed by. "Whose furniture is that?" Mrs. Beach asked. Her uncle replied, "Why, it's yours. Didn't you know it?" "No," she said. Her uncle told her, "Bradley is moving to Milton." He had bought the Hugh Welch house on the hill above his brother Almon's house without telling his wife.

He once spent 10¢ for a cigar to settle a bet. But there are other stories, like the one Fred M. Seelye told. Fred wanted a new gold dollar to give to his fiancée Elnor as a gift. The one he got at the bank was all tarnished, and when he showed it to Bradley Beach, Bradley said, "Hold on, Fred. Perhaps I've got a better one," and he went and brought back a perfect coin to trade with Fred. Another time he loaned money to Frank O'Brien, who couldn't pay the interest on a loan. Bradley took a fine colt, which he was to keep for the winter, in lieu of payment. Later he acquired the colt and sold it and put $30 in the bank for Fred Seelye who had advised him to sell the colt.

In November 1873, James Hutchinson borrowed $1500 from Bradley. Nearly four years later Lewis Hutchinson deeded a mill and land to Bradley, Elizabeth and her brother Beecher Perkins, along with another deed for house and land on the mill pond. Later Bradley gained full title to the grist mill. Samuel Bennett worked for him, and the business prospered.

Fred M. Seelye was fond of Bradley Beach and spoke well of him. He said of Bradley, "Old skinflint, hey? One of my best friends." Fred felt that Bradley's reputation for being stingy was misleading. He may have been "mean" and may have "lived closely," but when he died he was worth $75,000, a real fortune in those days.

James Birge

Born October 16, 1758, James Birge was the second child and eldest son of Elisha and Mary Mugleston/Muckleston Birge and grandson of Joseph Birge, one of the original proprietors of Litchfield, and his wife Dorothy Kilbourn Birge. In October 1780, James married Sarah (Sally) Palmer, daughter of Rev. Solomon and Abigail Foote Palmer. They had six children.

James was a soldier in the Revolutionary War. He enlisted in March 1776 and served until January 1777 as a private in Captain Bezaliel Beebe's Company, Col. Philip Bradley's Connecticut Regiment. He reenlisted in April 1777 and was at the Danbury raid.

Before 1790 he built the house which stands at the junction of Maple Street and Brush Hill Road (386 Maple Street) which was held in the family until 1941. His father Elisha lived with James and his family after James' mother

Mary died in a blizzard in 1786 at the old Elisha Birge home on the site of the present Joseph Italiaander house on Fox Crossing Road, off Milton Road.

It is believed that James was the first banker in Litchfield, although he may not have been formally associated with a banking institution in Litchfield. He held a number of mortgages in both Litchfield and Milton. He was also a Justice of the Peace.

James Birge died February 10, 1850, and is buried with his wife in Headquarters Cemetery in Milton.

Capt. William Bissell

He was called one of the two "gentlemen of Milton" by Walter E. Vaill; the other was Almon James Beach. His name was William Bissell, the son of Hiram and Beata Wetmore Bissell, born July 11, 1810, and died July 16, 1902. His father was the oldest Freemason in the State of Connecticut when he died in 1876. William married his third cousin, Amanda Jennette Bissell, daughter of John and Mary Dickinson Bissell and granddaughter of Anson and Sarah Dickinson. William and Amanda had at least three sons, Hiram, Warren and Jerome, and a daughter, Cornelia. Four children — three girls and a boy — died young and are buried with their parents in Milton Cemetery.

William was a Captain in the Civil War in the 19th Connecticut Artillery, the 2nd Connecticut Heavy Artillery. He worked for his father at the Welchs' iron works which Hiram ran.

Capt. William was a tall, slender man, handsome, with a long white beard which he had a habit of stroking, a "good dresser, very courteous, full of anecdotes, very kindly, good example of a gentleman of the old school," so wrote Walter Vaill about Capt. William Bissell.

The Bissells lived in the house on Shear Shop Road now owned by Malcolm Forbes, Jr., at number 109. Eventually, William owned this house, which had belonged to his father-in-law, John Bissell. Around 1858 William bought from Clarissa (Mrs. Gerret) Welch the house at the entrance to Milton, the present Col. Edward and Mary Raymond house in Milton Center.

The Bissells and the Welchs, besides being related, were very good friends.

Eli Bunker

Milton's resident Native American, whom we shared with Cornwall, was Eli Bunker. Eli was a member of the Schaghticoke tribe and lived at the foot of Mohawk Mountain, once part of Milton Society. His story was written for this history in the 1930's, when the Milton History was first begun, by Mrs. Andrew Clark of East Cornwall, who quoted from Rev. Edward C. Starr's *History of Cornwall*. Mrs. Clark wrote that Rufus Bunker and his white wife Rexa lived on a forty-acre farm near the foot of Bunker Hill in Cornwall. Rufus was "an old and honest man," whose name is associated with Bunker Hill.

Eli was their son. In 1842 he married Fannie Maria Watson. In 1854 he bought a little more than nine acres of land on the stream at the bottom of Mohawk Mountain from Sheldon Clark. The land is located where the road turns west off Milton Road, near the old West Goshen Cemetery and the Alfred Wright brick house, now called Eli Bunker Road. Sheldon Clark helped Eli build a sturdy cabin for his home on the bank of the hill where he lived.

Eli belonged to the North Cornwall Church. He was reputed to be a good neighbor, easy-going, pleasant, friendly and well-known throughout the county. He raised vegetables, sold maple syrup, collected herbs and roots for medicines in the tradition of his ancestors. He made and sold fine, long-lasting splint baskets for which he obtained the wood wherever he found it, and no one objected if he took wood from their property.

Eli Bunker was a tall, large man with piercing black eyes and copper-brown complexion. He reportedly wore an old overcoat and battered hat and was familiar to the people in Milton, Goshen and Cornwall.

He died in his cabin in the spring of 1888 and is buried in Cornwall Cemetery, Cornwall, Connecticut.

Anson Dickinson and his father, Oliver, Jr.

Born in Milton, April 19, 1779, Anson Dickinson (Dickenson) returned home many times until his death there on March 9, 1852. Between those dates he created a reputation as one of America's most esteemed miniature portraitists. Although Anson attained prominence throughout the nation, he came from a family that distinguished itself in numerous ways.

Anson Dickinson

Anson was the oldest of the ten children of Oliver, Jr. and Anna Landon Dickinson. His mother was recognized as an "authoress of considerable repute in ecclesiastical matters," quoting from a 1935 article by Ellen M. Doyle and Clarissa C. Deming in the *Litchfield Enquirer*. His father, a Revolutionary soldier, was a master builder, who is best remembered for his construction of Trinity Episcopal Church in Milton in 1802 which he copied from his memory of the second Trinity Church in Manhattan. A stained glass window in the church commemorates his pre-eminent role in its construction. Oliver is also credited with building the Welch-Vaill-Hart house at the corner of Cornwall Road and Saw Mill Road (127 Saw Mill Road), although his father, Oliver, Sr., may have been the builder.

Oliver, Jr., father of Anson, was the son of Oliver, Sr. and Mary Dickinson, and was born July 10, 1757. He died March 23, 1847. In 1778 he married Anna Landon, and he and his family lived in the house on Saw Mill Road where he raised his family. He was a prisoner during the Revolutionary War. He and his wife are buried in Milton Cemetery on Blue Swamp Road.

The earliest ancestor of the Dickinson family to settle in the Litchfield-Milton area was Ebenezer Dickinson from Hatfield, Massachusetts, whose estate was described in his will as in the "Great Blue Swamp," the early name for Milton. Ebenezer purchased the land from his son Reuben in 1753. As early settlers along this stretch of the Shepaug River, Ebenezer and his family members operated saw and grist mills and tilled the rocky clay soil. Son Reuben, who lived to the age of 102, lived in the "Thompson" house, presently 65 Saw Mill Road. Another Dickinson, Amos, at one time owned the former Wilbur and Amy Haviland house (37 Saw Mill Road), occupied now by the McKinney family. Oliver

Dickinson, Sr., another of Ebenezer's sons, built the house next door to Reuben's, where Anson was born. It was described as "a high, two-story gambrel-roofed red house," and is marked today by lilac bushes and the memorial marker placed by the roadside on the property of the Bernard Grendahls by the Milton Historic Sites Committee in 1984 to identify the spot.

Anson Dickinson's innate talent surfaced during the time he was apprenticed to a silversmith in the early 1800's. He had become intrigued by the portraits painted by the nation's foremost miniature portraitist at that time, Edward Malbone. Encouraged by those who viewed his work, Anson left for New Haven where he advertised his services as a miniature painter. Money realized from this endeavor, combined with his income from silhouette painting, enameling, framing and painting signs, enabled him to leave for New York with its wider field of clients. The highlight of this trip was a chance to view Malbone's manner of painting first-hand when he sat for Malbone in 1804.

Upon the death of Malbone, Anson Dickinson soon established himself as America's most prominent miniaturist. Miniatures were important as a link between the large portraits that preceded them and photographs which would be invented later. Miniatures were painted on ovals of ivory, imported from England, with paints mixed by the artist himself (at least in Anson's case) and were usually about three inches high and two inches wide. Dickinson's "hallmark" was the suggestion of a scene behind the subject, and also his distinctive use of blues and pinks. He carried with him all the materials he would need, including his paints, brushes, ivories, cases, magnifying glasses and reducing glasses. Around 1825 Anson began to use his second trademark, a satin case lining printed with his trade card.

Anson's reputation was well deserved as he was able to capture the essence of his model in the confined space of the miniature. His clients included Gilbert Stuart, Sam Houston, Charles Francis Adams, Governor Oliver Wolcott and many prominent people from his hometown as well as students at the Tapping Reeve Law School and Miss Pierce's Litchfield Female Academy. He spent his productive years travelling a circuit from Montreal in the north to Charleston, South Carolina, in the south, going by canal boat, foot and probably horseback, painting his miniatures in two to four days for a price of around twenty-five dollars. There were times when he didn't sign his work, but he kept a careful record, so we know he completed at least 1500 miniatures. Mona Leithiser Dearborn's book, *Anson Dickinson, The Celebrated Miniature Painter, 1779-1852*, shows ninety-four of his miniatures and details of their size, date painted, owner and origin. The years between 1812 and 1820 were busy ones for Anson in New York; he painted nearly three hundred miniatures during that time. In the following years he secured many commissions in Boston, Philadelphia, Baltimore, Washington, D.C. and Canadian cities. During his stay in Washington, Anson was asked by George Washington's step-grandson to paint a miniature working from the famous portrait by Charles Willson Peale. So successful was he that subscriptions for impressions were sold through newspaper advertisements.

In 1812 Anson married Sarah Brown in New York City where the couple took up residence. After twelve years of a childless marriage, Anson and Sarah adopted William and Mary Ann Walker who had been left motherless. Their happy family life is evident in portraits of Sarah and the children painted by Anson. The family returned to Milton from time to time to savor its peace and beauty, and finally in

1852, less than a year after painting his last miniature, Anson Dickinson died in the home in which he had been born.

Anson's reputation diminished somewhat during the next hundred years. Few of his miniatures were in museums; undoubtedly one reason for this is that they were considered family heirlooms to be worn in lockets, carried about in their cases or displayed in specially built standing cases. The aforementioned Mona Dearborn, a native of Bantam, Connecticut, took a special interest in Anson Dickinson. In her capacity as Keeper, Catalogue of American Portraits at the Smithsonian Institution, she arranged a slide show and lecture at Trinity Church, Milton, in 1983. This followed a major exhibit of Dickinson's miniatures by the Connecticut Historical Society in conjunction with the Stamford Historical Society and the Litchfield Historical Society, and coincided with the placing of the granite marker by the roadside where Anson Dickinson's birthplace stood. These two events were a fitting memorial to Anson Dickinson, one of Milton's finest sons.

Doctors in Milton

In a letter to Ellen M. Doyle, James (Jay) Gilbert wrote, in regard to doctors, "... perhaps the most important (character) of all in the community (was) the family doctor. Upon first thought, is it possible that this community could support a family doctor?" There were few resident physicians in Milton years ago. People tended to treat themselves with home remedies, and usually there were one or two people in the community who were natural healers, or knew the uses of herbs and plants and concoctions for various ailments. There were mid-wives, one would suppose, or at least women who helped one another through childbirth. Men were versed in animal husbandry and assisted each other in the farmyard.

Four men in the accumulated papers of the Milton History are mentioned as being doctors in Milton: Stanley Griswold, John M. West, Charles I. Page and Dr. Landon. Of these, Stanley Griswold may not have been a doctor but served as such and was called "Dr. Griswold." He lived at Headquarters where the John Dennisons had fourteen children, and the William Granniss family had eleven. Born May 9, 1804, and died in 1895, the son of Benjamin and Sally Wright Griswold, Stanley probably served Milton as doctor in the mid-1800's. He married Sarah Leverage and "had notions," Walter E. Vaill said — he kept his coffin under his bed, for one thing. He also wore a "Horace Greeley" hat covered with white fur.

John M. West, M.D., owned the house across from the parsonage, now gone, which he sold with about sixteen acres of land with dwelling house, barn and brewery thereon to John Welch in 1835. This land included the house later owned by the Worthington family, and still later by the Carroll Fischers on the East Cornwall road (606 Milton Road) and was the land which Clarissa Marsh Welch sold to Roswell Page who built the present house there. Dr. West was "a queer old dick" (Walter Vaill), and so many stories were told about him that when he died some of his heirs cut in his gravestone: "John M. West, M.D. Let the dead rest." This stone can still be seen in Milton Cemetery.

At one point Dr. West dumped the contents of his medicine chest into the well in the cellar of his house. No one dared use the well water after that, and a new well had to be dug outside in the yard.

There is another story about some young fellows who thought they would have some fun with the doctor. They stopped at his house claiming that one of them had "an arm out of business." When they left, the man had *two* arms out of joint.

Dr. West and his wife, Sophie, lost two children, a daughter Laura Ann, who died in 1813 at the age of three months, and a son who also died young.

There was a Doctor Landon who advertised in 1830 that he would attend people in Milton and Bradleyville.

Dr. Charles I. Page, son of Charles I. and Molly Langford Page, lived in the house on Blue Swamp Road now owned by the James Cropsey family (116 Blue Swamp Road). Dr. Page was born in 1868 and died in 1926 and is buried in Milton Cemetery. He is mentioned as being the attending physician at the death of Charles Clark in 1907. He is also mentioned in diaries of people living in Milton then.

In later years Milton people were cared for by doctors in Litchfield. Some names are included in the "Milton History Papers" and the memories of residents: Dr. Alfred Childs (the Health Officer), Dr. Marcy, Dr. Charles N. Warner, Sr., Dr. John Kilgus, among others. Within recent memory are Dr. Albert W. Dautrich and Dr. Charles N. Warner, Jr., along with one or two others. These were the last physicians to come to the house to treat the ill. For the past nearly twenty years Milton people have had to make the trip to Litchfield or Torrington to visit a doctor, or to the emergency room at the Charlotte Hungerford Hospital in Torrington when sick.

Ellen Margaret Doyle

Born in Torrington on January 28, 1883, to Terrence and Mary Harris Doyle, Ellen Margaret Doyle was destined to play a pivotal role in the development of Milton's children for the first half of the twentieth century. The Doyles moved to Torrington in 1883, according to Ellen Doyle, and later, the next year, bought the old Isaac Catlin place on Maple Street from Amos Bishop. Here is where Miss Doyle lived most of her life, a span of over ninety-one years. Her love for children developed as she mothered her three brothers, William, Edward and Francis, as well as her nephew, Neil, who lived with the elder Doyles, and her niece, Frances, who summered at the Doyle farm, and followed her aunt into teaching.

"Nellie," as she was known to family and friends, did not plan to pursue a career in teaching; in fact, she vowed not to do so. However, that vocation was thrust upon her when she agreed to substitute at the North Street School in Litchfield in 1901, when she was only eighteen years old. Six years later, in 1907, she was appointed to teach in the Milton District School, and she remained there for almost forty years, only leaving temporarily to nurse her ailing parents.

In the early 1900's the district plan called for a teacher to place pupils at the level determined as best suited to their age and ability. Miss Doyle adhered to this course of action until the new superintendent secured for her a syllabus of the curriculum in the New York schools. Adapting this to the requirements of a one room school, she was able to establish standards for the material to be covered at different grade levels. What a monumental task that must have been for one with little formal education in teaching, although she did attend Normal School later in her teaching career. She was wise enough to expand the curriculum to incorporate life experiences shared by students at all grade levels.

Former students attested to the fact that she was much more than a teacher; she was attuned to their individual capabilities and needs and the safe repository of family secrets. One student wrote to her, "I return thanks for the patience you have had in instructing my infant mind with wisdom and knowledge..." and later in the letter, "I love you next my parents, brother and sister and near relatives as every child ought to love those who have borne with their childish freaks and inexperience." Miss Doyle instilled moral values and fostered good study habits in her pupils, but was ready to temper discipline with humor when the situation called for it. She encouraged a love for music, arts and drama as well as serving as a referee in the children's games. Her depths of compassion were called into play when Virginia and Stephen Sutton, Mercy Birge's grand-niece and grand-nephew, came from England to escape World War II. They attended Milton School while living with their aunt and family. Miss Doyle's special attention to their feelings of fear and loneliness helped them blend into the school life, so that they still recall those years with great affection.

The chapter on "Schools" in this history is full of glowing memories by former students of their years under Miss Doyle's tutelage.

To illustrate what kind of individual she was we have only to look at excerpts from her list of things she liked and disliked. She liked: flowers, especially yellow; the smell of burning leaves; autumn and spring foliage; old people and children; pretty china; research; travel; theater; books and reading. On her "dislike" list were: big crowds; fussy things; drab surroundings; pretense; exploitation of children; social climbers; and parents who don't see that their children get enough sleep!

After teaching for thirty-nine years in Milton, Miss Doyle went along with her pupils to Litchfield Center School when the Milton School was closed in 1946 because of declining enrollment. In Litchfield she taught eighth-grade English and Social Science until her final retirement in 1952. Much of her time after retirement was spent poring over records in the town archives, the Litchfield Historical Society and the Connecticut Historical Society while researching information about Milton for this history. The writers are deeply indebted to her for the reams of material which she amassed and the enthusiasm she instilled in others, particularly the Milton Woman's Club, to finally complete a history of Milton. She also continued writing and giving radio talks on the history and folk lore of Litchfield County.

Ellen Doyle died on October 3, 1974, at the age of ninety-one, and is buried in St. Anthony's Cemetery in Litchfield. She gave an invaluable gift to those who knew her in her encouragement to see the goodness in all people, her joy in living and delight in learning. Barbara Gray Gill, who kept in touch with her until her death, recalls that in her last letter Miss Doyle wrote, "Live in my heart and pay no rent..." — a beautiful memorial to her indomitable spirit.

As almost an aside among the "Milton History Papers" is the following by Miss Doyle written before a Christmas program in the Hall, giving the teacher's viewpoint — in anticipation of Christmas exercises, children would ask, "Are we going to be on the stage?"

The stage was in the Milton Hall across the Green from the schoolhouse. Costumes, wings, halos, et cetera, were assembled year after year...

"Costumes to the right of us;
Costumes to the left of us;
Costumes in front of us;
Can we live thro' it?
Stormed at both noon and night,
'Would those pants be too tight?'
'This purple skirt all right?'
'Oh, I shall look a fright!'
On toward the festival!
We *had* to do it.

"One Nativity scene stands out in my mind - Setting - Creche - H.8. lighting - Stage suitable - Annunciation - Describe - Manger scene - Shepherds - Kings - David costumes - Perhaps a velvet tea cozy for a turban - spirit."

Those are the words of a weary teacher and stage manager! Often Miss Doyle would be up late, night after night sewing and re-fitting and mending costumes for the "show"; we never appreciated all the work and effort and energy she put into each year's production.

The Duggan Family

The James Duggan (pronounced Dug' an) house is on Saw Mill Road, number 21, at the corner south of the Wilbur Haviland-James McKinney house. Walter E. Vaill, Milton historian, said that this "corner house" was originally owned by Jeremiah or John Griswold, and owned by James Duggan in 1876. It is the Isaac Baldwin house. James Duggan also owned, around 1875, the Haviland-McKinney house as well as land around the Elizabeth Gauger house (49 Saw Mill Road). Some of the Duggan family still lived in the corner house in the 1930's.

One of James and Mary Duggan's five children was Amy — Mrs. Amy Duggan Archer Gilligan. She taught at Milton School and in early 1890 attended New Britain Normal School. Later she became a bookkeeper for a New Haven firm. She owned the Archer Home for the Elderly and Indigent in Windsor, Connecticut. The following is excerpted from an article in the February 1975 *Yankee Magazine*, entitled "Not That Sweet Mrs. Gilligan," written by Mary Louise Kitsen:

"Mrs. Gilligan was probably the most highly-respected, well liked and attractive homicidal maniac in the area of Hartford and Windsor, and perhaps in Connecticut. She was an attractive lady with dark hair and large dark eyes and a pleasing smile who was active in community affairs and attended church regularly."

Amy Duggan Archer Gilligan

The victim who put an end to her homicidal career, Franklin Andrews, died May 30, 1914. A day or two after his funeral his sister went through his personal belongings. She found a letter to him from Amy Gilligan requesting a loan of $1000. The sister decided that she had a right to the money and hired a lawyer. Amy Gilligan admitted that Mr. Andrews had loaned her $500, but the lawyer was never able to collect the money.

An investigation led by State's Attorney Hugh Alcorn, Sr. revealed that Amy Gilligan had purchased quantities of arsenic; it also revealed that forty-eight people died at the Archer Home between 1911 and 1916, including Archer and Gilligan, her husbands. The body of Franklin Andrews was exhumed and arsenic was found. Amy Gilligan was arrested for murder, pleaded innocent, was found guilty and sentenced to hang.

Because of a legal flaw, a new trial was held. In June 1919, Amy Gilligan changed her mind and pleaded guilty to a charge of second-degree murder. Both she and the State of Connecticut were ready to end the case without a hanging, if possible. Amy Gilligan was given a life sentence and taken to the state prison in Wethersfield where women were held. In 1924 she was again in court, this time for a sanity hearing. Several Milton neighbors testified to her mental instability. She was judged insane and committed to Connecticut Valley Hospital where she died in 1962 at the age of eighty-nine.

There was an unexpected sequel to this story: Joseph Kesselring, a playwright, decided to write a play based on the events. He made the woman older and gave her a sister and wrote it as a comedy. The play he wrote, which was based on Amy Duggan who once lived in the house on Saw Mill Road in Milton, was called *Arsenic and Old Lace*. It has become a classic and is a natural for summer theater.

Few houses and few villages have as colorful a history to relate as this one of the Duggan family of Milton, Connecticut.

Reverend Irving J. Enslin

Rev. Irving J. Enslin, pastor of Milton Congregational Church, ca.1959

A true man of God came to minister to the Milton Congregational Church in 1939. He came from Litchfield where he and his wife lived with their son, Francis I. Enslin, principal and English teacher at Litchfield High School. Rev. Enslin was retired at that time from a pastorate of twenty-seven years at the First Baptist Church in Derry, New Hampshire.

He came to Milton to fill the pulpit for the month of December 1938 after Miss Frances S. Walkley retired. He was hired April 1939 as settled pastor and stayed for twenty-three years.

Having no automobile, Rev. Enslin rode a bicycle up and down the Litchfield hills to Milton in the performance of his pastoral duties. However, on Sunday mornings his son Francis drove him to Milton for the service and stayed to take him home; that is, except on Children's Day when Francis went for a long walk. As an English teacher he found it too painful to listen to the singsong poetry recited by the children.

A quiet, sincere, well-educated, well-loved and caring man, Rev. Enslin gave inspiring sermons from the pulpit of the Milton Church. He had a thorough knowledge of the background of the Bible which he imparted to his congregation. His wife, the former Elizabeth Houston, joined the Ladies Aid Society and, although not active socially, supported its efforts.

While Mr. Enslin was here the church joined the United Church of Christ, the sheds alongside the church were removed, the church was electrified, two gas stoves for heating were installed, the parsonage was sold, the church was painted inside and out, and the roof was reshingled. He was here in August 1948 at the time of the church's one hundred fiftieth anniversary and led the celebration.

He retired from the Milton Church at the end of 1961. A farewell party was held for him February 1962 at the Milton Public Hall with nearly every member of the community in attendance.

Reverend William George Fennell, D.D.

William George Fennell (pronounced Fen nell') was born just over the line from East Cornwall in Goshen on November 15, 1859. His parents came from Wiltshire, England. He grew up in the East Cornwall area, attending District School No. 17. When he was seven years old his parents moved to a house at the top of Great Hill in East Cornwall, a house later known as the "Fennell Place." At thirteen he played the organ at church and planned to pursue a vocation in music. Instead he turned to the ministry.

He taught one term in the "Hardscrabble" school in Warren when he was seventeen for four dollars a week and board. At the end of the term he enrolled in the Connecticut Literary Institute at Suffield, Connecticut and graduated in 1880. Following this he taught for a short time in other schools in the state and entered Colgate University in the fall of 1881, graduating in 1885. He was helped financially by the Connecticut Baptist Education Society.

Dr. Fennell was raised up in the East Cornwall College Street Baptist Church and became pastor of the Baptist Church in Sidney, New York, staying there as supply minister for four and one-half years.

On June 30, 1885, Dr. Fennell married Inez Clarine Warner of Suffield and they had two daughters, Guinivere and Marjorie Lo. After his marriage, he attended Colgate Theological Seminary in Hamilton, New York, later going to Middletown, Connecticut as pastor, and then to the First Baptist Church in Meriden.

Dr. Fennell was a popular public speaker, a hard worker. He published a historical discourse and was editor of a series of lessons for the American Baptist Publication Society. He was a bright man, well-liked, with many accomplishments and honors, one of the foremost preachers in the Baptist denomination. He was elected President of the Connecticut Baptist Education Society.

In 1877 he began to preach an annual sermon at the East Cornwall Church and continued to do so for nearly forty years. The summer Sunday each year when he came to preach was known as "Fennell Sunday," a time of fellowship, old-home-day events, a reunion of old friends and neighbors including Mr. Fennell's boyhood friends, and a time to hear a delightful sermon. About two hundred people came to these services and stayed to picnic. They came from East Cornwall, Goshen, Milton, Litchfield and other cities and towns in the state, and even as far away as Philadelphia.

On August 21, 1894, a Wednesday, there was a special gathering at the College Street church, a roll call and prayer meeting at which Dr. Fennell, then of Meriden, gave the closing address.

From Meriden Dr. Fennell went to Newark, New Jersey, and then to the Asylum Avenue Baptist Church in Hartford. He died in Hartford, February 1917. At the time of his death he was chaplain of the Connecticut State Senate.

Instead of the usual Fennell Sunday on August 5, 1917, there was a memorial service to Dr. Fennell, attended by a host of his friends. Another memorial service, the last one, was held the summer of 1947.

The East Cornwall Baptist Church fell into disrepair and was not used for a number of years. Eventually it became too dilapidated to repair, and in 1949 the building was sold and taken down. A house now stands on the site.

The Fennell house at the top of Great Hill was the Baptist parsonage for many years. One family, Rev. Alfred H. Stock and his wife and three daughters, remembered it lovingly. Mr. Stock came to the church as pastor in March 1903. The youngest daughter, Caroline, said, "I loved that home." Another daughter, M. Adaline, in her "Recollections" described the house as "...a charming old white farm house from which ground studded with grey rock sloped away, later being transformed into an old-fashioned garden... Between the house and barn was the well with its long sweep." She went on, "The house was found to be made up of the usual large kitchen and pantry with the essential attached woodshed, a combined sitting and dining room, down a step to the parlor, but in addition a downstairs bed room and a small room for Father's study." This house was taken down years later.

The name of William Fennell is still held in high regard in these parts.

Information comes from Rev. A.G. Hibbard's History of Goshen and History of East Cornwall Area by Harriet Lydia Clark and Andrew Miles Clark Pikosky.

Jeremiah Griswold

Born in 1713, son of John and Mabel Boardman Griswold, Jeremiah Griswold married in 1734/5 Hannah Gibbs, and they had four children including sons Asahel and John. John, born in 1758 and married to Rhoda Wetmore, built the first model of an ironclad vessel which he tested on Milton Pond. He never secured a patent for this invention.

Jeremiah came from New Milford to Bantam where he bought land on or near Deer Island as early as 1730. He came to Milton around 1749 and bought one hundred acres of land from Joseph Gillette where the Welch-Vaill-Hart house is today. This was his first land holding here. He sold the property to Lt. Jehiel Parmalee who had the house built, probably by Oliver Dickinson, Jr., in 1774 and whose heirs sold it and the property to David Welch in 1784. Like Justus Seelye and David Welch, Jeremiah was a trader in land and anything else that sold well.

He was a wheelwright and miller, as were most of the Griswold family, and made wooden waterwheels, pulleys and power machinery and built dams on the Marshepaug for power.

The Griswold family has been traced back to 1300 in England. Jeremiah was the great-great-great-grandfather of Walter E. Vaill, and several families in Milton have Griswold ancestry in their lines.

Jeremiah Griswold died March 29, 1790, and is buried in

Milton Cemetery. His stone is missing, but he is listed in Charles Payne's book of burials in the Town of Litchfield.

Jeremiah Guild and Alban Guild

One of three children of Jeremiah and Elinor/Eleanor Evarts Guild, (rhymes with child) Jeremiah was born in Middlefield, CT, September 4, 1746, and died in Warren (then part of Milton Society) on January 30, 1822. He married first Hannah Hale/Hall, daughter of Ebenezer, on January 15, 1775. They had nine children, including son Alban, before Hannah died in Warren in 1800 at age forty-four. Towards the end of that year Jeremiah married Lucinda Fenton; four more children were born of that union. Jeremiah and his two wives are buried in Milton Cemetery.

When he was young, Jeremiah lived with his widowed mother in Middlefield. He loved the sea and studied navigation and became a sailor, making several voyages on trading ships sailing to the West Indies. Later he was owner and captain of a sloop in which he made several more trips to the West Indies. He served in the Revolutionary War and was taken prisoner along with his brother Samuel when the British seized and burned his vessel. He was imprisoned at Halifax, Nova Scotia and later paroled.

In the spring of 1793, he bought one hundred fifty acres of land in Warren, probably from Friend Frisbie, and moved there with his family. For several years he had a prosperous charcoal business for the iron works there. Later on he bought one hundred acres from Jedidiah Strong on Blue Swamp Road.

Jeremiah was the first Guild in Milton. All of the Guild

men were "splendid workmen," so said Walter E. Vaill. Ellen M. Doyle wrote of Jeremiah that he was "an honest and upright man." He was a member of Trinity Episcopal Church and for several years was one of the wardens. He was active in the building of Trinity Church. Ellen Doyle reported that he "loved its services and although situated more than two miles from his place of worship was very regular in his attendance." She added, quoting from the Guild book, that, "the solemn rites of the burial service were performed, when on a cold blustery day, February 2, 1822, his body was committed to its last resting place, the Rev. Isaac Jones officiating, who said in his funeral discourse, that a pillar had been removed from the church militant."

Descendants of Jeremiah Guild have lived in the Milton area for several generations, and some still live here.

Alban Guild

Born in 1784 and died May 2, 1874, at ninety years of age of heart disease, Alban Guild was the son of Jeremiah and Hannah Hale/Hall Guild. He was a wagon and cabinet maker, builder of sleighs and carriages, a farmer like others in the family, and played an important part in many community activities such as charcoal production, lumber business and milling.

On June 19, 1807, he married Roxanna Dickinson, daughter of David. They had three daughters and a son David who married as his second wife Sarah Strong. She bought the Guild house on the Mill Pond in 1868, one of the oldest houses in Milton, now 122 Saw Mill Road, home of the Craig Litwins.

Alban Guild ran the Guild Tavern from about 1862 until his death. This is the house now owned by the Webster Janssen family at 542 Shear Shop Road, and the original house may date back to 1788. This was a stop on the Hartford-Poughkeepsie Turnpike. The Tavern was completely renovated in 1876 after Alban's death. He also owned land behind the store (now the house at 541 Milton Road) where he had a dam and woodworking shop on the river and where he ran a tavern, before the Guild Tavern, a "quiet respectable place," according to Walter E. Vaill. When Alban died in 1874 the Guild Tavern was run by Horatio N. Griswold, husband of Alban's granddaughter, Augusta R. Johnson. After Horatio died in 1892, the Tavern began to fail.

Alban and his wife, and Horatio Page Griswold and his wife, Augusta R. Johnson Griswold, are all buried in Milton Cemetery.

Reverend George J. Harrison

"A history of Milton would not be complete without a biographical sketch of the Reverend George J. Harrison..." This sentiment was voiced by his relative, Miss Sara Harrison of New Haven. In perusing Milton's history, one is inevitably led to the same conclusion.

New Haven claimed Rev. Harrison as a native son, as his roots went back to his birth there on March 22, 1823. His childhood was spent in New Haven where his "scholarly attainments" (again, Miss Harrison's words) were noteworthy. A Bachelor of Arts degree from Union College, followed by preparation for the ministry at Princeton Theological

Seminary, form an impressive résumé. His interest in pedagogy surfaced early as he spent some years after Seminary in teaching positions in New Haven and New York.

At the age of twenty-six, in 1849, George Harrison was wed to Elizabeth Jewett of Ridgefield, Connecticut. Again in Miss Harrison's words: "...(he) always felt himself indebted to her for a happy and successful life." She bore him eight children including a set of twins of whom one, Mary Jewett Harrison, died in 1864 at the age of less than four months. Another child, Benjamin N. Starr Harrison, was almost fourteen at the time of his death in 1873. These two children are buried in Milton Cemetery.

George Harrison accepted a call to the Milton Congregational Church in 1854 and remained there until his death nearly forty years later on Christmas Eve 1893. Early in his ministry he would walk from Litchfield to Milton via Brush Hill Road. Later his family moved into the parsonage in Milton which had been purchased from the Gibbs family by the church for his use. The parsonage remained church property until 1953 when it was sold. Noteworthy besides Mr. Harrison's long tenure was the high regard in which he was held by his wide circle of friends within the church and without. Virtues attributed to him included compassion, vivaciousness and a wonderful sense of humor which showed up in the stories he related.

His advice was often sought by the young people as well as by their parents, which was an asset when he founded the Milton Academy in 1856, only two years after coming to Milton. The diligence and scholastic fervor with which he pursued the founding and maintenance of the Academy is evident from a reading of the chapter on "Schools" in this history. The building which housed the Academy later became a blacksmith shop. It is still standing on the southeast side of the Milton Green.

It would not be fitting to conclude Mr. Harrison's biography without reference to the "Pound Parties" which were popular during his time as minister. As was the purpose of the "Wood Spells," when firewood was donated to the pastor, the "Pound Parties" were intended to augment his meager earnings as pastor. These "donation people... unsectarian and undenominational," appeared at intervals with pounds of certain food items, as well as perhaps a handmade quilt. Less welcome items included cast-off clothing, household articles and furniture. Fred H. Seelye recounted one of the Reverend Harrison's prayers, which always followed receipt of the goods. As he was kneeling, the Reverend was struck in the back by a large codfish flung at him by one of a group of rowdy, perhaps tipsy, boys who antagonized the community with their antics (their names shall remain anonymous!). The boys really felt no animosity towards Mr. Harrison and their subsequent apology was received by him with tolerance, and they became good friends. His reaction typified his generous, placid nature.

To summarize the Rev. Harrison's life one has only to review his works. The church flourished under his long and devoted pastorate, and his impact on the education of the area children was held in high regard. Walter E. Vaill described him as a "very human and lovable man, small, with snow-white hair and a short beard." Perhaps the best tribute to his life came at the time of his death: "Mr. Harrison was a Christian scholar of broad and catholic temper, the peerless Christian husband, Christian father and Christian friend, and from first to last a Christian gentleman."

Thomas Hinchliffe

Born November 29, 1832, Thomas Hinchliffe of Sheffield, England, married Anne Morris and fathered one son, who died young, and six daughters: Alice, who moved to New York; Anne, who married William Hall; Emma, who lived with her parents; Florence, married to Walter E. Seelye and mother of Norris and Fred H. Seelye; Kate, wife of Austin Page; and Mary, who went to Colorado. Alice and Emma are buried in Milton Cemetery with their parents, as are Florence and Walter Seelye. The Hinchliffes were "nice people, the daughters handsome."

Thomas Hinchliffe came from Hoadleyville to Milton in 1873 and operated the Aetna Shear Company on the site of David Welch's iron works and puddling furnace on Shear Shop Road. He was, according to Walter E. Vaill, "a great scholar with a fine library." He was also an altruistic man, interested in the welfare of his adopted hometown. In 1900 he was the largest contributor to the fund for the building of the Milton Public Hall, and he helped support other ventures and organizations in Milton.

The Shear Shop brought a number of families to Milton which increased the area's prosperity and added to the social and economic life of the community, bringing here families whose descendants remain nearby. The Sheffield-steel-lined shears produced by the Aetna shop were among the finest in the country. Several innovations which the factory introduced led to its success. The Company operated in Milton for some thirty-seven years, employing as many as thirty-seven men at a time.

Thomas Hinchliffe made business trips to New York periodically and was there when the Brooklyn Bridge had its grand opening; presumably Mr. Hinchliffe witnessed that event.

Several houses were refurbished or built for the employees of the Shear Shop and their families. The Hinchliffes themselves lived originally in a small factory house on Shear Shop Road until 1880, when Mr. Hinchliffe built a large gracious house on the hill across from and overlooking beautiful Shear Shop Pond. The house was owned by Beatrice M. McKechnie in later years and eventually fell into such disrepair that it had to be taken down.

In 1909 Thomas Hinchliffe sold the factory, house and other buildings on Shear Shop Road. He died August 12, 1912.

James H. Hurley and Jesse H. Derby

James H. Hurley came to Milton from Elizabeth, New Jersey, around 1873 to work in the Aetna Shear Shop for Thomas Hinchliffe. He was one of several men who came to work in the Shop and stayed in Milton. Born in 1850, he died in 1929 and is buried in Milton Cemetery. His wife was Theresa M. Maher, and they had a daughter, Mary F., also called May and Mamie.

When James Hurley first came to Milton he lived in the house at 541 Milton Road now owned by the Paul Deerings. Later he and his family moved to the Hugh Welch house (556 Milton Road) which is the present home of the Nesbitt family. James bought this after the death of Anson Bradley Beach in 1885. The family lived in that house for years.

Mary married Jesse H. Derby, known locally as Jet Derby, a master carpenter who built the Milton Public Hall. He was hired by the Milton Public Hall Association on October 30,

1900, to build a hall on the foundation which had been laid on October 5. The shareholders voted to "finish the building on the inside." On December 18, Edwin Dickinson took a note from the Association for $175. Jesse Derby also reportedly had a large number of glass photographic slides of scenes of Milton which were in the house on the hill where he lived but have since disappeared.

Walter E. Vaill expressed the sentiments of the Milton community when he wrote about James Hurley: "He and his wife were a welcome addition to Milton." Of Jesse Derby Mr. Vaill said, he was "a man we all liked."

James and Theresa Hurley and Jesse and Mary Derby are all buried in Milton Cemetery.

The Leatherman

The Leatherman, who is believed to have been a Frenchman named Jules Bourglay, for thirty-one years walked a three hundred fifty mile circuit so regularly that clocks could be set by his arrival at a specific place. He walked from New York to Ridgefield, Connecticut, through Danbury to this area, down to Old Saybrook and back to Ridgefield. The trip took thirty-four days. Both the papers in the Milton History material and memories of local residents document the periodic passage of the Leatherman through Milton. The "Milton History Papers" record, "...and he is known to have stopped at a rock shelter on Cat Hole Road in the Milton section." Older people have recounted seeing him and feeding him over the years.

He was dressed all in leather, his outfit weighing some sixty pounds. People speculated that he came to America from France after an unfortunate affair in which he lost a large amount of money belonging to the father of the girl he loved. The father was in the leather business. As a self-imposed penance the Leatherman took the life of hardship and wandering.

People along his route left food for him which he sometimes ate outside their homes, carrying the remains to eat later at rough fireplaces near the caves and overhangs which sheltered him. He seldom spoke, and then only in French.

He developed cancer of the mouth, was hospitalized for a short time, but left the hospital surreptitiously and continued his walking. He survived the blizzard of 1888, but not long afterwards, on March 24, 1889, was found dead in a cave near Mount Pleasant in New York. He was buried in Ossining, New York, carrying to his grave the secret of his identity and the reason for his thirty-one year ordeal.

Reverend Truman Marsh

The first rector to serve the Trinity Episcopal Parish in Milton was Rev. Truman Marsh, 1799 to 1810. He was rector here when the church was raised in 1802. He came originally in 1795, newly ordained, as visiting rector to preach part-time, five Sundays a year in the schoolhouse or private homes. St. Paul's, Bantam, shared Rev. Marsh with Milton.

Born in Litchfield on February 22, 1768, he married Clarissa Seymour, daughter of Major Moses Seymour (per gravestone in East Cemetery, Litchfield). Two of their children are buried in Litchfield's East Cemetery — Truman, who died at the age of nine months, and Delia, who was a little more than two and one-half years old when she died.

Rev. Marsh preached in New Milford and Litchfield, as well as in Milton. While at Litchfield, in 1829, he said of the Milton church, "The congregation is generally large and attentive — services half of the time," meaning that services were held half of the time in Bantam and half in Milton at that time.

By 1837 when Trinity Church was consecrated, Rev. Marsh was in ill health. He died March 27, 1851, and is buried with his wife in East Cemetery in Litchfield.

Beatrice M. McKechnie

Beatrice M. McKechnie and John O'Neill

A former Milton resident who left an indelible imprint on those who knew her from the 1920's to the 1960's was Miss Beatrice M. McKechnie. Born and raised in Scotland, she retained her Scottish burr and speech mannerisms all her life. To her, insects were "wee beasties" and "aye" was pleasanter than "yes." Her early history we know only from bits and pieces she imparted to eager listeners. She was known to have been a nanny, which could have been the reason for her coming to the United States, but in what year no one knows for sure.

Miss McKechnie said she crossed the Atlantic Ocean thirteen times. Vital statistics on her are scarce; she was born probably in the late 1870's. But we know she came to America as a young girl, perhaps in response to a job offer. Her demeanor and obvious love of art objects, reading, language and history suggest a cultured background, but that can be only speculation. Her acquisition of "objets d'art" could have resulted from her service in wealthy American homes. Her longest employment was as a nanny for Jack O'Day in New York, whose family requested that she raise him "as her own," which she did for many years. He was the brother of the three O'Day girls. Miss McKechnie treasured a life-size marble statue of Jack O'Day which occupied a prominent spot in her home.

Thomas Hinchliffe/Beatrice M. McKechnie House

She retired to a stately old home on the hillside across from Shear Shop Pond in Milton, built originally by Thomas Hinchliffe and owned then by his son-in-law, Walter Seelye. The house, which she called "Ecclefechan," was accessible only by climbing a series of stone steps. Flowers flourished in her yard with the help of local children to whom she paid pennies in return for weeding and carrying water from Shear

Shop Pond. At one time, after Miss McKechnie bought the house, Carrie Duggan of Milton lived there in the three-room apartment on the north side. Others who lived there were Charles and Delia Beeman, Jacob and Alice Ackerman, Stewart and Nettie Rydehn and Henry and Enid Lockwood.

She was not a recluse, often walking the half-mile or so to Milton Center to the Congregational Church. Walking was made even more difficult for her as she had broken her leg (she said she slipped on a banana peel) in New York. The leg was never set, or set improperly, and remained twisted for the rest of her life. This required her to rely on her cane or "sticks" for walking. Nevertheless, vanity prompted her to walk in high heels and to hide her deformity by always wearing long skirts.

She enjoyed having visitors and was famous for her New Year's Day open house "tea" when she showed off her beautiful china and goodies. Also, to the consternation of some, she was very generous in dispensing alcoholic spirits which were not normally offered in staid New England homes, especially early in the morning.

Her New Year's galas or other celebrations were usually held in the first floor dining room where she had, among other seats, a hammock. Those who attended remember the potbellied stove burning brightly in a vain effort to warm the cold corners of the highceilinged room. The room itself was a veritable museum of lovely knickknacks, embroidered pillows and doilies, books and fine china. She served delicate cookies, fruit cake and candied fruits in the continental tradition. Always present were her cat (Toby?) and bulldog, Brownie, her only children. She was a colorful entertainer, telling stories indicative of a former life strange to her audience, and quizzing the children to keep them alert. She is also remembered for the homemade candy (penuche) she gave out at Halloween.

As she was failing, she carefully marked some of her precious china pieces for Milton children, and the notes in her scratchy handwriting are treasured.

As more years went by, finding herself unable to live alone, especially with the daily task of carrying water, she eventually entered a nursing home in Warren in July 1951. Neighbors visiting her found her extremely unhappy; so the Howard Sheldon family, Edna and her son Walter in particular, took her into their home in the Center, allowing her to live out her last years there.

Jack O'Day had married a Page, and the Pages were charged with the care of Miss McKechnie. They were very glad to have her go to the Sheldons. She died there around 1964. Her body was sent to New York and was cremated after a service conducted by Reverend H. Waldo Manley, late of the Bantam and Milton Episcopal churches. Several from Milton attended the service including Lena Haviland, Edna Sheldon, Karolina Rydehn and Walter Sheldon.

Although her ashes repose in New York, Milton people claim her as their own, including the "big boys" whom she taught in Sunday School and kept in line despite being only about four feet tall and rather frail. They, like all of Milton, respected and loved her.

Jehiel Parmalee

Builder in 1774 of at least one of Milton's oldest houses, the Welch-Vaill-Hart house at 127 Saw Mill Road, Jehiel Parmalee was born in 1718, son of Joshua. He and his wife

Mary had ten children, five sons and five daughters. Jehiel died January 15, 1776, of smallpox in the Welch house where he lived.

In 1767 he came from Farmington to Milton, receiving a deed for ninety acres of land from Jeremiah Griswold. He was a Lieutenant in the Revolutionary War.

When he died, Jehiel left so many heirs that the property was split up to such an extent that it was of little use to any of them. For example, the barn was divided among three sons. Then, in 1784, the heirs sold the property to David Welch who came there to live.

Jehiel Parmalee's gravestone is the oldest one still standing in the Milton Cemetery.

Justus Seelye

Justus Seelye was one of the three earliest settlers of Blue Swamp, later called Milton. He was born in Newtown, Connecticut, around 1724, son of John and Martha Seelye. The family moved to New Milford when Justus was four or five years old, and he grew up there.

On March 10, 1746/7, Justus married Elizabeth Gibbs, daughter of Benjamin and Abigail Marshall Gibbs of Litchfield. The couple was married in Litchfield by Reverend Thomas Collins and apparently moved to New Milford where their first three sons were born. It appears that Elizabeth died sometime between 1751 and 1756 because of gaps in the births of Justus' children. He married as his second wife Phebe Bissell, who survived him. In all, Justus Seelye had twelve children. His daughter Elizabeth, married William Sprats, the well-known architect.

Justus was in Litchfield by April 13, 1752, when he purchased land from Daniel Barnes, Jr. That year he also bought property from Jeremiah Griswold, and two years later bought from George Isaac and John Marsh what is probably now the Edward A. Raymond property. He shared with the heirs of Benjamin Bissell a division of land, as recorded in the Litchfield Probate Court. Throughout his life he carried on numerous land transactions; his name appears on many documents in the Litchfield Town records.

In 1762 Justus Seelye enlisted in the Connecticut Forces, Col. Archibald McNeil's Company, in the French and Indian War. He appealed for compensation from the General Assembly in early 1775 for hardship due to the service. Three years later he was awarded £50. Following his discharge, he built a saw mill at the corner of Saw Mill and Blue Swamp Roads in 1769. He also dammed the river to form the pond known then as Seelye Pond.

Seven of Justus Seelye's sons served in the Revolutionary War. The family left Milton before 1800.

From his saw mill Justus Seelye supplied building materials in 1771/2 for the Tapping Reeve house on South Street in Litchfield where the first Law School was located.

Justus Seelye died in 1795 and is buried in Milton Cemetery on Blue Swamp Road. His tall reddish stone, which is missing, read simply: "Justus Seelye 1795."

Reverend Hiram Stone

Rev. Hiram Stone, rector of Trinity Episcopal Church

One of this area's best loved ministers was the Rev. Hiram Stone, who resigned as Army chaplain in February 1876 to ascend the pulpits of St. Paul's Episcopal Church in Bantam and Trinity Episcopal Church in Milton. He had charge of these two parishes for thirty years, from November 1873 to September 1874 on an interim basis, and then from July 1875 to November 2, 1903, as full pastor.

Born in Bantam on July 25, 1824, he spent his young years in that community. He studied at Trinity College and was one of the earliest graduates of Berkeley Divinity School. In October 1853 he was ordained as Deacon of the Episcopal Church by Bishop Brownell, and Priest the following year by Bishop Williams. His earliest parish was St. John's Church in Essex, Connecticut.

In 1855 he was the first missionary of the General Board of Missions to be sent to Kansas to the first Episcopal Church in that part of the country. Because of ill health, he returned to New England, whereupon he took charge of the Bantam and Milton parishes.

Described by Walter E. Vaill as being "tall, (with a) long black beard; liked by everyone," he was married first on February 21, 1864, and had at least one son, Lewis H., born in

1866, and a daughter, Carrie L., who married John Brock and died about seven years later leaving three small children. He married a second time while he was rector here, and of that marriage he reportedly said that his (new) wife was "so much in love that when she was married she turned to stone!"

Rev. Stone was a School Visitor (an official school evaluator) in 1894. At various times he gave interesting lectures on the Mound Builders of the west, from his own experience.

At the time of Trinity Church's one-hundredth anniversary in 1902, Rev. Stone gave the Centennial address, remarking that though Trinity was "in feeble condition now, the Church has witnessed the passing away of three generations who have worshipped here." He also stated that, "not a single word or unfriendly altercation" had passed between him and "any member of the Church or community," a remarkable assertion.

It was said of him that the friendship and respect felt for him in both Bantam and Milton was not confined to any class or denomination. At the Centennial celebration at Trinity he was presented with a silver loving cup, much to his surprise, on which was inscribed: "Rev. Hiram Stone. A loving token from his brethern of the Litchfield Archdeaconry, on the centenary of Trinity Church, Milton, and on the 25th anniversary of his rectorate, September 3, A.D., 1902."

In his daughter Carrie's obituary are the words, "...it is no exaggeration to say that there is no man in this vicinity who is more loved and respected." The Milton community was most fortunate to have Rev. Hiram Stone and Rev. George Harrison here at the same time, two exceptional, upstanding gentlemen.

Rev. Stone died April 3, 1911.

Reverend Herman Landon Vaill

The Vaill family figured prominently in the history of Milton. One of its early members in this area was the Rev. Herman (pronounced Harmon) Landon Vaill, son of Benjamin and Sylvia Landon Vaill, who was born December 7, 1794. His marriage to Flora Gold, daughter of Deacon Benjamin Gold of Cornwall, in January 1823, produced at least six daughters and three sons. Two of his sons ran the *Winsted Herald*, as did another member of his family in later years.

The Rev. Vaill taught in the Foreign Mission School in Cornwall, the Goshen Academy in Goshen, Connecticut, and the Morris Academy in Morris, Connecticut, where John Brown, the abolitionist, was one of his scholars and later wrote to Rev. Vaill from prison. At one point in his career Rev. Vaill lived on the Torrington Road where he had a school. The Vaill house there became one of the stations on the Underground Railroad. For awhile he was a School Visitor in this area. He served as third pastor of the old Torringford Meetinghouse and first pastor of the new church there, before coming from Cornwall to Milton in June 1849.

During the two years that he was at the Milton Congregational Church he lived in the house presently owned by Walter C. Sheldon. In later years he lived in the old Vaill home, built in 1744 and considered one of the oldest houses in the Town of Litchfield, on the corner of Brush Hill Road and Knox Road.

The following anecdote is found in the "Milton History Papers": "Mr. Vaill's white horse roamed the Milton roads at will and one Halloween night received a coat of green paint at the hands of some of the more daring of the village young men. The next morning, the pastor's son, Joseph, who later became the editor of the *Winsted Herald*, was out 'with a pail of soapsuds and a broom' in an effort to clean the poor animal."

Known for his piety and elocution, it is said of him that, "The eloquence of Herman Vaill / Would make the stoutest sinner quail."

Walter E. Vaill, his grand-nephew, spoke of him as a thin, homely man but witty. Upon his death in 1870 he was buried in West Cemetery in Litchfield.

Walter Edward Vaill

One of Milton's best known historians and genealogists was Walter Edward Vaill. He was born in Marquette in Upper Michigan "on top of a copper mine" (his words) on July 21, 1865, son and only child of Dr. Charles H. and Rosa Peebles Welch Vaill. He

Walter E. Vaill, Milton historian

died in Milton on May 24, 1960, when he was nearly ninety-five years old and is buried in Milton Cemetery in the Welch lot. His great-great-grandparents were David and Irene Marsh Welch. David Welch of New Milford was one of the three earliest settlers of Milton around 1740, and its first nailmaker. Walter was the great-great-great-grandson also of another early settler, Jeremiah Griswold; this made him the sixth generation to own the Milton land where the house is located, at the "Y" of Saw Mill and Milton Roads, and the fifth generation to live in the house, which is still owned by Welchs — Reeves Welch Hart, Jr. and his sister's family. The house was built by Jehiel Parmalee in 1774 on land originally owned by Jeremiah Griswold. David Welch bought the house from the heirs of Jehiel Parmalee in 1784.

While the family lived in Michigan, Walter remembered seeing deer and bear, killed by hunters, on the Vaill front veranda. When he was five years old the family moved back to Milton, and this is where he spent most of the rest of his life.

Dr. Charles Vaill was an assistant surgeon in the regular army with the rank of Captain in the Civil War. He was connected to the well known Rev. Herman L. Vaill. Walter was also descended from the Landon, Griswold, Marsh and Seymour families. He was particularly proud of his Griswold line which connected him to several families in Milton and to an ancient British family. He later traced the Welch family back to 1637, to Thomas Welch of Hertfordshire, England, who was one of the first to settle both in New Haven, 1638, and in Milford, 1639. The Welchs were prosperous people.

As a boy Walter started his formal schooling at the Milton Academy. He was a lively child, a bit of a troublemaker, though never malicious, enjoying woods and fields and rivers more than the schoolroom. For a short time he attended the Yale Art School where he studied art ("for my own amusement") and drafting. Besides history, local and world, Walter was a prolific reader, professional commercial draftsman, pattern, design and mold maker, talented artist and genealogist, as well as citizen of the world. His memory was amazing because his interest in the world and in people was so large. He also had a great wit, sometimes caustic and a bit devious, but always present, with a deep hearty laugh, which helped him through sad and difficult times in his life.

He married Sarah A. Murray of Waterbury on October 30, 1892; she died September 1934. Although they never had children of their own, Walter, known affectionately as "Uncle Willie," enjoyed the youngsters of Milton. He used to have wiener roasts for them and would have the boys help set fire to big brush piles and burn them, something he enjoyed himself. He spent time in the summer cutting weeds and brush in Milton Cemetery, letting the children help to keep the cemetery neat. His family has its own lot surrounded by a fence of large granite slabs.

Not only did Walter Vaill have an immense interest in history at all levels, he also left behind extensive handwritten records and genealogies, all painstakingly copied out by hand, and many fine, intricate scale drawings of houses and other buildings. In his house he had several portraits of Welch and Griswold ancestors, as well as wonderful French engravings, a number of rare Latin books (some printed as early as 1500 A.D.), and excellent pen and ink drawings of Milton buildings and places which were prized. Unfortunately, some of these treasures appear to be gone now.

He experimented with designs etched in pieces of oak tree fungus with a steel point. As the fungus aged, tannin from the fungus came through to make the pierced pictures appear to be sepia prints. His lively mind led him to this sort of innovation.

He was eclectic, fascinated with all facets of life and learning, and his love for and understanding of Milton and its people was often quite touching. Those of us who knew him will never forget him. Others have benefitted from his accomplishments. Much of this history comes from records which he kept.

Frances Sarah Walkley

Frances S. Walkley, pastor of Milton Congregational Church, ca. 1940

A remarkable woman came to Milton in June 1924 as minister to Milton Congregational Church, a woman none of us who knew her would ever forget, Frances Sarah Walkley. She stayed here as pastor for more than fourteen years, until December 1938, serving not only the Milton church but the whole community with much ability and success, and she left her special mark on a generation of youngsters in Milton.

Miss Walkley was born in Plantsville, Connecticut, December 16, 1859; she died January 28, 1951. She was the daughter of Jonathan and Frances Marie (Hayes) Walkley. Her mother died when she was three weeks old. Her father, who enlisted in the Service, died on the Fourth of July, 1862, when his daughter was two and one-half years old. At first she was cared for by different relatives until after her father died, when she was raised by his favorite sister, Sarah Walkley Stow, who cherished her as a daughter throughout her life.

Following an accident when she was young, Miss Walkley had trouble with her eyes, which continued the rest of her life. As a child, she was in delicate health and therefore had no regular schooling. She did attend Sally Low's Academy for a short time. Remembering those days, she always spoke of a phrase in a prayer which the principal, Mr. McLaughlin, used again and again: "Help us to live this coming day as we shall wish we had lived when we meet Thee in Thy Kingdom." At another period of her life when she was not well, she said the Twenty-third Psalm over and over and credited it with helping restore her health.

She was a student at the New England Conservatory of Music for two years, afterwards teaching piano as an avocation as long as she lived. She continued to practice one-half hour a day until her final illness. Her favorites included "The Moonlight Sonata" and Mendelssohn's songs, such as "Songs Without Words." She and her sister, Mrs. W. H. Cummings, enjoyed playing two-piano pieces together.

At sixteen she showed signs of being an excellent teacher. She caught the attention of a lively Sunday School class of boys in Plantsville by teaching them basic astronomy. She could always make learning a pleasure because she never "recognized the philosophy of drudgery," as her niece, Frances Walkley Cummings wrote.

One of her methods of teaching Sunday School was to have her pupils memorize Bible verses and the books of the Bible, a method she used in Milton with much success, judging from the memories of those who can still recite them. She also devised a "Brief Outline of the Life of Christ" in the form of a cross, and another in the form of steps, which were used in Milton and elsewhere.

Miss Walkley was a student at the School for Christian Workers in Springfield, Massachusetts, later Springfield College, graduating in 1895. She stayed on to teach there for two years, then began the church work which she continued for the rest of her life. She was traveling secretary in Sunday School work in Erie County, New York; for five years she was caller and Sunday School worker in the United Church of

New Haven. The years 1904 through 1907 were spent in New York with the State Sunday School Association. At that time she developed a long and serious illness and was unable to work until 1910, when she became Superintendent of the Junior Department of the Church School in Center Church in Hartford.

During her lifetime she kept notebooks of her travels and of what she saw. She made three trips abroad: 1912 to Italy from January to September; 1914 she and Miss Minnie Dougherty (life-long friend) traveled through Palestine on donkey-back; from August 1926 through January 1927 she was in England, Western Europe and Poland, where her nephew, Earle R. Cummings, was comptroller of the YMCA.

In the summer of 1915 she began preaching at a parish in Belfast, Maine, and spent three summers there, and four winters in the Blue Hill, Maine, church. She was also in Robbinston, Maine for the summers of 1916, 1917, and two years in the parish of Gayesville, Vermont.

She came to Milton in June 1924 and stayed here until her retirement in 1938, except for the summer in Poland. The church here in Milton presently opens Palm Sunday through the end of December, so Miss Walkley had the winter months for her own pursuits. It was her custom to start a library wherever she went to preach, and Milton was no exception. She began it with contributions from friends and others, and it grew well. Housed at first in the parsonage, it was later moved to the gallery of the church and open to the whole community. She also grew a multitude of flowers at the parsonage and established the memorial friendship garden on the east side of the Milton church with plants which parishioners gave in memory of loved ones. The church was thoroughly renovated early in her ministry; it was reopened August 1925 with a special service.

Though never ordained, Miss Walkley did calling, gave excellent and uplifting sermons, took an active part in social organizations and events in the community and worked with the children and young people who were her special interest. Social activities for them were centered in Milton while she was here. Well remembered are the "cootie parties" and hot dog roasts and other entertainments at the parsonage. She had the Honey Bee Club for the children, Camp Fire Girls, Boys' Club, Sewing Club, among others, and Children's Day programs which were original and wonderful. For years she led a choir of village girls, an excellent one. She always had the ready ear for anyone in trouble.

To Miss Walkley there were no juvenile delinquents, just restless, sometimes naughty, children who needed something to do; she gave them something to do.

She spent the last years of her life in her girlhood home in Plantsville, caring for her sister who died in 1944. She then kept the house for her nieces and nephews and their children who loved to come home to "Aunt Fan." Retirement kept her busy; she was active in the Plantsville church, doing calling among other things. She also kept up her music and worked in her gardens. Her niece Frances Cummings said she had an "amazing capacity for friendship" and knew no barriers between herself and others. She loved people, loved having friends and was herself a good friend.

Her niece, Florence Cummings Persons, lived with her in the Plantsville home, taking care of her, until she was hospitalized with her final illness. Her sight was failing in the last months of her life, but she never became bitter about it. She was survived by two nieces and three nephews, and countless friends.

David Welch

As early as the year 1753 David Welch, along with Jeremiah Griswold and Justus Seelye, came from New Milford to the western frontier area, West Farms or Blue Swamp, later called Milton.

Son of John and Deborah Ferris Welch, David was born in New Milford January 3, 1725. On December 6, 1758, he married Irene Marsh, daughter of Captain William Marsh of Litchfield. They had one son, John, born in 1759.

David Welch's first land here in Milton was probably the piece he bought from Justus Seelye in November 1753. He also bought fifty acres from Jeremiah Griswold sometime after 1749. In 1765 he bought fifty acres from Jeremiah Griswold where the present Reeves W. Hart, et al, house stands. This Welch deeded back to Griswold the following year; and in 1767 Griswold sold it, with dwelling and barn, to Lt. Jehiel Parmalee. This dwelling is not the one standing now, which is believed to have been built in 1774. Later, around 1784, David Welch bought out the heirs of Lt. Parmalee, including the present house, and moved there. He lived there some twenty years.

Earlier, about 1756, he built the house now known as the Edward A. Raymond house. When he moved to the house at the fork of the Milton-Cornwall Road and Saw Mill Road, David Welch gave the other (Raymond) house to his son. After his father's death, son John gave the Saw Mill Road house to his son Garrett P. Welch upon his marriage in 1823/25.

The Welchs were prosperous people who valued

learning, books, manners. David was the first nailmaker in Milton; he started the iron business here, procuring from Salisbury the finest quality of iron ore in the country, from Ethan Allen. David Welch had a puddling furnace (forge) on Shear Shop Road. He also had a store in his house in the Center. He was a land dealer, as were Jeremiah Griswold and Justus Seelye.

Before the Revolutionary War, David Welch held a Captain Commission from the Legislature. In April 1775 he was appointed Captain of the 4th Company and Second Major of the 1st Connecticut Regiment. He was in New York the summer and fall of 1775 at Lake George, Lake Champlain and St. Johns. He was called out with other Milton men in the French and Indian War.

His interest in politics led him to be Selectman of the Town of Litchfield five times. He served the Milton community and Town of Litchfield in several capacities, among them the drawing up and signing of the petition which set Milton apart as the Third Ecclesiastical Society of Litchfield. He was also State Senator, Justice of the Peace and Judge.

He died March 26, 1815, and is buried in Milton Cemetery.

Jonathan Wright

Jonathan Wright was born March 13, 1746, and died April 15, 1836, aged ninety. He was the son of Samuel and Martha Knowles (Shaw) Wright. In 1764 he came from East Haddam to Litchfield when he was eighteen years old. He settled in Blue Swamp (Milton) where he had a deed in 1798 from Moses Barn(e)s. Three years after coming to Milton he

Ens. Jonathan Wright

married Leah Bissell by whom he had eight children. After Leah's death at age thirty-five, Jonathan married Tryphena Tracey in 1784. They had two daughters. Tryphena died in 1786 when the second daughter was born. Two years later Jonathan married as his third wife Thankful Landon. Four children were born of that union, so Jonathan fathered fourteen children in all.

He built and lived in the house where Harold and Frances Bunnell live (489 Maple Street). He also built and lived in another house, the present home of Dewey and Elizabeth Kizzia on the west side of Saw Mill Road at the corner of Blue Swamp Road, which Jonathan owned in 1816. In the west corner of the garden at that house there was a forge where nails were made, probably by the last nailmaker in Milton, Captain Gross.

Jonathan was an Ensign in the Revolutionary War. Among the "Milton History Papers" is a copy of a tax imposed on a chaise owned by Jonathan Wright, who had the first horse-drawn chaise in Milton.

When he died he left a chest of papers, accounts and letters which are of much interest locally and to which this History is indebted. Family members emigrated to New York State and Ohio and were instrumental in building up those states.

Jonathan served on several committees and commissions in the Town of Litchfield. He and his wives are all buried in Milton Cemetery.

Reverend Asahel Nettleton, D.D.

A letter dated October 5, 1976, to Milton Congregational Church member Ingrid Nesbitt from John Thornbury of Winfield, Pennsylvania, gives a brief insight into the career and importance of one of Milton's early ministers, Asahel Nettleton, born in 1783, died in 1844.

Mr. Nettleton, an evangelist, was sent to Milton by Rev. Lyman Beecher in 1813 to rouse the church from an apathy into which it had sunk. He came at a time when the Milton Congregational Church was floundering, the result of poor ministering by preceding pastors, loss of members and financial problems. During his time in Milton he brought twenty-seven converts into the church and helped to revitalize it.

Dr. Nettleton was considered one of the great preachers of his day, counting among his close friends the Rev. Lyman Beecher, who said of him, to quote from Mr. Thornbury's letter, "I regard him as beyond comparison, the greatest benefactor which God has given this nation; and through his influence in promoting pure and powerful revivals of religion is destined to be one of the greatest benefactors of the world." The words are somewhat extravagant, but they show the high esteem in which he was held during his career.

A biography of Rev. Nettleton published in 1844 reports that initially few came to church after his arrival here, and there was even a question about his being invited to one of the parishioner's homes for dinner following the service, an embarrassing situation. However, "a gentleman," per Mr. Thornbury's letter, unnamed, finally did ask him to his home.

There was a revival of spirit and a renewal of faith and increased church attendance while Dr. Nettleton was in Milton. In 1832, he was among those who founded the Hartford Theological Seminary.

Reverend Wesley Eugene Page

The Rev. Wesley Eugene Page, born in Brownsville, Maine, graduated from Bates College, Maine, and from Yale Divinity School. While attending Yale, he served as a student minister in the Milton Congregational Church, coming from New Haven on Saturday and returning on Monday. He was ordained in Milton in June 1897. He came to Milton as pastor in May 1896 and stayed until December 1903. On May 28, 1896, there was a reception for him to which the community was invited.

He married Mary Page, daughter of Milton's Samuel D. Page, deacon of the Congregational Church, on May 31, 1899, and they lived in the parsonage.

He was pastor here when the Church celebrated its one hundredth anniversary in August 1898, and the pamphlet on the Church's history which Rev. Page wrote is still in use.

He left Milton to preach in Ellsworth, Connecticut, in December 1903, and retired in 1936.

Reverend Solomon Palmer

The son of Daniel and Elizabeth Hillyer Palmer, Solomon Palmer was born in 1709, a native of Branford, Connecticut. He graduated from Yale in 1729 and married Abigail Foote. They had at least two daughters, Sarah (Sally) who married James Birge, and Anna who married William Ward.

Although he never ministered here, Rev. Palmer lived in Milton on Milton Road in the old house on a rise of ground across from what is now Floren's Pond. He was pastor of the Congregational Church in Cornwall in 1741 and was ordained in August of that year. He remained there for over twelve and one-half years. Then, to the complete surprise of his congregation, one Sabbath in March 1754 he declared that his ordination was invalid because he was an Episcopalian, and he renounced his ministry among them.

At that time there were few Episcopalians in Connecticut. Rev. Palmer went to England where he was ordained as a priest of the Episcopal Church by the Bishop of Bangor. Returning to the United States, he was appointed missionary by the Society for the Propagation of the Gospel in Foreign Parts. He carried on his work in Goshen and New Milford and Litchfield and as an itinerant pastor in various areas of the western section of Connecticut.

He was the first regular rector of St. Michael's Episcopal Church in Litchfield, coming there April 23, 1749. In 1763 he went to New Haven's Trinity Church, then returned to St. Michael's in 1766 where he remained until his death.

He died December 8, 1771, and is buried in West Cemetery in Litchfield.

Reverend Joseph Dyer Prigmore

The close proximity of Yale Divinity School to many small Connecticut towns made it feasible for the churches in those towns to be supplied with student ministers to fill their pulpits. One among many of those students was the Rev. Joseph Dyer Prigmore, a native of Missouri, who came to Milton first as a student minister, and then from 1904 until 1906 as minister of his first parish. While student minister, he traveled by train from New Haven to Bantam and then walked the back way to Milton, "whistling all the way," his daughter records.

Born in Reeds, Missouri, May 6, 1871, he was a delicate child. It was said of him that he was always "at home" with everyone, easy, comfortable. Children loved him and loved to listen to his stories. He is remembered for the Boys' Club which he organized, for which he "fitted up" the room over the Milton church vestibule, closing off the gallery and putting a stove up there for winter use. Also, he started a fund for the renovation of the church which was accomplished later on.

He brought his bride, Amy Secor Davis, here in June 1905. They later had a son William and a daughter Edith Elizabeth. Rev. Prigmore and his wife were good friends with the younger members of the Milton congregation.

The Prigmores left Milton in 1906 and went to Ellsworth Falls, Maine. Rev. Prigmore died in Springfield, Massachusetts, on July 16, 1951.

Thumbnail Sketches

Isaac Baldwin - son of Horace and Rachel Marsh Baldwin, born July 15, 1800, died June 22, 1882; married Rachel who died aged forty; may have married Abigail as his second wife; Isaac and Rachel are buried in East Cemetery, Litchfield. Around 1850 Isaac owned the place at the south corner of Saw Mill Road (21 Saw Mill Road); was one of signers of first Temperance Pledge; was attorney, member of the Legislature. Isaac and Rachel had daughter, Louise, who was nurse in Civil War, was married twice and was a great friend of Rosa Vaill, mother of Walter E. Vaill. Isaac's son, Samuel, S., was attorney in Pompey, NY. Isaac belonged to Methodist Church.

Nathan Bassett - son of William and Lydia Fisher Bassett, born 1769, died October 6, 1862. Parents were from Norton, MA. Nathan married on October 29, 1793, Mehitable Buell, daughter of Ira. Their children included Samuel. Nathan was a very large, handsome man, according to Walter Vaill — a stern man, leader of the Milton Presbyterians. His land abutted the David Welch property on Milton-East Cornwall Road, and the two men had a quarrel over a small piece of land which involved lawsuits. Later on they became close friends, although they continued to argue every day. Nathan and Mehitable are buried in Milton Cemetery.

Samuel Bassett - son of Nathan and Mehitable Buell Bassett; had property on crossroad east of Malcolm Forbes' place; the house burned down and the road is overgrown now. Samuel had a saw mill there. He was "an enormous man, something of a hermit," wrote Walter Vaill.

Capt. Heman Beach - born June 23, 1813, died March 25, 1881; married twice Eliza Thomas (?) and probably Mary Kesler (?); lived on upper Maple Street at present 641 Maple Street, which was a Frisbie house, later Herman Perret's. Capt. Heman was a very quiet man, much respected in Milton. He was father of a number of children including Heman, Jr., who was tax collector for Town of Litchfield. Heman, Eliza and Mary are all buried in Milton Cemetery.

Wadham Beach - brother of Mrs. Ambler with whom he lived, lastly in house on site of present Todd residence (11 Headquarters Road), formerly schoolhouse; he played the fiddle, and when his sister would get up to dance to the music, he would put fiddle away. After sister's death, he continued to live in the house until it burned up — with him in it.

Reverend Benjamin Birge - son of Joseph and Marcella Ward Birge, born in Milton July 24, 1795, died in Lexington, KY (some records say Ohio) March 29, 1820; great-grandson of Rev. Solomon and Abigail Foote Palmer; member of St. Michael's Episcopal Church, Litchfield; was taught religion by Rev. Truman Marsh; attended Episcopal Academy, Cheshire; was accomplished scholar in several languages — Greek, Latin, Hebrew. The *Litchfield Monitor* said of him that he was "possessed of a sweetness of disposition, urbanity of manners, and amiability and dignity..." He lived in house his father built, now 499 Maple Street; was minister in Lexington.

Amos C. Bishop - son of Amos and Lois Cornwall Bishop, born June 14, 1810, died November 1, 1881; married Almira; both buried in Milton Cemetery. He was called "Deak" because his father was deacon of Milton

Congregational Church. Walter Vaill remembered him as a "little old man, kindly, with a sense of humor, very caustic." He enjoyed playing poker with friends, even when he was an old man. His place was sold to Terrence Doyle in 1883.

Hiram Bissell - son of Benjamin, born 1783, died March 6, 1876; married Beata Wetmore; they had ten children: Capt. William, Rufus, Jerome, Capt. Hiram, Garry, Benjamin (who died at age sixteen), Lucy, Lyman, Joseph and Nancy. Hiram was a "goldmine of traditions"; the oldest Freemason in the state when he died; a man of great strength who ran the iron works for the Welchs as did his sons. He and his wife are buried in Milton Cemetery.

John Bissell - son of Joel and Mercy Bishop Bissell, born December 28, 1761, died July 27, 1819; first married November, 1781 Mary Dickinson, daughter of Oliver, Jr.; they had eight children and lived in house at present 109 Shear Shop Road which he may have built; remarried on December 2, 1807, to widow Huldah O. Chapel; they had three children. John was Revolutionary War soldier. He and wives are buried in Milton Cemetery.

Warren Bissell - son of Capt. William and Amanda Jennett Bissell, ran a Sleigh Shop on Shear Shop Road for a time; bought from Jaggers and Cartelege "premises occupied for cutlery works"; lived at Seelye-Sheldon house, now 557 Milton Road.

Capt. William Bissell - son of Hiram and Beata Wetmore Bissell, born 1810 and died July 16, 1902; married third cousin, Amanda Jennett Bissell, daughter of John. William was in Civil War, 2nd CT heavy Artillery, 19th CT Infantry;

bought old David Welch house (now 530 Milton Road) from Clarissa Marsh Welch around 1858. He was a "small snappy man who had spent time in Paris — slim, handsome, had a long white beard which he had a habit of stroking, good dresser, always very courteous and kindly — grand example of gentleman of the old school, full of anecdotes" (Walter Vaill). He had several sons; four daughters and a son are buried with him and wife in Milton Cemetery. Before he bought the Welch house he lived at 109 Shear Shop Road; worked at the Welch iron works which his father, Hiram, ran.

James Blake - son of Albert and Harriet Morey Blake, born May 18, 1825, died August 14, 1916 (dates per gravestone); married May 8, 1847, Jane Seelye; lived in East Cornwall at junction of Flat Rocks Road, South Road and College Street in house now owned by Dorothy Moseley; was member of Litchfield and Cornwall Turnpike Corporation; post office was in his house for a number of years; ran large farm on property; loaned money to neighbors and evidently took land in payment, thus acquiring much more land than the original farm; sold farm to Benjamin and Ethel Bailey; had three children; was a musician and their house, which had a ballroom, was a "place to enjoy life." He was affectionately called "Uncle Jim" and was, according to Walter Vaill, a "fine man, generous, shrewd — the soul of hospitality, everybody's friend, no one better..." In later years he lost his sight and was cared for by the Baileys.

Joseph Bradley - son of Leaming and Anna Bradley; married May 24, 1798, Lucy Stoddard; daughter, Louisa, married Leonard Kenney; they were the great-grandparents of Ernest Kenney Smith. Joseph's grandfather, Abraham Bradley, was from Guilford, CT.

Capt. Solomon Buell - son of John and Mary Loomis Buell, born August 30, 1715, died March 22, 1795; married January 19, 1737, Eunice Griswold, the daughter of Jacob. Eunice was the first white child born in Litchfield; had children; second wife Jerusha (Jewett) Gillett; owned house now owned by Esty Foster at 615 Milton Road, but may not have lived in Milton; was in French and Indian War; he and Eunice are buried in West Cemetery, Litchfield. Son, Ira Buell, born 1745, died March 4, 1778; married 1767 Prudence Deming, sister of Julius. Ira inherited property on Milton Road 1768 where he lived. After his death his widow and her sister ran a tavern there according to tradition, which also states that General Lafayette stopped there.

Charles Clark - known as "Nobby"; one of the Shear Shop workers from England; "good honest citizen," per Walter Vaill; fiddler; he bought the old Carriage Shop property on Blue Swamp Road; dances were held at old paint shop; lived across the road in house, gone now (26 Blue Swamp Road), with two other families. Wife's name was Emma.

Edwin Perry Dickinson - son of Amos and Sarah Perry Dickinson, born 1821, died 1922, over one hundred years old; married Harriet E. Gilbert; one son, Gilbert A., died at age ten; another son was Ithamer; lived at present 499 Maple Street on large farm which he bought in 1849 and family maintained for over a century; came from most distinguished family in Milton, per Walter Vaill. Edwin, Harriet, Gilbert A. are all buried in Milton Cemetery.

Ithamer Dickinson - son of Edwin P. and Harriet Gilbert Dickinson, born 1854 and died 1925; married 1878 Celia A.

Pratt; one son, Gilbert E., died young; one daughter, Lulu, married William Ravenscroft; another, Edith, married Henry Ernest Axford and lived on farm. Ithamer, wife and young son are buried in Milton Cemetery.

Terrence Doyle - bought the Amos Bishop place about 1884; moved there from Torrington 1883; married Mary Harris, daughter of Moses who owned the present 43 Potash Road.

Thomas Doyle - one of Irish immigrants, came to Goshen, CT; in early 1870's bought the old Bissell, later Forbes, place (109 Shear Shop Road). In later years family owned the Catlin place on the ridge above Milton, present 566 Maple Street. This is family of Ellen Margaret Doyle.

Deacon Samuel Dudley - "Inventor of considerable renown," so say the "Milton History Papers." He invented the original diagonal roadscraper; patent model was made of this invention, which he manufactured in his barn for several years on his property just off Maple Street.

Charles Ferris - born 1804, died December 15, 1883; married Mehetible Parsons, daughter of Eliphaz; lived in house on Blue Swamp Road (now number 15); tailor by trade. He was paralyzed and used a wheelchair in later years; he and wife are buried in Milton Cemetery.

William Ferriss - lived at house now 15 Blue Swamp Road; worked at Smith's Carriage Shop; drove the hearse which was stored in a shed on the Green; born 1836, died 1905; married Almira Monroe; both are buried in Milton Cemetery.

Friend H. Frisbie - son of Noah, from Roxbury, born 1768, died August 20, 1843; married February 1, 1795, Lucy Bishop, daughter of Noah; he and daughter, Betsey, died 1826, are buried at Headquarters Cemetery, Milton. Joined Baptist Church from Episcopal Church, November 13, 1817.

John Gardner - carpenter; lived 1850-1860's up Shear Shop Road just over the line in Goshen in house, last owned by Svante Sture (Stuart) Rydehn and Karolina Rydehn (house burned in September 1946). The Gardners kept summer boarders; wife chose the difficult words for spelling school; since she always chose the same words, everyone learned them after awhile. John drowned with others off Bridgeport when boat sank.

Benjamin Gibbs - from Windsor; born 1675, died May 10, 1767; married September 16, 1708, Abigail Marshall, daughter of David; fourteen children including Gershom. Both Benjamin and Abigail are buried in West Cemetery, Litchfield.

Gershom Gibbs - son of Benjamin and Abigail Marshall Gibbs, born in Litchfield July 28, 1721, died December 29, 1776, on board prison ship *Martyn*; first white male child born in Litchfield; was soldier in the Revolutionary War, Capt. Beebe's Co.; married Tabitha Moore; lived in Milton; had at least six children. Both husband and wife are buried in Milton Cemetery.

Moore Gibbs - son of Gershom and Tabitha Moore Gibbs, born January 12, 1757, died April 15, 1834; married June 29, 1786, Patience Skeel(s); had eight children; he built house which was parsonage for Milton Congregational

Church, 563 Milton Road. Moore was a soldier in the Revolutionary War. Both Moore and Patience are buried in Milton Cemetery.

Abner G. Gilbert - born April 29, 1816, died January 20, 1906; married Roxanna O. Guild, daughter of Alban; two daughters are buried with parents in Milton Cemetery. Abner was a noted fox hunter in Milton, an exclusive class of men who hunted only foxes; lived at present 556 Milton Road.

Hobart DeLos Gilbert - son of William Henry and Ellen Gibson Gilbert, born September 25, 1858, died June 19, 1935; married first October 5, 1904, to Lucy Benson, daughter of Morton; one son died in infancy; wife died young. Hobart, called DeLos, married second March 31, 1910, Mary (Blackburn) Pepper; lived in old Granniss-Morton Benson house on Prospect Mt. Road, number 321, where her son, Gordon, and wife, Irene Benjamin Pepper, had an apartment; both DeLos and Mary were active in Milton affairs. DeLos and Lucy and infant son are buried in Headquarters Cemetery.

James Birge Gilbert - known as Jay; son of William Henry and Ellen Gibson Gilbert, born August 16, 1862, died December 10, 1935; married April 28, 1885, Lena Merriman, daughter of Joseph; lived in house his great-grandfather, James Birge, built at junction of Brush Hill Road and Maple Street, last of family to live there; was very moral man, literate, interested in and versed in Milton history, fund of information on Milton old times and people; could be relied on to play for dances at a moment's notice; pleasure to talk with; he and wife were a great asset to Milton.

William Henry Gilbert - son of Truman and Selima Birge Gilbert, born May 13, 1820, died 1884; married August 25, 1841, Ellen Gibson from Pennsylvania; was scholarly man, good conversationalist; lived in James Birge house, present 386 Maple Street.

Horatio Page Griswold - called Rash (pronounced as in ratio), son of Jarvis and Susan Page Griswold, born 1836/7, died June 29, 1892; married Augusta R. Johnson, daughter of David; 1876 lived behind house now 541 Milton Road; built annex to woodworking shop; had dam at Alban Guild's; ran Guild Tavern and was the last innkeeper in Milton. He and his wife are buried in Milton Cemetery, Blue Swamp Road.

Howell Griswold - born September 24, 1834, died January 31, 1913; married Thankful J. Smith, daughter of Anson. Howell was an expert blacksmith; made hardware; lived in Terryville in later years; two sons. He and Thankful are buried in Milton Cemetery.

Jarvis Griswold - son of John and Rhoda Wetmore Griswold, born 1800/1, died January 16, 1881; married Susan Page; he was an excellent wheelwright, skilled workman; went about country helping set up mills; both Jarvis and Susan are buried in Milton Cemetery.

John Griswold - son of Jeremiah and Hannah Gibbs Griswold, born June 29, 1758, died December 22, 1847; married August 23, 1782, Rhoda Wetmore, daughter of David; he built model of first ironclad vessel which he tested out on Milton Pond; never did anything with invention; was wheelwright; lived present 37 Saw Mill Road; soldier in French and Indian War and Revolutionary War. John's gravestone recently replaced in Milton Cemetery; Rhoda's stone is missing.

Julius Griswold - son of John and Rhoda Wetmore Griswold, born January 11, 1783, died May 13, 1868; married, first, Betsey Stewart/Stuart; married second, Asenath Hall; lived in old house on corner of Saw Mill and Headquarters Roads, gone now, on site of house formerly Malcolm P. Seymour's at 4 Saw Mill Road. Julius had "shaking palsy" and was called "Shakespeare Griswold." When he died he was buried at Headquarters instead of Milton Cemetery. Later his family decided to move his remains to Milton Cemetery. This was done by ox cart, and he now lies beside his wife.

Truman Guild - son of Jeremiah and Lucinda Fenton Guild, born April 19, 1806, died March 2, 1890; married Lamira Catlin; had at least four children; was surveyor for Perambulations of 1849. He and his wife are buried in Milton Cemetery.

Daniel Hall - son of John and Damaris Everett Hall, born August 8, 1777 and died May 22, 1862; married November 21, 1802, Desire Dickinson, daughter of Oliver, Sr.; had three sons and four daughters, including daughter Jennet/Janet (Jennie). Daniel and Desire are buried in Milton Cemetery. Daniel was a farmer.

Salmon C. Hall - son of Daniel and Desire Dickinson Hall, born November 9, 1809, died April 10, 1895; laborer; was First Lieutenant in Civil War, Co. F, 1st Kansas Volunteer Infantry; buried in Milton Cemetery.

William J. Hall - son of William and Mercy Barn(e)s Hall of Guilford, born probably 1738, died November 25, 1777; married February 9, 1758, Mary Smedley and had children. According to sources in "Milton History Papers," he lived in house at 65 Saw Mill Road which he may have built in 1758-1760 when area was "practically a wilderness." Information in other sources indicates that house was built and lived in by Reuben Dickinson; both premises are described in this book. On bank of river behind house was located the largest nail forge in the area. There was also a grist mill there and cheese was made on that property. William was in Revolutionary War and French and Indian War, in Capt. John Marsh's Co., 2nd Regiment, 1757; in 5th Company, Col. Smedley's Regiment, 1761; in 4th Company, 2nd Regiment, 1761; a man "full of original humor." He is credited with planting the maples along Maple Street and the spruce trees in front of Milton Cemetery. He and his wife are buried in Footville Cemetery, Lakeside, CT.

Wilbur A. Haviland - born August 1872, died September 16, 1951; second wife was Amy Ogden, born November 3, 1883, died May 25, 1971; they had daughter, Elizabeth, and son, Clifford; Wilbur's son by first marriage, Harry, was brought up by Wilbur and Amy; came to Milton from Stamford, CT, around 1904 when Harry was eight years old; lived in Roswell Kilbourn house (37 Saw Mill Road). Wilbur was Sunday School Superintendent at Milton Congregational Church from September 1921 until April 1950; grew strawberries north of his house; local children picked for him, taking home money as well as berries. Amy was Sunday School teacher for years. Haviland is oldest and most complete pedigree of any in Litchfield, going back to

1000 A.D. in Normandy, France, and Dorsetshire and Guernsey, England (Walter E. Vaill). Wilbur and Amy are buried in Headquarters Cemetery along with Elizabeth and her husband, Harry James Bristol; Harry Haviland is buried in Milton Cemetery which he tended for years.

Frederick T. Jennings - a man who was never too busy to stop and carve a toy, a boat or windmill for a child in Milton — they loved him; married and had son and a daughter, Irene; painter; was in Civil War, Company A, 2nd Regiment, Heavy Artillery, C.V.; kindly man, tall, bearded; brother was T. Leander Jennings; Frederick lived in house now 49 Saw Mill Road; died December 16, 1878, and is buried in Milton Cemetery.

Truman Leander Jennings - in 1850 he owned what is now called "Raymond Cottage" at 529 Milton Road, which he may have built; sold to Ithamer Page; was surveyor for 1850 map of Milton; tall, bearded man, kind and scholarly; served often on School Committee; was in State Legislature where he introduced bill to make schools absolutely free; married Jane Page, daughter of Albert Page; their daughter married John Ravenscroft.

Abner Landon - son of Capt. Abner and Martha Youngs Landon, born March 10, 1739/40, died before 1812; married Eunice Gibbs, daughter of Zebulon; owned and ran saw mill at junction of Saw Mill and Blue Swamp Roads with brother, Daniel; owned much other property in Milton; sold to Welchs in 1790 "Pond Meadow" at corner of Saw Mill and Milton Roads, where present home of the Gerald Napolitano family is located.

Augustus Morey - called "Squire Morey"; born around 1794, died April 19, 1867; married Harriet Birge, daughter of Joseph and Marcella Ward Birge; lived in small red house at present 606 Milton Road; he was carpenter; made coffins in small barn/garage on property. Augustus and Harriet are buried in Milton Cemetery.

Gilbert Page - born January 13, 1835, died December 3, 1884; married Mary M. Dean; lived on Goodhouse Road, north of old Beach place. Ira Page brother of Gilbert, born 1832, died December 11, 1885; married Elizabeth and had children, son Austin and daughter Ella; lived in former William Woodington, later Hubert Hubbell house on Hemlock Hill Road; both Ira and Gilbert were very active in Milton Congregational Church, and both, with wives, are buried in Milton Cemetery.

David Parmalee - born 1747, died November 12, 1815; owned land south of Mill (Milton) Pond including house later owned by Harry and Lena Haviland known as Mill House, Saw Mill Road, later moved to Blue Swamp Road. David had bar there and was in charcoal business; lived later, and perhaps built, place now owned by Paul Goss family, 53 Blue Swamp Road, once planned to be site of Russian Orthodox Church, David had several sons in Civil War, two killed: William and Willard H.; Willard killed at Cold Harbor, VA; built old Stock/Birge/Winn house at present 81 Headquarters Road. William, brother of David, ran Vaill farm on shares when Walter Vaill was young.

Capt. Eliphaz Parsons - from Middletown, CT; married Abigail who died 1799, aged 56; no record of his being buried in Milton Cemetery, but wife, son and son's wife are. Son,

Eliphaz, Jr., married Lois Bishop, daughter of Noah, and had eight children; lived in house father, Eliphaz, Sr., probably built on Potash Road (number 43).

Dr. Edward Holman Raymond and Grace Isabel Raymond - he was born December 4, 1879, and died September 8, 1958; she was born January 8, 1885, and died September 2, 1960. He was former professor of oral pathology at Columbia University; practiced dentistry, an early leader in use of Novocaine in that field; served in France in World War I; bought David Welch house in Milton in mid-1920's; retired here 1928; they had four children, two sons and two daughters. Both served Milton well for many years in many ways, leaving an indelible mark on the community. Dr. Raymond headed several organizations over the years and was active in Trinity Episcopal Church; was a leader here, as was his wife. Both were loved and respected in Milton.

Herbert T. Register - born September 10, 1844, died January 18, 1927; came from England; worked in Aetna Shear Shop for Thomas Hinchliffe; later ran general store in Center, afterwards owned by Jacob Ackerman, which was the meeting place in the evening for men of the community; they sat on boxes or benches inside and out and visited, swapped stories and argued. Herbert was well known and liked in the area. He is buried in Milton Cemetery.

Anson C. Smith - son of Horace and Sarah Smith, born September 8, 1813, died March 26, 1883; married Clarinda Frances Birge, daughter of Harvey and Thankful Griswold Birge; lived at old Smith house at Headquarters, now gone; had at least two daughters and one son; noted for wit and hearty laugh, as was his grandson, Ernest K. Smith. At one time Anson ran Welch-Vaill place for Walter Vaill's grandmother; lived for a while in Dr. West's house across from parsonage, also long gone now; bought present Smith farm on upper Maple Street (588 Maple Street) from Wallaston Wadhams.

George Anson Smith - son of Anson and Clarinda Birge Smith, born April 16, 1847, died February 8, 1913; married Josephine Louise Kenney, daughter of Joseph, parents of Ernest Kenney Smith. Smith pedigree comes down from both Edward and Michael Griswold, as well as Gibbs and Marshall families. Anson, Clarinda, Josephine, Ernest and his wife, Mary Benjamin Smith, are all buried in Milton Cemetery.

Chester and Palmer Smith - from Massachusetts; started Carriage and Sleigh Shop on Blue Swamp Road, 1840/50, below Blake's Grist Mill; thriving business until went bankrupt; house across the road, later a boarding house burned down. Chester married Helen Griswold. More information of Chester and Palmer in "Industries" chapter.

William Sprats - born William Pretcell in Edinburgh, Scotland around 1757, according to letter from granddaughter, Polly Maria Goodrich, 1904, died 1810 and buried in Vermont; married before April 1782, Elizabeth Seelye, daughter of Justus; had several children before she died in 1800; married second Martha Waterhouse, who died in 1807 after having four children, bringing total children for William to thirteen; he probably married third Phoebe. He fought with British in Revolutionary War; escaped from British and later took name Sprats; was quartered in Litchfield, per tradition. He was an architect in Scotland and carried on tradition in this area; built fine houses including what is now 49 Saw Mill Road, Milton; had very good reputation; was joiner (did finish work as well as being architect and contractor); went to Massachusetts 1797 for year or so, then to Hampton, NY; had acre of land here in Milton, gift from father-in-law Justus Seelye, probably what is now 122 Saw Mill Road, or that vicinity.

Seymour Stevens - born 1801, died January 15, 1873; married Emeline L. Guild, daughter of Alban; tanner, and wagon maker, had tannery behind present 541 Milton Road with several large buildings, pits and big building to hold tan bark; millstones used to grind bark are now, (1) at Milton Public Hall and, (2) in front of Academy building. He used to toll the bell when someone died and for funerals, for which he was paid 50¢; when someone objected to cost, Seymour said, "I will toll bell for nothing when you die!"; was short, fat, good-natured man, kindly, liked by children in village to whom he gave apples; tannery blew down 1874/75; lived at present 49 Saw Mill Road house where he had shoe and coffin business; died of apoplexy and is buried with wife in Milton Cemetery. He was proprietor of Guild Tavern for years.

Jared Stewart/Stuart - son of Nathan and Martha Stewart/Stuart, born January 8, 1760/61, died in NY January 26, 1777; also known as Jirad; was fifteen years old when he died, a soldier in Revolutionary War, Col. Bradley's Regt.; is buried in Milton Cemetery with parents.

Supply Strong and Jedediah Strong - Supply died 1796; second wife was Anna; lived in old Osborn house, farm on south side of Milton Road just above Duck Pond Road; owned much land on Potash Hill in Milton but no record that he lived there. Son, Jedediah Strong, born 1738, died 1802, only lived in Milton in old age; Justice of Peace, 1779; Associate Judge County Court, 1780; Representative for number of years; member of Governor's Council, 1789; Town Clerk, 1773 to 1789; his beautiful handwriting can be found in Town records; probably Congressman; held important offices during Revolutionary War. "Mortal homely man," says Walter Vaill, "very brilliant man but very queer"; married a Wyllis; marriage didn't work out; divorced, and when old he lived with sister, Anna Strong (who married Jacob Osborn); buried near sister's house in private lot. Small man, with limp; loved his daughter and left everything to her when he died.

Marie-Louise Thompson - daughter of William Waldron and Mary Louise Guion Thompson, born in NY; mother died when she was one year old and father raised family of two sons and two daughters, among them Guion Thompson and Léonie Thompson; Marie-Louise lived in Milton from around 1900 until her death, at house now 65 Saw Mill Road and house now 530 Milton Road. Known as "Miss Tommy," she was one of the world's greatest women horseback riders; won Ladies Hunter Class four successive years in New York, an unequaled honor; taught riding as one of nation's top instructors; barn on Saw Mill Road (now 58 Saw Mill Road) across from house was located where garage of Blaine A. Cota, Jr. is now; it was moved south to present location; later, small buildings from property across road were added as ells to barn, which was originally intended to be riding academy where Marie-Louise would teach; never materialized.

Abram Edwards Welch - son of William Henry and Henrietta Edwards Welch; born ca. 1838; always called "Edwards" or "Ed"; lived in Milton for a number of years with Welch family; a Milton boy who fished streams and hunted woods in Milton; brought up by uncles, David and John Welch. His father, youngest son of John and Rosannah Welch, a lawyer, was the last Welch to be born in the old Welch house (530 Milton Road). Edwards Welch left the University of Michigan when Civil War began, 1861; was Capt. of 1st Company, 1st Miner Regiment; wounded and imprisoned at first battle of Bull Run; escaped prison after thirteen months, was recaptured. Wounded again by Indians when in command of Fort Snelling, Minnesota; Major 4th Minnesota and badly wounded at Vicksburg, perhaps lost an arm; appointed Lt. Col., but may have died before he received it. Died at Nashville, TN, February 10, 1864, aged 26; buried in Red Wing, MN; well liked in Milton, tall, outdoor man; face badly pitted by smallpox.

Garitt/Gerrett Welch - son of Hugh P. and Helen Williams Welch, born 1795, died 1847; married 1823 Clarissa Marsh, daughter of Rev. Truman Marsh; she lived fifty-five years in old David Welch house where he had store before he died; was first Milton postmaster. Both are buried in Milton Cemetery.

Hugh P. Welch - son of John and Rosannah Peebles Welch, born 1793, died at Lawrence, Kansas, 1869; married Helen Williams, daughter of Edwin; built house on hill above Milton Congregational Church, now Nesbitt home at 556 Milton Road; trees from the property which were cut for lumber for the house were so huge that the logs had to be taken to New Haven to be sawed because no mill in the

Milton area was large enough to do the job; was Justice of Peace and Associate Judge of County Court, 1826-1838; had fine voice and was lay reader at Trinity Episcopal Church; was great-grandfather of Walter Vaill.

John Welch - only child of David and Irene Marsh Welch, born in Milton September 3, 1759, died December 26, 1844; married November 8, 1784, to Rosannah Peebles of Island of Half Moon, New York; Revolutionary War soldier, Col. Sheldon's Dragoons, a Lt. in Sappers & Miners (Engineers) and served almost continuously from August 1779 to 1781; graduate of Yale 1778; was Judge in Courts, Delegate to Constitutional Convention 1819, State Senator 1825-1827; lived in old David Welch house, present 530 Milton Road, after parents moved to Welch/Vaill house; had store at house now 541 Milton Road. He and wife are buried in Milton Cemetery.

David Wetmore - son of Daniel and Dorothy Hall/Hale Wetmore, born 1729, died June 15, 1774; married October 24, 1763, Sarah Stanton, only child of Henry and Mary Jenckes Stanton; name changed from Whitmore to Wetmore several generations back; five children including Rhoda who married John Griswold. Both David and Sarah are buried in Milton Cemetery, although stones are missing.

Wheeler brothers - three Wheelers in Milton: David (never married), Christopher (married a Collins) and Charles D. (married a Guild); Charles was last man in Milton able to brew beer; lived halfway to Litchfield. Christopher lived at present Malcolm Forbes' place, 109 Shear Shop Road. Wheelers came from Stonington; all were "shrewd, jolly men, quite stout," according to Walter Vaill; before

Revolutionary War, family sold two hundred acres here to David Welch while still living in Stonington.

Seth Whiting - born 1842, died January 26, 1887; married Abbie J. Smith, daughter of Palmer; was one of owners of Carriage and Sleigh Shop which he and Homer Smith lost; he was a trimmer there; was soldier in Civil War, Corp. Company A, 2nd CVHA, was wounded in hand; good fellow, "big, handsome bearded man, liked by everyone," so wrote Walter Vaill who admired Seth as a boy, who also said Seth made toys for children; when old was in a hospital in New Haven; just before he died, offered to marry a woman so she could receive his pension; she declined. He and Abby are both buried in Milton Cemetery.

Wolsey Woodin - son of William, born 1825, died January 18, 1875; lived with mother at what is now 23 Blue Swamp Road; Woodins from Warren; mother wove rag carpets. Wolsey's sister, Abby, married John Candee. Wolsey was one of best carriage painters around; was Civil War soldier; handsome man, good friend to young Walter Vaill, who said, "Wolse died about 1875, and I cried very bitterly. I had lost a friend"; Walter was nine and one-half years old then. Wolsey is buried in Milton Cemetery.

Capt. Samuel Wright - born 1788/89, died March 12, 1878; married Desdemona Guild; lived where Zelim Richard family lived for years at 401 Milton Road; son Everett Wright lived at present Harold Bunnell house, 498 Maple Street, as did Capt. Samuel. Samuel was a "tall man who always wore a stovepipe hat on Sundays" (Walter Vaill). The monument raised on the Wright lot in Milton Cemetery was the first granite stone there.

"...And so we leave them all, with charity for their faults, and great respect for their accomplishments."

(From talk by Ellen M. Doyle at the Litchfield Historical Society, ca. 1954)

Chapter IV

SOCIAL LIFE — How We Lived and Played

❖

In the early days of the settlement of Milton, social life consisted of going to church, trading at the general store, attending weddings and funerals and occasionally going to a dance or social.

The days, which began before daybreak and ended in the early evening, were full and busy. At times, outside work such as haying was carried on at night when the moon was full, which made for an even longer work day.

There were chores to be done all year round. Almost everything the family needed and used was made at home. Some chores were shared by the whole family; others were the specific province of the father or mother. Commonly included in the father's responsibilities were the building of the dwelling house and outbuildings using lumber from trees on the property. Sons helped as soon as they were old enough. There was always wood to be cut and split and brought into the house for the fireplace, or for the Franklin stove, a later convenience. The tools used were made by hand, as were nails, shingles, flooring and furniture. Plowing was an early spring chore, and planting of the crops was done by father and sons, sometimes with help from the whole family. Harvest was a time for neighbors to help one another, as was raising a house or barn. Fences had to be maintained after they were built. Stones, logs and water all were hauled by hand or with oxen or horses.

In the house the mother was in charge, along with her daughters. Their jobs included making cloth for the family's clothing, putting up food for winter, making butter, baking, braiding rugs, making quilts — all things pertaining to the family's physical welfare.

Auction Poster, 1897

Life, however, was not all toil in those days. People had diversions also — fishing, trapping, hunting, swimming, skating, going nutting, gathering apples and probably taking one's girlfriend to search for arbutus. Besides church socials there were singing groups, occasional lectures, ballroom dances (as far back as 1783) to teach grace and manners, and kitchen dances. Young people enjoyed boating, horseback riding, roasting nuts, playing games such as backgammon and checkers, rolling hoops, jumping rope. Corn was popped, apples were candied, molasses taffy was pulled. In winter there were sleds and rippers (which held a number of youngsters); there were books which households shared and often read aloud, and newspapers, which consisted of one folded sheet of paper. Entertainment was centered in the home, church and at the neighbors'. Women enjoyed sewing circles, quilting bees, teas with visiting, and probably working in their flower, herb, or vegetable gardens.

Fathers made toys for their children — "hoe-boys" (wooden figures with moveable parts), small wagons, hobby horses. For daughters, dolls were fashioned of corn husks, straw and rags; small dishes came from acorns and other nuts or wood.

Sabbath began at sunset on Saturday and ended at sunset Sunday; work, except for essential chores, was suspended for that time. Church attendance was mandatory, the journey made with horse and wagon or sleigh. Neighbors often shared holydays (now called holidays), such as Easter, whose arrival then, as now, signified the end of the long winter. The twenty-fifth of March was the New Year Day and the beginning of the farmer's spring. Rogation Sunday in mid-May was the day when boundaries were paced off along the fields — which the pastor blessed that day — a day shared with neighbors. The Fourth of July was more of a celebration then than now, with firecrackers, cannons and bells announcing the birthday of the new Republic. The family went to the village center to join neighbors, and there were often auctions, picnics and other diversions on the Fourth. Lammis Day, on the first day of August, began the harvest with the blessing of the crops. This was also the early settlers' day of thanksgiving, a holiday not officially proclaimed until 1863, when it was moved to November. At Christmas the house was decorated with strings of greens and berries; exchanged gifts were handmade; a big meal was prepared and often included "candy" for dessert along with pies and cakes ("candy" was broken up pieces of loaf sugar and maple sugar). The family made its own fun and good times, and neighbors were very important people, indeed.

Photograph Courtesy of Litchfield Historical Society

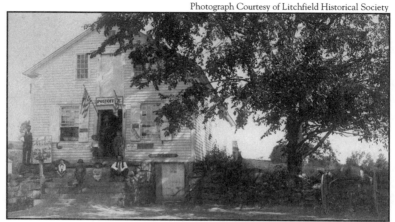

Barnes & Earle Store

The General Store

The general store gave the community a center, heart and nerves. The storekeeper was our great civilizer, for the crossroads might get along without a doctor or lawyer but no scattering of houses could hope to become a village without a store.

The Milton general store was originally located in the east wing of the David Welch home (now the Raymond home at 530 Milton Road). The east wing was added in 1790 and the store was kept by Walstein Wadhams. An advertisement stated that he had on hand "a good and selected stock of dry goods, hardware, boots and shoes."

Later, before 1854, the store was situated where the Milton Hall now stands on land belonging to Garrett Welch. There were a series of owners of the store from then on — A.J. Beach, Tom Beach, later Frank and John Barton. In 1885 Frank Barton moved to Watertown and the store closed for several months. Elmore and Granniss then bought the store, followed by Frank Barnes and Frank Earle. The store burned in January 1894.

"The store was a long, two story wooden building with a magnificent set of stone steps leading to the door. In my youthful eyes they were a high as the pyramids and as splendid as the stones in Solomon's temple.

"Inside on the left was the post office. A stove stood in the center of the room. At the rear was an office with a safe and large accounting books were on a table with a high stool behind it. A lavish display of goods was on the shelves and show cases of everything the community life demanded.

"Commodities were sold in bulk: flour went out in barrels or big sacks, sugar the same way — twenty-five pounds for a dollar. Hams were sold whole, salt pork in big chunks and molasses was carried away in brown jugs.

"It was a charge and carry system. The farmers carried away their purchases and the storekeepers charged the goods, hoping against hope that sometime they might see some cash.

"A stone wall ran from the store to the Episcopal church. Lined in front of it were a number of hitching posts. When this parking space was occupied with 'nags' and 'rigs' and the steps were overflowing with sitting citizens, business was good. At such times there was always sure to be a quoit game going in front of the store, a rifle shooting contest in the lot back of the store and, across the road on the green, a baseball game.

"Advertising signs adorned the sides of the store, and a large one in front was colorfully illustrated and lettered 'Do you smoke the Rip Snorter? If not you oughter — Five Cents each — or six for a quarter!'

"The daily break in the town's routine was the arrival of the stage that ran from Litchfield to Cornwall and carried mail and passengers. During the summer, life flowed in and out of the store. In the winter, life ebbed. The store telephone, the only one in the village, called the doctor as a new life was coming into Milton or an old life was passing on, or a child was ailing and needed more than Granny's remedies.

"One winter's night in 1894 the store caught fire and burned to the ground. It was a tragedy to the storekeeper but a grand spectacle to my boyish eyes. My mother took my sister and me over to Rash Griswold's house opposite the burning building. We stood huddled in awe on the veranda. The fire roared and the flames lighted the village. There was no fire department; the heat was so terrific that the men could not get near it with buckets of water so it burned unchecked with exploding rifle cartridges adding to the noise and the supply of kerosene oil adding to the flames.

"The fire ruined my father and changed my own destiny but my little sister vented her childish emotion with a comment that momentarily lifted the calamity from my Mother's heart when she said, 'Now all that nice candy is burned up'." (Written by Clarence Barnes, son of Frank Barnes who owned the store).

The old stores usually sold liquor. That our ancestors did not suffer from thirst is proven by a deed in 1885 to John Welch who owned property, now Paul Deering's at 541 Milton Road across from the Congregational Church, which speaks of dwelling, barn and brewery.

Walter Vaill remembered when the store was the general meeting place at night for all the local men who sat around telling stories. One night, when the stories got too lurid, his uncle John Welch sent him home — much to his disappointment. He also told that Michael Sepples, who worked for Barton, described the importance of the Milton store to a wide area of Litchfield County: For example, it was quite common for Seymour Johnson who lived at the foot of Bunker Hill in Cornwall to take home $200 in payment for veal and farm products that he had sold at the store. Mr. Sepples made two weekly visits to Waterbury with those products, delivering them to stores such as Pierpont's. He then put up his horses at the old Scoville House and spent the night there. He was paid in silver which he put in a shot bag — it was very heavy. Upon being asked if anyone had ever attempted to rob him, Mr. Sepples said, "No, I just threw the bag under the blankets and covers."

Hiram Bissell, formerly of Milton, related the story of a so-called "Raggy" (a person from the Mt. Riga area of Salisbury), who came into his store, slipped off his coat and picked up a whole dried codfish, hung it down his back with a piece of string and put on his coat over the fish. Bissell, peeking through a hole from his back room, came out, engaged the man in conversation and suggested that he should wear a longer coat or appropriate a shorter fish. The story is also told of a Milton man who was light-fingered and was known to lift eggs and put them in his pockets. Some of the cracker barrel crowd would make a point of sitting very close to the culprit or accidentally stumbling and falling against him — with predictable results.

Perhaps as good a date as any for the closing of one age and the opening of another would be 1909, when Henry Ford's first Model T rolled off the assembly line. What the railroad did to the buffalo the automobile did to the country store. "You have a car, I see, but no bathroom," remarked a Department of Agriculture investigator to a farmer's wife. "You can't go to town in a bath tub," the lady replied. The inexorable changes of the Automobile Age had begun.

Reports from Headquarters

James Birge Gilbert, writing for the Bicentennial of Litchfield, described a journey to Headquarters in the early days of Milton.

"We will begin our little journey into the past starting in the western part of the town of Litchfield, at the section known as Headquarters; the reason perhaps is because it is the least known of any section. We have the Bantam, Milton and Northfield sections, but this community has practically passed into oblivion. As we wend our way among bushes, briers and forest, looking for the past, we find between 25 and 30 old cellars which once had houses on them and families living in them.

"Among the cellars was one of an old inn where a four-horse stagecoach on its route from Hartford to Poughkeepsie stopped to feed the horses, and passengers to obtain refreshments. If you entered the old inn before it was completely demolished you would see a small room where a deep depression in the floor was made by countless feet standing before the bar."

The original name of this section known as Headquarters was the unfortunate appellation "Nigger Quarters." At the end of the eighteenth century a few slaves were owned by farmers, such as David Welch, in the Milton area. Due to the small scale and limited agricultural production of properties such as Welch's, slaves became an unprofitable burden to the farmer. Under the law, however, slaves could not be freed by their owners without provisions made for their support, lest they become dependents of the town or state. Several acres of land were purchased in the Headquarters area to start the slaves on their way to independence and self-sufficiency.

There is a record of two slaves, Elizabeth and Joseph, being set free in Milton. The documents for Elizabeth follow:

"Elizabeth, Negro of David Welch — Litchfield County.
This certifies that David Welch Esq. of s^d Litchfield did on the 14th day of Jan'y AD. 1797 make application to in the subscribing informing us that he was desirous of Emancipating a certain femal slave to him belonging Named Elizabeth whereupon we made enquiry respecting the age and health of the said Elizabeth and do find that she enjoys good health and is between the age of twenty-five and forty-five and we also find by enquiring of Said Elizabeth that She is Desirous of being Emancipated from her S^d Master"

Tapping Reeve   Justice of Peace
John Welch   Justice of Peace

David Welch's affidavits stated:
"Know all men by these Presents that I the subscriber do make free and Emancipate a certain female negro slave to me belonging named Elizabeth being the same Elizabeth mentioned in the above Certificate in Writing where of I have here unto Set my hand this 14th day of Jan'y AD. 1797"

David Welch
Recorded Jan 14, 1797   Moses Seymour, Register

One character living in Headquarters many years ago was a lowly man who somewhat resembled the "Leatherman" (see "People" chapter), not in dress, but in character. He lived in an old hut, on charitable contributions, and when spring came he started out on his travels, returning after several weeks. Little was ever known about his history. He was called "Old Tater John," as he never begged for anything except potatoes and salt, which he cooked in fireplaces of stone made along the wayside.

Fourth of July celebration on Milton Green

Independence Day Celebrations

Walter Vaill wrote of the Fourth of July when he was a boy: "Fourth of July in 1876 was a great day in Milton. Someone was roaring out songs over in Rash Griswold's tavern. This was before the little addition was put on the north side of the house for a barroom. Business was unusually good that day.

"Frank Earle had sent off and bought masks which the young men dressed up with (and anything else they could lay their hands on). Nellie Doyle's grandfather's Knights Templar regalia, black velvet trimmed with silver, two swords and other items lent by the family were worn. They formed a parade and called it the Antique Horribles. Dr. North played the cornet and there was a picnic in the grove near the Jay Gilbert place. The little girls wore white dresses while the little boys threw firecrackers under the horses. There were addresses made and someone read an original poem. Everyone had a fine time except the dogs and horses." Nellie Doyle said, "Being only 11 years old, I suppose I missed the best part of it — the evening — which was quite lively, according to reports."

Fourth of July picnic and ballgame, 1920

From the *Litchfield Enquirer* of July 12, 1883, we obtain the following account: "The Fourth of July came in clear but very hot, the thermometer indicating 90° in the shade. Bells were rung and cannon fired at an early hour. At about 9:45 AM the Antique Horribles moved out on the line of march, but owing to the intense heat, a part of the proposed line of march had to be abandoned about noon. A game of baseball was played at 2 PM between two picked teams, the result being 14 to 13, married over singles.

"Everything passed off in a pleasant and orderly manner to the satisfaction of all, until evening, when a heavy thunderstorm arose, to the disappointment of a large crowd of people who had congregated to witness the display of fireworks. The display was postponed until Saturday evening when a fine show was presented. Some of the oldest inhabitants say they never saw a finer Fourth of July celebration in Milton before.

The Antique Horribles, around 1905

"The Antique Horribles returned thanks to James Duggan, Thomas Hinchcliffe, William Bissell, F.N. Barton and H.P. Griswold for their kind hospitality to them during their march in the hot sun, and many, many thanks to the ladies for the bounteous collation set before them on the Green on their return from marching."

The picnics continued until the mid-1930's. The "Appendix" contains a list of committees for the 1931 picnic.

Courtship, Weddings, Anniversaries, and Cow Dowries

In Milton, around the year 1860, Anson Smith gave his daughter Elizabeth a variety of things when she married Benjamin Griswold and moved to New Preston. We have the list first-hand from her brother George, who wrote in his diary:

"What Father got for Lib: one counterpane $4.00; 1 wash stand $2.50; 1 wash bowl $1.25; 8 yds carpeting $3.20; 2 tablecloths $3.00; 1 melodeon $62.00; 1 lamp $1.00; 1 set dishes $14.00; 1 Brittania teapot $2.25; To 5 dollars cash — Total $107.48."

Anson was a farmer and also raised horses; not a rich man, he did pretty well nevertheless.

In connection with weddings, the dowry always seemed fascinating. "When I (Nellie Doyle) was a girl I thought it very comical that great-grandfather gave grandmother a cow when she and grandfather were married a century and a quarter ago in Ireland. In later years I've always been glad that he was well off and able to give her a cow."

The following story has come down through the years about a local man named "Uncle Harvey":

When Uncle Harvey reached the age of nearly three score (aged 56), his wife died. Soon after he started a "campaign of courtship" to secure another mate. He was successful in a promise of marriage from a woman known as "Aunt Ann," who lived alone in a home just this side of Litchfield. The wedding night was set, with the ceremony to take place at Aunt Ann's home, where the newly married couple would reside.

The evening was cold and rainy, but everyone, including the minister and guests, arrived on time — except Uncle Harvey. Time passed into late evening as Aunt Ann became more and more agitated, convinced that poor Harvey must have met with some terrible accident. A party of men was dispatched on horseback to scour the roads searching for the bridegroom. Eventually, they ended up at the door of his house. The house was dark, but their loud knocking caused a window to open on the second floor, and Uncle Harvey's head appeared.

"What is wanted?" said Harvey.

"*You* are wanted at your wedding; what is the matter, are you sick?" replied the men.

"No, I'm fine, but the weather is so terrible. I thought it just as well to marry in the morning," replied Harvey abruptly.

He was told that all the guests were present, and he could ride back on one of their horses, but he said stubbornly, "No; tell Ann that I will be over in the morning to fulfill all my obligations promised."

The men returned to Aunt Ann with Harvey's message, and as the reader can imagine, Ann was furious. She vowed that morning would be too late and that "she would not marry him now if he were the last man." In the morning the storm cleared, Uncle Harvey harnessed up his old horse, rode over to Ann's and went inside. Tradition doesn't tell us what happened inside that house; but after a time, the door opened and Uncle Harvey and Aunt Ann came out, arm in arm, grinning like Cheshire cats. They climbed into the old buggy, drove to Litchfield and were married. Surely, this must have been true love; at least we will record one more victory for it.

Another victory for true love was recorded by the *Litchfield Enquirer*:

"The golden wedding of Mr. and Mrs. Almon James Beach was celebrated on Wednesday, October 15, 1890, by a gathering of children, grandchildren, other relatives and friends at their residence in Milton. It was a complete surprise, Mr. Beach having taken his gun and dog, going out into the fields to celebrate the day in the sport which he enjoys so much.

"Among the many presents received were two large pictures handsomely framed; one entitled 'The Wedding, Fifty Years Ago' and the other 'The Golden Wedding' represented the old couple dancing. They were the gift of their children. A handsome crazy quilt was a gift of their daughters and grand-daughters. There were other beautiful presents but space forbids our particularizing.

"Thirty-eight guests sat down to a bountiful supper provided by the guests. About eight p.m., while the group were quietly enjoying the evening, there came a ring at the door and in marched three men, two carrying chairs, one each for Mr. and Mrs. Beach, designed for comfort not for show; the third man armed with a center table; followed by a large crowd of people and a more surprised man or woman than Mr. and Mrs. Beach were, it would be hard to find.

"The Rev. Mr. Harrison, pastor of the Congregational Church, in his pleasing and peculiar style made a few remarks, among other things thanked Mr. and Mrs. Beach for getting married fifty years ago, in order to give the company the pleasure they were now enjoying.

"At about 10 p.m. the Goshen Cornet Band was discovered on the lawn in the front of the house in full uniform with lamps and instruments just ready to give a serenade. At the first note out rushed the dancers and all to hear. The band was a surprise to the surprisers, and were at the same surprised, as they were invited to serenade Mr. Beach because of his love for music. They expected to find a small party instead of a house filled to overflowing.

"There were nearly 200 guests present, a large part of

whom sat down to tables bountifully supplied with refreshments furnished by the surprisers. The remaining hours were spent in dancing in the attic, and conversation, with music by the band, until two o'clock, when the guests returned to their homes feeling that they had a very enjoyable time and satisfied that it was possible to have a genuine surprise party, yes, three of them at the same place at the same time. We cannot wish Mr. and Mrs. Beach many happy returns of the day, but hope that they may live to celebrate their Diamond Wedding."

Bicycles and Funerals

When bicycles became the rage in the "Gay Nineties" most of the young people in Milton had them. It was a common sight to see a group out for a ride after supper, perhaps down Maple Street or "around the square" from the center. That was when the Milton Wheel Club was organized with Tom Doyle, President; Lewis Osborn, Secretary; and Mary (Mamie) Hurley, Treasurer. The Griswold House (tavern), which was owned by William J. Hall at that time, was rented by the Club for a very small sum. Card parties and dances were given there regularly on Tuesday nights. At one time a whist party was given one week and a dance the next; later when the partitions were removed upstairs, dancing was enjoyed on the second floor with card playing reserved for the lower floor. The musicians for the dancing were from Milton or nearby towns: William J. Hall, Theron Loveland, Austin Page, Byron Hall, Dan Young and Clark Dodge were among them. On very rare occasions a magic lantern show would come out here. Once

Charlie Carter had a tent on the green and took tintypes. A.J. Beach had an orchestra here at one time, including among others Charlie Blake, violin; Seeley Hart, bass viol; Tim Carter, drums.

The Wheel Club during its existence sponsored many activities for the young people and raised money for worthy causes. It was dissolved sometime after 1901.

The Milton hearse was housed in an enclosed space in the south end of the Episcopal sheds which stood on the east bank of the river, south of the bridge. It was a one-horse vehicle with five "urns" on the top. In the latter days of its use one of horses from the Barnes and Earle store was used for funerals and Frank Earle drove.

Upon the death of an individual in the community, the Episcopal Church bell was tolled immediately. This was an old English custom and was called the "passing bell." Those within hearing distance would count the strokes — corresponding to the age of the deceased — and perhaps figure out who had died. Walter Vaill remembered hearing the bells when his grandmother died. Warren Bissell stood in the road beyond the parsonage and signaled to someone down by the church that the funeral had left the house of the deceased. The bell was then tolled again. Seymour Stephens, the tanner, used to toll the bell, for which duty he receive fifty cents.

Another custom was to remove the coffin plate at the graveyard and present it to the chief mourner. Mr. Vaill had a key labeled "Key to the coffin of Rosanna Welch," his great-grandmother. Looking glasses (mirrors) in the mourners' home were removed or covered and the clock was stopped at the hour of the passing. In connection with these remarks, it is interesting to note the cost of what was probably one of the more expensive funerals:

Rev. Truman Marsh Estate
To D.C. Bulkly
To Mahogany Coffin $25.00
Box for same & Coffin Plate   5.00
                             $30.00

Rec. pay
D.C. Bulkly

Milton Hall

The Milton Public Hall Association was organized for the purpose of erecting a hall for improving the social life of those in the community. Real estate was purchased

Milton Public Hall, built 1900

and subscription papers were circulated with September 30, 1900, as the deadline for determining whether sufficient funds could be raised to erect a weatherproof building. The chosen site was next to the Episcopal Church on the site of the second general store. Included in the "Appendix" is a list of original subscribers to the Milton Hall Association.

Interest in the Hall was such that money, labor and materials were pledged generously. The foundation for the Hall was laid in October 1900, and work went ahead with volunteer workmen. The Association hired a carpenter, Jesse H. Derby, and it was voted to "finish the building on the inside." Edwin P. Dickinson took a note for $175; the endorsers were Ithamer T. Dickinson, Thomas Hinchliffe and Walter E. Seelye. The Milton Wheel Club whose members had sponsored dances in the Griswold house for some time donated fifty dollars to the building fund.

The Dramatic Club, which had been giving plays in the schoolhouse under the direction of Miss Julia Peacock, bought a drop curtain for the stage. Ten of the club's members who took part in the five-act drama *Under the Laurel* on the evening the hall was opened (December 18, 1900) were Lillian and Lewis Osborn, Lulu Dickinson, Willis Perkins, Thomas and Edward Doyle, Roy Baker, Fred Plumb; the Doyle boys' sister, Nellie, was the persecuted heroine.

The play had everything — a contested will, a penniless maiden, a haunted cabin, a sheriff's posse, a precarious mortgage, thunder, lightning, moonlight and romance. Mrs. Michael Driscoll loaned the family piano for the festivities and she "received a complimentary ticket." The net proceeds for the evening were $61.25. Farm teams did the trucking for the entire project; a last minute job having been to bring chairs from Torrington.

For many years there was an "Annual Ball" in December. Each Christmas the school children gave a program in the Hall for the community. At this time, each child received a gift — a box of hard candy and an orange. Card parties, dances, plays and entertainments were given quite regularly to raise money. Local people played for the dances; Turrill's and Hyland's orchestras, both of New Milford, sometimes furnished the music. The "Baldheaded Band" was no doubt one of the most famous groups that played the Hall.

Fifty years later, in 1950, the *Litchfield Enquirer* noted: "At the end of fifty years of existence the Milton Public Hall Association has a great sense of satisfaction that it has served the needs of the people of the Community."

Milton Library

Milton Library grew from an idea by Miss Julia Peacock, a teacher in Milton School when it was located on East Cornwall Road in the late 1800's. Miss Peacock loved books and thought them important for her pupils to have — in fact, she brought her own books to the school and made them available to the children. Ellen Doyle was one of her pupils and later became a teacher at the Milton School, and a great lover of books, as well. When the new school was to be built at the end of the Green, Miss Doyle urged the builders to include some bookshelves. The school children helped by selling "Hawthorne Certificates," cards bearing a portrait of Nathaniel Hawthorne. These were sold for ten cents each to fund the purchase of new books to add to the school collection. When Frances S. Walkley came to the Milton Congregational Church, she gathered a small collection of books which were kept at the parsonage and borrowed by the children. Gradually, more books were added, for adults, too, and the Milton Library was born. It was housed for years in the parsonage, and when that was sold, in the gallery of the church. The Milton Library is gone now. It ceased to exist in 1969.

Fresh Air Fund

In 1904, when Mrs. Shepherd Knapp gave a farm in Milton to the Herald Tribune's Fresh Air Fund to establish a summer camp in memory of her husband, she gave the beginning of the Fresh Air Fund's camping vacations.

Since 1877, the Fresh Air Fund had been arranging for deprived, underprivileged children from New York City's slums to have summertime visits with families in the country. With the founding of the Shepherd Knapp Camp the program could be extended, and for half a century thereafter this camp — and friendly, interested people in Litchfield — welcomed needy boys and girls to the clean beauty of Milton summers.

"On July 5, 1910, The Shepherd Knapp Memorial Home opens at Milton with an enrollment of 200 children," said the *Litchfield Enquirer*. The camp provided many activities for the campers. They were taken to Bantam Lake for swimming, and for long walks "around the block" which provided opportunities for lessons in flora and fauna. There was a pavilion at the camp where programs were held; once a circus came complete with elephants, which the children were permitted to ride.

Across the street from the camp was a huge garden, with Zelim Richard as gardener. The camp raised potatoes and many different kinds of vegetables (at one time the garden yielded two bushels of peas at one picking). A meadow next to the vegetable garden provided huckleberries. Of course, there was fresh milk but the city children did not like the "yellow" milk; they preferred the "blue" milk they had in the city.

The camp was sold in 1951 when all the Fresh Air Fund Camps were established in the wooded hills of nearby Dutchess County, New York.

The Milton Post Office

The Milton Post Office, established in the 1820's, was located in the general store on the site of what is now Milton Hall. The property was given by Garrett Welch, and the post office was run by the owner of the store. After John Barton sold the store in 1885, the post office appointed Frank Earle as assistant postmaster. When the store burned in 1894, the post office was moved to Mrs. Earle's dining room/kitchen and remained there until Rural Free Delivery was instituted in 1906. "Though Milton people have been enjoying the benefits of Rural Free Delivery for the past year the post office was not discontinued until Monday, April 30, 1906," said the *Litchfield Enquirer* in May of that year. There had been a post office here in Milton for over 81 years.

An article in the Sunday magazine of the *Waterbury Republican* (January 5, 1915) stated, "When the first delivery of mail took place May 15, 1905 with the Rev. Alfred Stock at the reins, there were just five rural carriers in the state." In May 1914 Joseph D. Coffill, Milton Road, Litchfield took over the delivery of the mail. For forty-two years Joe made his appointed rounds on RFD #1 Litchfield.

Joseph D. Coffill, R.F.D. mailman

When Joe Coffill made his first circuit in May 1914 in horse and wagon the roads were dirt tracks — all twenty-five miles of them, except for about a mile of what was to become Route 25 (now Route 202). This mail carrier provided many extra services for patrons on his route even though it had expanded to fifty-one miles. In 1916 he bought his first automobile, a Model T roadster, but true horsepower continued to play a major part in distribution of the mail until 1920. When the 1955 flood slashed through the area and destroyed bridges and roads, Mr. Coffill covered more than one hundred miles each day to service his route. He retired in 1956 after a job well done for all those years.

Milton Woman's Club, late 1930's

The Milton Woman's Club

The Milton Woman's Club was started in June 1927 at the home of Mrs. Ernest (Mary) Smith (see "Appendix" for list of original charter members and elected officers). It was voted to meet once a month on the third Saturday; dues were 10 cents per meeting.

The object of the Club is to promote the social, cultural and civic interests of the women of this community; a limit of twenty-eight members was set, probably in consideration of the size of the hostesses' parlors and geographic boundaries were loosely set.

Early programs were conducted mostly by the women themselves. They read and reviewed books, acted out plays, sometimes in costumes; they had debates, musical programs, played games, showed slides and gave talks on trips taken, and hosted yearly summer picnics. Among the many projects undertaken by the Club were a flower show and tea in August 1928, which raised almost $100 for the benefit of the Milton Public Hall; in 1935, care of the two Milton cemeteries was embraced by the Club, which eventually resulted in formation of the Milton Cemetery Association in 1940; in May 1932, the Club planted a Norway maple tree at the Milton Congregational Church in honor of the two-hundredth anniversary of George Washington's birthday. In June 1930, the Club began its most ambitious project — the writing of a history of Milton — which resulted in publication of this book.

Money has been given for many worthy causes, such as the donation of books to the local schools and the High School. A math prize is awarded each year at the Litchfield High School awards banquet.

In 1947, the Club marked the twentieth anniversary of its founding by having a special program, "bringing to our minds former members and delightful times we have enjoyed together." For June 1956, there is an entry by Dorothy Earle in the minutes about the resignation of Carrie Peck, who had been treasurer of the club for twenty-one years. Dorothy wrote, "with regret we accepted her resignation and the thanks of the club go with her, a competent officer and a loyal member."

In the summer of 1977, the Club celebrated its fiftieth anniversary. Two charter members, Mercy Birge and Mary Smith presented a loving trip back in time with their memories — only two other charter members were then still alive; Sarah Dudley and Alice Phillips.

Changes, of course, have taken place over the years. One of the first was to divide the office of Secretary/Treasurer into two offices. Another was to change the meeting day to the third Monday of the month. Dues have risen and by-laws have been amended and updated; but through all these years the Milton Woman's Club has maintained its essential character and has remained a service of social, cultural and civic interest for each woman in our community.

Three Ancedotes: Little Cats, Big Cat, and "Little Bill"

Mattatuck Press; February 11, 1915 — "Town Topics": "George Derby of Prospect Road in the Milton district Thursday caught in a large steel trap one of the largest wild cats ever captured even in that wild section. The animal was over 4 feet long from nose to tip of tail and weighed nearly 40 pounds. The cat closely resembles the tiger and its death has brought relief to the scattered residents of that part of Litchfield. It had been the means of frightening many children in the past few months while on their way to school...Arnold Cone of Bantam bought the big cat and has mounted it."

*　*　*

In the 1860's, when the charcoal business was flourishing in nearby Cornwall, the charcoal burners used to come down to Rash Griswold's saloon to spend the evening — they always had plenty of money. Walter Vaill used to tell the story of one night's adventure when some of the local boys were invited to return to the bush for a celebration. The charcoal burners had two casks of cider and a supply of liquor in their wagon. As they went along home over Blue Swamp

Road they robbed a farmer's henhouse of turkeys and chickens. Further on down the road they stopped in the dooryard of a fellow named "Little Bill," cut off the heads of their purloined fowl and plucked their feathers, before continuing on their way. "Little Bill's" reputation was notorious in the neighborhood, so the farmer, Charles Page, who most certainly suspected this particular ruffian of the crime, got the constable Anson Smith to look into the incident. It turns out that "Little Bill" was not even home that evening, having spent the night in Cornwall where he was working by the day. As for the charcoal burners, whenever they were in danger of being apprehended for anything, they left for elsewhere. And we suspect Mr. Page was never recompensed for the charcoal burners' "fowl" deed.

* * *

From the oral history, as told by Ernest Smith:
"Electa Griffin Goslee, a cousin of mine, was quite a lady in her time. After her young husband Chester died, she ran the farm; drove the oxen, did the plowing and milked the cows. When her two boys Fred and Hiram were old enough they took over the work but they fought so much they couldn't stay at home.

"Electa decided to make a fur cape. She went around Milton asking for kittens, preferably black. Some were given to her, some she picked up as strays and the rest she brought from anywhere she could get them, about a dozen in all. When they had grown she killed them, skinned them herself and dyed them to make a cape, black as coal; there weren't a white hair in it. She came up to the house in July with it on. Yeah, she was a grand old gal."

"Cotillon" Invitation, 1848

Chapter V Part 1

DWELLING HOUSES — Where We Lived

Eighteenth-Century Rural Dwelling Houses and Typical Family Life

This contribution, based upon independent sociological study of Colonial New England, with specific attention to the Connecticut Colony, emphasizes the inextricable bond between rural dwelling houses and family life therein during this period in history. It should be understood that the development of early domestic architecture is a specific technical study in itself, but for this particular purpose, only simplistic coverage will suffice.

The initial monumental effort to clear the land was impeded by encounters with black bears, wildcats, wolves and rattlesnakes. Human strength and endurance were confronted by enormous trees to be felled and disposal of residual stumps. Outcroppings of glacial deposits and vast accumulations of heavy brush were obstacles to progress, as well. However, compensating resources discovered here — pure water, virgin timber, wild game, fish and fowl, all for the taking in abundance — were the prerequisites for settlement in this vast, uninhabited wilderness.

But eventually with hand tools, unfailing fortitude and the incredible power of oxen, it was possible to haul timbers to sawmill facilities to be stockpiled for later construction. Fieldstones retrieved in the process were transported, as well, by ox-drawn stone boats for raisings at selected sites.

In time, physical trials were rewarded by a wilderness yielding slowly to cleared fields and boundaries defined by fences of piled stones. At still greater length, soil was prepared roughly for planting survival crops for anticipated farms in this remote place called "Blue Swamp," named after the Blue Gentian discovered there in abundance.

Understandably, it took years — until the 1750's — before dwelling houses, per se, began to appear in what was now designated "West Farms." During this interim period land speculation was heavy throughout the East and West Tiers of one-hundred acre lots.

Timbers felled for framing were oak or chestnut, hand-hewn for traditional post and lintel construction of early dwellings. It is obvious that training and skill — including handling tools, felling, debarking, hewing, squaring, adzing and much more — were necessary to produce huge framing timbers such as the "summer-tree," a massive burden-bearing beam located at the center of each room. Accuracy in measurements and deft shaping to specification were essential also, especially for mortise and tenon joints.

Many first habitats were simple, utilitarian central- or end-chimney structures of one, one and one-half, and sometimes two stories, with a gable roof. They had a "down-hearth" kitchen, a parlor and a bed chamber. A connecting passage ran across the front into which the front entry opened. Often a steep ladder-like stairway led from the kitchen, usually to loft space above. A two story plan accommodated a kitchen chamber over the kitchen, a parlor chamber over the parlor, and an upper connecting passage across the front. A "winder" stairway led from the lower passage, climbing upward along the chimney wall to join the upper one. The loft, in this case, was enlarged to a "garret" accessible from a "winder" leading from the upper passage.

Sites for raising house frames were chosen on hills or high ground for adequate drainage. Water for wells was sought without delay by the ancient art of "dousing" with a "divining rod." By virtue of the area's high water table, manually dug wells were shallow, shored up by fieldstones and capped by a large flat stone cover with chiseled-out center through which buckets could be drawn to raise water to the surface by the reciprocating action of a "sweep."

It was a custom in Connecticut to face dwelling houses south or toward a road (highway) leading to or passing by them. For most, cellar holes were excavated to fit beneath only one room, with the balance merely crawl space. Many of these early foundations can be discovered today in abandoned locations, partially buried and lost to all but the discerning eye, marking evidence of long forgotten productive lives. These foundations, laid up without mortar, were of fieldstones until late in the eighteenth century when cumbersome granite blocks were employed (in Milton), cut at a quarry located on the "Kent Road" (now Blue Swamp Rd.).

At the center of early foundations a tall free-standing single-flue stone chimney stack (chimneys were known as "smokes" in the seventeenth and eighteenth centuries) was erected to accommodate a stone fireplace for each room to be framed against it. In order to ease discomfort while cooking or baking during excessive summer heat, a "down-hearth" was constructed in the base of the stack in some cellars. One dating ca. 1756-58 exists in the Major David Welch dwelling on the Milton-Cornwall Road. A brick oven ("beehive") for kitchens was constructed in the back wall, at one side or the other, depending on the right- or left-handed ability of housewives for whom these were intended.

Traditional "raising" of frames necessitated an assembled band of strong men. Using long iron pikes, they simultaneously raised one preassembled segment after another from the ground to standing position. All segments were pinned together securely with "trunnels" (tree nails) to complete the frame of the dwelling.

When the frame was finally assembled, all participants seated themselves on the sills (already in place) to focus attention upon a small pre-cut pine tree as it was hoisted to the roof peak. At the anticipated climax all joined with rousing enthusiasm to celebrate, often by consuming a quantity of good Jamaica rum. The efforts of raising such a dwelling house were possible only by the reciprocal sharing of expertise, service and time — a way of life at this period which enabled people to accomplish phenomenal results for their dwelling houses, barns, farm layouts, burying grounds, mills, dams, roads, and bridges.

From this initial phase of house construction, an additional one and one-half to two years was often required to complete the dwelling, depending upon conditions and circumstances. After a roof was shingled with hand-riven cedar, the new frame had to be enclosed quickly for protection. If only an insufficient quantity of clapboards was available for the immediate purpose, wide pine "weather boards" were applied for siding. Although many times exteriors remained untreated for long periods, fish oil was often applied for protection. Painted surfaces were not used until later; a red pigment, discovered by accident as the oxidization of yellow clay, became "Venetian Red," the color widely accepted in paint for barns, dwellings, sheds and even for furniture.

Wide boards of oak, chestnut or sometimes pine, were used for flooring, nailed to joists, never pegged. Occasionally a double layer was installed to prevent sifting dirt from reaching rooms beneath. When floors were permanently set, hearth stones cut to specification were laid in hearth openings. An inner one served for the fire bed and an outer one protected surrounding floors.

By 1720 windows had changed radically from leaded casements to double-hung sash of which only the lower portion was moveable. Six-over-six, or nine-over-six quarrels of expensive poured glass, imported from England, were set into wide muntins for two windows per room in the simple five-window facade. Small openings in garrets and later in lean-to upper spaces held four-over-four quarrels or sometimes only two-over-two in a single window. As the need and desire for better indoor light increased, larger sash with twelve-over-twelve quarrels and narrower muntins were set into a nine-window facade.

Sash weights were not introduced until approximately the 1770's or later; before that the drop of a raised sash presented a potential hazard. An accident of this kind happened at the old eighteenth-century Solomon Buell house in the nineteenth century. A truant Milton schoolboy, in his haste to avoid detection of his absence, attempted to gain entry to his room from a ladder through such an unsupported window. The result was his unfortunate demise. A prop of any kind was useful for supporting a sash, and could be as simple as a dried corn cob. A common locking device was a sawn bar placed diagonally across an upper sash or one set tightly against one side or the other of an upper sash and the window frame.

If interior shutters were used — designed either to slide or fold — they were used as barriers against wind and cold in unheated rooms, and not intended to preserve privacy, which was of little concern in such remote areas. Exterior shutters, often believed to be correct for early windows were, in fact, quite late as substantiated by a letter of inquiry in 1798 written by George Washington when he was interested in having them for Mount Vernon ("...as in the latest fashion").

Exterior doors of heavy batten construction, similar to their English prototype, were for protection. These were suspended by long, heavy wrought-iron strap hinges nailed to the inside, and swung from iron pintles. An impenetrable entrance was secured further by a heavy removable oak locking bar engaged from the inside. Early interior doors of simple design had three separated horizontal battens nailed to the back side. Wrought iron hardware, per se, was either imported or sometimes forged locally. Hinges available in "H" and "HL" shapes and thumb latches in the arrowhead design were widely used, along with other styles available as time went on.

An interesting custom prevailed regarding the use of doors, which was to close one upon entering or departing from a room, encapsulating inner space. This logical practice prevented drafts from sweeping into cold rooms, causing burning candles to sputter and casting grease over furniture and fabrics nearby.

The most important concern for the dwelling house was function. The great "down-hearth" kitchen was the heartbeat of the house. Its commodious fireplace with bake oven was the central source of energy for cooking, hot water, and baking. It provided minimal, yet appreciated, creature comfort in frigid temperatures, especially while dressing, undressing and when bathing. Wet clothing from inclement weather, and small light laundry, were hung up to dry by the welcome warmth of the hearth fire, which never was allowed to die out. If such was the unfortunate case, it had to be rekindled by use of flint, steel and tinder, the ancient method often found to be a long and troublesome chore.

Most of the day the kitchen was filled with bustling activity, with the housewife, and her small girls at times, moving about among equipment of iron, copper and brass pots, pans, kettles, and such, as well as necessities such as mortars and pestles for various uses, a butter churn, apple peelers, a "steelyard" or two, wire greens washer, trivets for all purposes, toaster, baskets, to name only a few. Equipment hanging from overhead joists never seemed a threat to the housewife, whose average height was about five feet.

Storage cupboards and wall shelves held articles of "treen" (woodenware) such as a "trencher" or two, bowls, plates, paddles, scoops, spoons, funnels, egg cups, lemon squeezer, along with choppers, jagging wheel and knives and the like. An iron dough scraper, birch whisks, and pewter and horn measures were among the necessary items.

Forged nails driven into the leveling boards of the lintel held cooking utensils such as skimmers, ladles, flesh forks, spatulas, skewers, tasting spoon, potato rake, etc. — for easy access. A large iron crane installed within the hearth opening was equipped with trammels and "S" hooks in various sizes for adjustment of height and distance from the fire bed of whatever had to be tended. At one extreme end of the crane a large cast iron water kettle, with attached "tilter," placed over its independent fire bed, maintained a continuous supply of boiling water, replenished as needed.

Down-hearth cookery — with a well controlled fire, fed by a good coal-producing back log and maintained by a deep ash bed — provided sustenance until the invention of the cook stove in the nineteenth century. It required quantities of dry hardwood, cut and split into lengths not greater than whatever was to be set before it. Small coal-fires on the outer hearth stone were set beneath iron trivets, creating supplementary cooking space. Cooking methods included spit roasting, rotary trivet broiling, boiling, braising, stewing, steaming, toasting and baking — in the brick oven and/or in the cast iron "Dutch Oven" set on a trivet fire or hanging from the crane near the main fire.

Heating the brick oven was by a fire built directly on its floor. The fire was kept burning briskly for about an hour and a half, until reduced to bright coals. These were crushed down and spread evenly over the oven floor, there to remain until the bricks soaked up maximum heat. When the temperature was right, the coals were raked out with an oven "hoe," the ashes swept clean with a turkey wing and, for bread, corn meal was cast over the oven floor. It now was prepared for loading in the order of required baking time while "stopped-up" by a stout removable wooden door. Small oven iron trivets were set under certain baked goods to elevate them slightly to prevent burning.

The "beehive," used for weekly baking, consumed the better part of a day, and never was used for cooking meats. By the late 1750's its position was placed forward about half-way in the fireplace opening, retaining use of the chimney flue. Toward the end of the century it was changed again to a position almost flush with the jamb stones, with allowance for its own flue through which smoke was drawn out and upward, exhausting into the main flue. During firing, this oven had a rolled iron door to prevent flying sparks from endangering the kitchen. These "improvements" did little more than reduce the size of workable space within the hearth itself.

A huge kitchen work table was used as well for serving family meals, at which time father, or the eldest male, seated himself in a "great chair" at the head of the "board" (table).

This ancient custom is the origin of the term "Chairman of the Board," so commonly used today.

An indispensable appurtenance was a large stone sink, a receptacle only, chiseled out of solid rock, with high sides and a long deep trough which ran directly through an exterior wall to channel waste water to the ground below. A large stave "keeler" (tub) was placed on its floor and used for washing soiled kitchen and tableware (and sometimes very light laundry) in hot water and homemade lye soap. Water had to be carried in from the well in stave buckets hooked to "shoulder yokes" worn by the women and often by children. Reserve water was stored temporarily on a "water bench" standing nearby.

At the close of a long hard day in the fields, the house, barn and elsewhere, the kitchen was the gathering place where the family could enjoy a brief spell of leisure near the fire before early bed-time. At that time the fire was "banked" with ashes to hold for the night, to be uncovered the following morning and rekindled for the new day.

The kitchen chamber above was a household work room which contained necessary equipment, hand tools and supplies with which to create homespun fabrics to be hand-sewn into clothing and household items for the entire family. Fleeces were processed for wool to be carded, spun, skeined, reeled and either woven on a huge harness loom, or knitted, into clothing items. Preliminary processing of home grown flax usually was handled outdoors or in a barn, but final preparation and spinning of the fibers for linen thread often took place in this chamber.

Other hand-work included decorative stitchery, applique work, quilting, simple laces and braid, crocheted trimmings, "bed rugs," household sewing and the never-ending mending essential in order to prolong fabric use.

Housekeeping, per se, was regulated despite primitive methods and means. For example, bare wood floors were swept with a "besom" — a bundle of birch twigs tied to a wooden handle. A wet mop was merely a bundle of discarded fabric fragments of worn out useful items, tied to a handle. A scrub-brush was made from corn husks drawn through bored holes in a block of wood. Used with homemade lye soap, this was harsh but effective treatment. Seasonal house cleaning was accomplished by what was called a "wang." Friends and neighbors would gather together to make short work of a major undertaking in one another's houses; eventually, each household would benefit by the combined efforts.

Heavy duty laundry was a difficult quarterly obligation, handled outdoors in good weather, either pounded on rocks in a flowing stream, or in huge cast iron caldrons hung over an open fire pit or in huge stave wash tubs. Rinsing required quantities of water carried from a well or stream. Starching was slapped in by hand and drying methods varied from spreading items over grass, to draping them over sturdy bushes, to pinning them to supported lines of cord. Ironing, known as "smoothing," was by "sad irons" heated at the hearth fire, a requirement for almost all fabrics, which then were folded carefully — even sheets and pillow cases of which there were dozens. Each piece was neatly embroidered with identifying initials and also numbered to keep accurate count of the clean supplies on hand between wash periods.

Each housewife produced her own supply of lye soap for which she had produced the liquid lye by the "leaching" process in the spring. A bottomless barrel, usually a hollowed out tree trunk supported by a large elevated flat "leach stone," was filled with alternate layers of straw and wood ashes over which quantities of boiling water were poured repeatedly. The seepage, liquid lye, drained into an incised circular channel in the stone's surface, from which it dripped into a bucket set beneath its overhang.

The entire household bedding supply was made by the housewife. A woven "rush" mat was placed on top of the "bed cord" laced through the bed frame for sturdy support. The mat prevented bed clothes from sagging into the interstices. A straw or corn husk mattress placed on top was covered by a feather bed dressed with hand loomed sheets, blankets and feather pillows supported by a bolster. This followed the traditional custom from ancient times, when the sleeper was elevated to a half-reclining position as a precaution to avoid vulnerability at the hands of an enemy. When a clean casing was needed, the mattress was emptied of its contents and after laundering was refilled with fresh straw or husks.

Pre-Revolutionary period dwellings almost never were designed to include closets as we know them. Clothing was hung from wall pegs between wearings, but seasonal articles, linens, bedding supplies and the like, had to be put away in a variety of storage chests, chests of drawers, trunks and boxes.

Sanitation was primitive at best. The "necessary" or "privy" was housed usually a fair distance from the dwelling house and "draw-well." It was designed for single and/or communal occupancy and sized for children as well as adults. Indoor facilities were mostly glazed earthen pots, some of which were set into chamber chairs for comfort and convenience.

The smoke house, a valuable "appurtenance," held hams, bacon, fish and fowl suspended over a fire bed strewn with dry corn cobs used for curing.

Earthen cellars were utilized for keeping-over binsfull of fall harvest vegetables and certain fruits, barrels of cider, home brews and wine along with a keg of molasses for sweetening and a "powdering tub" filled with meat curing in brine.

The spring house, simply a small housing built over a natural spring, provided protection for perishable cream, cheese, butter, milk and such in warm weather (milk was not used for drinking at this period).

Garrets held storage sacks and barrels of flour, grain, sugar and salt. Confined summer heat was excellent for drying herbs for winter use. Space was available as well for general storage, including supplementary facilities for sleeping.

Responsibility for all household work and its upkeep fell on the women's shoulders. However, a lighter side to such demanding schedules was enjoyed in the exchange of gossip or the latest news to reach the settlement by the arrival of the "Post Rider" on one of his infrequent trips passing through — or perhaps from an occasional traveler in need of sustenance for himself and rest for his horse.

By tradition, the parlor was the best room in the dwelling and was reserved for special occasions. Bible readings and prayers were held here without fail. Weddings and funerals were observed with traditional customs, handled by the family with help from friends and neighbors when possible. The minister or special guests were welcomed, always in the parlor. Except for such use, this room always remained closed to the family.

Furnishings included the best and cherished pieces, many being heirlooms — especially the family Bible with its vital statistics inscribed. An architectural feature of the parlor was a barrel-back corner cupboard with open upper display shelves for valued items of export porcelains, blown glassware and whatever other precious items were in need of protection. Although rugs, per se, were not used on floors at this period, deer hides, bear skins, and later eighteenth century hand-painted canvas "floor-cloths" were placed where needed. However, imported woven "table rugs" were used, especially in the parlor. If a family possessed a timepiece, it usually was a "lantern-clock," often inherited from the seventeenth century. Its hourly strike was so loud it resounded throughout the dwelling. A timing glass filled with sand was necessary for just that purpose.

The parlor chamber overhead was considered the second best room, but it was shared by babies in cradles, very small children in a "truckle bed" (or underbed) and, in large families, children also slept on "pallets" for the floor. "Tester" bedsteads for adults were prevalent. One special one, originally set up in the parlor during the seventeenth century, was removed to this chamber in the eighteenth century. This was completely dressed with hand-worked and embroidered curtains, valences and "coverlid," the pride of the housewife's needlework proficiency. Although intended, as before, only for heads of the family, this chamber was relinquished for honored guests whenever necessary.

At this period, the lighting of interiors was a problem of major concern, owing to the time and effort expended in procurement and preparation of fuel — gathering rush grasses; processing animal and vegetable tallow; collecting and extracting wax from honeycombs and bayberries; preparing residual hard fats from cookery; and spinning and plaiting wicking for candles that would be dipped or molded and cured before use.

Valued fragments of waste paper were saved and rolled into tapers called "spills" which were essential until matches were introduced in the nineteenth century. After a spill was ignited at a hearth fire and its flame transferred to a lighting device, it was quickly extinguished and the burned end folded over to be saved for further use until completely consumed.

Lighting devices included a variety of "fat lamps," candle

holders, beams and sconces; chamber sticks; "lanthorns" and chandeliers. These were crafted in wood, brass, pewter, wrought iron and tinned, rolled iron. These came in many different forms to be stationary, portable, or hanging, and were put to use only when necessary — during early morning before sunrise, early evenings for short periods and on dark or stormy days. When necessary to read small print, work on intricate stitchery or use quill penmanship, it was best to wait for the brilliance of sunlight.

When extra space was needed in the dwelling, an added lean-to was achieved by downward extensions of the original gable roof rafters. These were joined to a separate frame previously attached to the standing frame. This created four additional rooms and greater storage possibilities. This idea was adapted to one and one-half story gable and gambrel dwellings, as well. It gave the advantage of a new larger kitchen, centrally located with the hearth flue cut into the existing stack, or with a separate flue constructed along the exterior of the stack. This plan also offered a convenient adjunct to the kitchen — a shelf-lined buttery with northern exposure, if possible — where cooler temperatures prevailed for keeping foodstuffs. Butteries usually were whitewashed for cleanliness and better light.

At the opposite end of the kitchen, a "kitchen bedroom" was included to serve whatever function would have to be handled. Proximity to the down-hearth, where the housewife could be found a good part of the day, made this the practical room in which to care for injuries, illness, childbirth and infirmity. Between crises, however, the bed was used at night by an untroubled member of the family.

At one end of the upper level of the lean-to a children's chamber was framed, with the balance of space to the far end reserved for storage of grain, and so forth. Access to these parts was through the kitchen and parlor chambers of the original second story.

There were barns and sheds for the family "creatures" — surrounded by barnyards not far from the dwelling — and additional sheds for farm equipment, tools, tack and conveyances. A chopping block and woodshed usually stood at a convenient distance from the kitchen doorway, with quantities of wood to be split for supplies needed throughout the seasons.

Close to the kitchen doorway a "kitchen garden" was cultivated for culinary and medicinal herbs as well as a variety of small vegetables. Strongly aromatic herbs were grown to ward off insect pests, moths and especially fleas. Tansy, one of several strewing herbs, was used at the down-hearth to discourage ants attracted to grease and spills from cooking.

In addition to culinary use, rosemary needles were burned over coals and carried in a "sensor" to refresh household air, especially in the sick room. The Apothecary Rose was favored since ancient times for its beauty and highly fragrant petals gathered in quantity for distillation of rose water, a special flavoring in cookery. On high poles, heavily laden hop vines yielded blossoms used in flavoring home brewed beer. Pumpkins, a staple in the settlers' diet, was grown in profusion, along with cabbages, squash, onions, and other vegetables. Outlying fields were planted with crops of corn, wheat, rye, barley and hay, with space set aside for fruit trees and berry bushes.

When, presumably, there was more time to tend and enjoy ornamental flowers, a "parlor garden" was laid out on that side of the dwelling where perennial favorites could delight the senses with their changing bursts of color and wonderful perfume.

Daily routine for young boys included much practical education relating to farm labors — care and feeding of livestock, crop culture, hunting, fishing and so forth, and well rounded general knowledge which, along with mandated early schooling, was to take them through life.

Young girls, from a tender age, were instructed in the ways of housekeeping, including cookery, care of younger siblings, needlework, and the production of homespun fabrics. They also sewed for their dowries, which parents expected to be completed by the time of early marriage.

Despite such pressures, children were instilled with respect for the wisdom and advice of their elders, but there was a time for simple outdoor games. Toys, as such, were teaching devices, in effect, for future practical application.

Among many superstitions which played a role in the lives of the settlers, one commonly known is the planting of "mugwort" near doorways to ward off "witches." Another was to place shoes behind a wall near a chimney stack in order to prevent a fire in the house. Another very different example is an account of a happening in a farm house not far from Milton. A pair of women's cloth shoes was discovered years later nailed to the top step of the garret stairs, in the form of a cross. This was believed to prevent the return of the spirit of a suicide/hanging victim in that garret. To date the shoes have remained undisturbed since that event.

Changes in architectural styles and details slowly emerged in remote areas like West Farms. Innovative refinements and structural differences appeared in some new dwellings while some older ones were updated for outward appearance. The familiar "feather and bead" interior sheathing was displaced, in some cases, by hip panelling and more sophisticated moldings. There was a greater choice in paint colors for interior finish with dark ones lightened in value by a mixture with white. However, white paint, per se, was not used until the Greek Revival Period of architecture. Whitewash was used from very early times for cleanliness and better light, as previously mentioned. Hand painted decorations and murals also came into favor preceding the nineteenth-century period of stencilling on walls and floors — the latter having been preceded by hand painted patterns which simulated carpeting.

The winder staircase was abandoned after a time, in favor of a steep vertical one which ascended directly from the front entry, behind which a smaller brick chimney was erected with small brick fireplaces.

By the late eighteenth century a radical change came in the central chimney stack, which was divided into two separate flues at the base, allowing a straight-run staircase to rise between to the second floor. Above the ceiling, the flues joined to emerge at the ridge as a single smaller brick stack. Its smaller brick fireplaces were less likely to waste heat, even though dampers were not used at that time.

Wide-board flooring, prevalent in early dwellings, now, of necessity, was abandoned for narrow boards. Front entries differed in style and "strength" by about the 1760's. Panelled doors came into favor, over which some had poured-glass lights set into separate framing — allowing welcome light to enter the passage where only darkness had been known before. Security bars were now less cumbersome than they were before.

In the chimney stack of later dwellings a smoke chamber was constructed at garret level, a convenience compared to the old separate smoke house.

Outdoor sanitary facilities of the past now were being included in a line of attached sheds extending beyond dwellings.

During the early years, house lots were enclosed by high board "paling" fences to prevent damage from intrusive creatures. As the problem became less troublesome, fencing became more decorative than protective. However, the "fence viewer" continued to serve the town by inspection of outlying fences in need or repair.

THE DWELLING HOUSES OF WEST FARMS-MILTON

The eighteenth-century dwelling houses considered here lie within a limited peripheral boundary of "West Farms" (Milton).

Seelye/Larned/Cohen House

Ca. 1752
72 Blue Swamp Road
On the Kent Road (now Blue Swamp Road) the 4th part of Lot 5, or one-fourth of the one hundred acres set to Jeremiah Griswold, was conveyed by him to Justus Seelye with appurtenances thereon standing in 1752. From the

premises Seelye could look east to a parcel in part donated by him for early burials. The dwelling house to which said appurtenances belonged stands on a rise looking east — a two-story center-chimney lean-to with five-window (originally) facade. One extra window is a late addition. The barns could be of early date as well.

David Welch/Edward and Mary Raymond House

Ca. 1756-8
530 Milton Road

Opposite "Birch Swamp" (recorded name in 1744) on the north side of the Milton-Cornwall Road, a two-story center chimney dwelling house stands east of the East Tier boundary. It is believed to have been a wedding gift to David Welch and his bride Irene Marsh from her father John Marsh, Jr. One hundred and eighty of Marsh's acres in Blue Swamp were included.

In 1784, David's only child, John, newly married and attending Tapping Reeve's Law School in Litchfield, was in need of financial assistance. That year the east portion of the structure was added to serve as a store for this purpose and the whole property was given to John. Major Welch, an enterprising land speculator, held numerous mortgages in the area. He also served in a number of civic offices and was chosen representative to the General Assembly in Hartford. Shortly after having come to West Farms from New Milford in 1749-50, he established the Welch Puddling Furnace northwest of this dwelling house.

1756
566 Maple Street

Isaac Catling (Catlin), son of John, a proprietor and a first settler in Litchfield, raised on fifty-five acres a two-story center-chimney lean-to dwelling house which has an unusual feature. The architecture never included a front entry because of precarious placement of the dwelling on the steep incline where it stands on the West Goshen Road. The house faces west toward the village, and is located just south of the westward turn of the old highway (Cornwall Road, now Potash Road).

Isaac Catlin/Doyle/Stevens House

1759
65 Saw Mill Road

In 1759, Reuben Dickinson received of his father, Ebenezer, twenty acres in Lot 6—East Tier on Saw Mill Road. Here he raised a one and one-half story gambrel dwelling house with gable-end chimneys and a center hallway with straight-run stairway, architecturally ahead of its time. Having come from Hadley, Massachusetts, Dickinson was aware of the advanced domestic styles there. Many changes have come to the structure since the nineteenth century, when a cheese factory operated on the premises. Following Reuben's death, the William Hall family acquired the dwelling — William having purchased the land prior to that time.

1759
127 Saw Mill Road

Jehiel Parmalee /David Welch/ Reeves W. Hart House

In 1759, Jeremiah Griswold raised a center-chimney dwelling with hewn overhang on the northward turn of the Cornwall Road in Lot 4—East Tier. Although one of the first to settle in West Farms, by 1765 he sold the house, barn and ninety of his acres to Jehiel Parmalee who died of smallpox in 1776. In 1784, Major Welch purchased the property from the heirs of Parmalee, and at the same time deeded his first property to son John.

1759
(house gone)

Ebenezer Dickinson conveyed most of his residual acreage in Lot 6—East Tier to Oliver Dickinson who, as a master carpenter, was responsible for the design and building of Milton's Trinity Church edifice — patterned after Trinity in New York City, as he remembered it from being held there as a British prisoner of war. Oliver was married in 1778 and raised a two-story red gambrel dwelling on Saw Mill Road north of Reuben Dickinson's dwelling house. Oliver's son Anson, born in 1779, became a noted prolific miniature portraitist during the nineteenth century. Unfortunately, in the late 1800's, this dwelling house was demolished. A large memorial stone marks the site with surviving cellar hole.

1764-66
615 Milton Road

Capt. Solomon Buell raised a dwelling house in Lot 3—East Tier on the Cornwall Road, on part of land set to Jeremiah Griswold in 1759. It survives today, a two-story center-chimney structure with hewn overhang, north of the Griswold place. In 1737, Solomon married Eunice Griswold, daughter of Jacob, one of the original proprietors of Litchfield. She was the first white English child born in Litchfield, on March 21, 1721. Their son Ira received this house, barn and fifty acres in 1768 upon his marriage to Prudence, sister of Julius Deming, the prominent, wealthy Litchfield merchant. As a widow in 1778 Prudence "kept tavern" here where, it is said, Lafayette supposedly stopped over one night. In 1793, their daughter Mehitable married Squire Nathan Bassett, Milton's Presbyterian leader.

1767
498 Maple Street

In 1767, Leah, daughter of Benjamin Bissell, and Jonathan Wright married — their ages twenty and twenty-one, respectively. Although he probably worked on the construction of their house, it is recorded to have been owned by Leah until her death in 1782. Jonathan as a widower at age thirty-six remarried and his daughter, Sally, became her mother's heir.

In 1795, Sally conveyed the entire sixty-four acre farm, situated along the Milton-Cornwall Road east of the East Tier, to "Jonathan" living in the house at that time. However, no distinction was made whether he was father or brother — both of whom were named Jonathan.

Ca. late 1700's
115 Saw Mill Road

To further complicate the above picture, Capt. Jonathan Wright (which Jonathan?) is associated with late eighteenth-century real estate matters and also with the small one and one-half story lean-to dwelling on the corner of Saw Mill and Blue Swamp Roads in the East Tier of Lot 5 — property deeded by Justus Seelye to David Welch in 1753. This dwelling is an example of a "half-house," with chimney and front entry on the north end, and appears to have been raised in the late 1700's or possibly early nineteenth century. The last nailer in Milton was one Capt. Gross who forged his work in the west corner of the garden in the nineteenth century.

Bissell/Seelye/Sheldon House

Ca. 1770
557 Milton Road
A one and one-half story center-chimney dwelling in the central part of the village, in Lot 4—East Tier, has a "cockloft" above the garret — an unusual feature in architecture of this period. It is a reminder of ancient times when a live cock was kept high under the roof to herald the arrival of dawn. An original porch was removed from the north facade in the 1960's or before, revealing horizontal sheathing, an example of "weather-board" siding. On the south side, a "Dutch Eave" allows the advantage of a modified lean-to. In 1790, Aunt Hannah Seelye held school sessions here.

Ca. 1770's or later
181 Blue Swamp Road
At the western end of Blue Swamp Road where it turns north, a small one and one-half story, center-chimney dwelling with a cellar kitchen, a typical style, stands on large farm acreage in Lot 5—West Tier. This, in 1753, was owned

by Justus Seelye, half of which he conveyed to David Welch. In 1852, one Hall owned the small dwelling which, it is said, was raised by John Hall in the 1770's or so.

John Bissell/Malcolm Forbes House

Ca. 1770
109 Shear Shop Road

On the "country road" (now Shear Shop Road), north of the Welch Puddling Furnace, a one and one-half story center-chimney dwelling was raised ca. 1770 on part of one hundred acres set to Isaac Bissell in Lot 1—East Tier around 1761. The summer kitchen ell is indigenous and the eighteenth century "windlass" still raises water. This acreage, set to Jacob Griswold in 1730, was owned by Lt. John Bissell following the Revolution. It was inherited by Capt. William Bissell who served in the Civil War.

1774
116 Blue Swamp Road

Prior to the outbreak of the Revolutionary War, John Cotton of Middletown raised a large two-story center-chimney farm house on fifty acres in Lot 5—West Tier, acquired from Justus Seelye in 1768. It stands on Blue Swamp Road where from 1776 to 1923 it was held by the Page family.

Ca. 1774
695 Milton Road

Nathan Stuart had a dwelling house (now gone) on Page Road in Lot 2—West Tier, on land received from Isaac Marsh, son of Capt. John Marsh. However, it is unclear where Stuart resided when his sons Jared and Nathan Jr. were born in 1761 and 1764. Lt. Jared died aboard a British prison ship in New York in 1777 and Nathan Jr. appears to have been living in the old dwelling standing on the Cornwall Road, close to the northern Town line of Litchfield in 1787. This simple structure has the basic appearance of mid-eighteenth-century architecture with added lean-to and five-window facade.

Prior to ca. 1778
8 Blue Swamp Road

On Saw Mill Road, just north of the bridge, a parcel of land formerly owned by Justus Seelye was conveyed to John Collens in 1778 and deeded back to Seelye the same year — one acre, a dwelling house and blacksmith shop thereon, in Lot 5—East Tier. This was a small one and one-half story gable structure with cellar kitchen, standing near the Seelye pond which serviced his saw mill diagonally opposite. It was occupied by Harry Haviland and his wife Lena and later moved to a lot on Blue Swamp Road, part of land owned in 1749 by Jeremiah Griswold, Lena's ancestor.

Prior to 1783
99 Saw Mill Road

On the west side of Saw Mill Road in the 5th Lot—East Tier, a small one and one-half story dwelling house stands south of the bridge. Although the land was set to John Collens in 1753, the house is believed to have been raised by Lt. John Hall, a Revolutionary War veteran who married in 1776. A transaction between Hall and one Judson Guitteau conveys a small house and eight acres to Guitteau on February 10, 1783. It is very probable that Hall could have lived here for a time prior to this date. An early barn still stands.

Ca. mid-1780's and possibly later
67 Litwin Road

According to a twentieth-century abstract of title, it has been assumed that a date of 1767 applies to the dwelling on the south side of the road (now Litwin Road) when in fact the Highway Committee for the Town of Litchfield in 1767 laid out a road running past Eli and Theodore Catlin land conveyed to them by their father, John. Eli is believed to have had a dwelling on the north side of said road, the foundation of which exists just west of the present barn.

The committee's notation, recorded in Vol. 7, p. 9R, Litchfield Land Records, "past Eli and Theodore Catlin's land...whereon they now live," may have led to a misunderstanding of the architecture of the dwelling house standing on the south side. It would appear that the style and construction of the dwelling, including the proportions and chimney design with divided flue, do not conform to the 1767 period, but to that of the 1780's. Much, however, depends upon the interpretation of early deeds: "whereon they now live" indicates a dwelling house there in April 1767 but does not specify where. There is also evidence in the original section of the house of construction earlier than that of the 1780's. This is the property of Peter and Eileen Litwin.

The large acreage originally was set to John Catling in 1727 and before the 1767 date of conveyance — all lying east of the East Tier of the West One Hundred.

Ca. 1785
37 Saw Mill Road

Roswell Kilbourn purchased three pieces of land in 1785 from joint ownership by Capt. Solomon Buell, Justus Seelye and Beriah Stone, who had purchased the one hundred acres of Lot 7—East Tier set to John Catling (Catlin) in 1759. One-third of the whole, the southern parcel, went to Justus Seelye whereon the one and one-half story brick-center-chimney dwelling was raised by Kilbourn upon the birth of his first child. It is believed he finished work in the summer of 1786, but because he was experiencing financial difficulties he sold the farm to Noah Westover and departed from Litchfield in 1787.

A deed from the Tax Collector for Litchfield conveyed to William Sprats five acres, lately belonging to Roswell Kilbourn, bounded southerly by land which the Tax Collector had attached and sold as the Estate of Kilbourn to raise £2 for taxes due. This was where the Kilbourn dwelling house stood.

Westover sold this piece to Elizabeth, wife of James Wright, son of Jonathan and Leah. It was then mortgaged to the Benjamin Talmadge Co. after the panic of 1787 and two years later sold to David Welch. In 1789, John Griswold, Jeremiah's son — a Revolutionary War veteran who had married in 1782 and experimented with his own design for an ironclad vessel prior to the work of Ericsson on the *Monitor* — purchased the property. This dwelling, an unspoiled example of Milton's early farmhouses, survived without alterations or modernizations until well into the second-half of the twentieth century.

Ca. mid-1780's
49 Saw Mill Road

William Sprats, a British soldier of Scottish descent, came to Hartford and to Litchfield as a paroled war prisoner following the defeat of General Burgoyne under whom he had served prior to 1779. He met and married Elizabeth, daughter of Justus Seelye, in whose employ he was for a period of time. As a trained architect and joiner, Sprats built on the five acres (mentioned earlier) on Saw Mill Road in Lot 7— East Tier his own small gambrel dwelling with chimney and front entry on the original north end (a typical "half-house"). In the twentieth century the present north was joined to the original. Sprats created many mansions in Connecticut between 1793 and 1796, including his work on North Street in Litchfield. By 1798, he sold his entire farm in Milton and moved out of state.

Moore Gibbs/Parsonage

1786
563 Milton Road

In 1786, a small one and one-half story dwelling house with brick center-chimney was raised on the Milton-Cornwall Road in the center of the Village in Lot 4—East Tier by Moore Gibbs, son of Gershom, the first white male child born in Litchfield, on July 28, 1721. Moore was grandson of Benjamin of Windsor, a first settler in Litchfield.

The "Dutch Eave" construction on the south side perhaps was suggested by that of its next door neighbor. Following Gibb's death and the demise of his wife fourteen years later, the house became the parsonage for the Milton Congregational Church in 1854, which it served for many years. A book collection placed here by minister Frances Walkley became the nucleus of a small library which followed. The granddaughter of Henry Ward Beecher lived here with her family in 1921.

Joseph Birge, Jr./Edwin Dickinson/Goldring House

Ca. late 1700's, possibly 1780's
499 Maple Street

Opposite the farm of Leah and Jonathan Wright on the west side of the Milton-Cornwall Road, a two-story dwelling with brick center-chimney bears elements of late eighteenth-century architecture indicative of a raising date of that period. In the nineteenth century the south end with chimney was an addition which served for a time as a shoe shop. In 1726-7 Benjamin Boardman owned this land, his second sixty-five acre pitch lying east outside of the East Tier. Edwin P. Dickinson purchased the property in 1849 from builder Joseph Birge, Jr., and it remained in his family for the next one hundred years. To the present day the farm still maintains its original function. A serious fire in the 1960's necessitated interior refurbishments and construction.

1786/1790
386 Maple Street

James Birge, grandson of Joseph of Windsor, a proprietor and a first settler in Litchfield, became the first banker there and held many mortgages in the area. His dwelling house, a two-story

James Birge House on Maple Street

brick-center-chimney structure stands on its original large acreage, north of the junction of Maple Street and the present Brush Hill Road, east of the East Tier boundary line. This dwelling also has the late style divided-flue chimney construction as described earlier.

Ca. 1790's
21 Saw Mill Road

On the southerly end of Saw Mill Road in Lot 8—East Tier, a two-story brick-chimney dwelling house with Classic Revival architecture is believed to have been raised ca. 1790 for Isaac

Isaac Baldwin/James Duggan House

Baldwin Jr., grandson of the Rev. Timothy Collens, and that he lived there in 1831.

The Guild Tavern, after 1883

1793
542 Shear Shop Road

On January 23, 1793, Jedediah Strong of Litchfield conveyed to Jeremiah Guild of Middlefield, Connecticut, one hundred acres in Blue Swamp. The bounds defined indicate the location of the old Guild Tavern which stands at the corner of the Milton-Cornwall and Shear Shop Roads. This two-story center-chimney structure was at first home for the Guild family. By 1833, it had become a tavern which served the Hartford-Poughkeepsie stagecoach line until 1877. Jeremiah's son Alban, born in 1784, ran the establishment until three years before it ceased to function, when he was ninety years of age. H.P. Griswold became the proprietor who had the building repaired and altered. Two fires in the twentieth century damaged much of the eighteenth-century architecture, which had to be replaced with new. The old building by this time had reverted to a private dwelling, which it is today.

Ca. 1795
606 Milton Road

Jeremiah Griswold/Morey/Worthington House

In what was a subdivision of Lot 3—East Tier, a small red one and one-half story brick-chimney farmhouse stands southeast of the old Solomon Buell dwelling (owned by his son-in-law Squire Nathan Bassett by 1793). It is believed to have been raised ca. 1795 on land owned by Jeremiah Griswold in 1767, who conveyed it to his son Asahel of Newtown, Connecticut. Asahel Jr., born December 22, 1775, was married in 1797. Given about the average of two years for construction, it is possible that this was raised for him. Benjamin, his brother, born in 1779, married Sally Wright in 1799 (daughter of Jonathan and Leah Wright). Their son Sylvester, born in 1814 — and possibly his parents, as well — lived in this dwelling in the late nineteenth century. Augustus Morey, born 1793, lived here in 1852 and died in 1867.

It is uncertain when the Worthingtons bought the place, except that the "Misses Worthington" lived in the nineteenth-century dwelling standing on the adjacent property just south of it, in the early twentieth century. The gambrel structure on the south side formerly served as a "toll house" on the Milton-Cornwall Road (now the West Goshen Road), somewhere between the Wright farm and the twentieth-century Fresh Air Fund camp.

1798
641 Maple Street

A large two-story farmhouse with end-chimneys was raised in 1798 on land originally set to the heirs of John Baldwin in 1767, on the road to "Canada," as West Goshen was known by early inhabitants. This large family farm, established by the Beachs, stands east of the East Tier layout in Milton, and continued to function as such well into the twentieth century.

Ca. Nineteenth Century
122 Saw Mill Road

Guild/Kenney/Litwin House

An interesting subject is the so-called "Meeting House" on Saw Mill Road. Information from the "Milton History Papers" indicates an early date of construction of about 1750, and according to the Milton Historic Study Committee report, the house was raised about the mid-1700's. Research of the property, however, has revealed the following background: In 1780, this one-acre corner piece on which the structure stands, north of Justus Seelye's 1778 one acre, was conveyed to Eli Smith by Moses Barnes. In 1782, Seelye deeded one-fourth of his one acre, south of it, to his daughter Elizabeth and her husband William Sprats. In the description the northern bounds was that of Eli Smith (no house). In turn, the Sprats conveyed to Henry Plum the same, bounded on the north by Eli Smith. In 1797, Eli conveyed his one corner acre to Elihu Wetmore. In 1798, Wetmore conveyed the same one acre to James Birge. Birge had his own dwelling ca. 1790 elsewhere.

The architecture of the meeting house does not appear to reflect the period of 1750. Remains of a brick oven on the outside of the wall (covered over in the 1960's) seem not to be compatible with eighteenth-century fireplace (chimney) design and function. However, tradition has long stated that this is one of the, if not the, oldest houses in Milton.

This one and one-half story center-chimney house, recently enlarged by a two-story addition on the east side, stands on what was part of Lot 4—East Tier of the West One Hundred in the eighteenth century.

Four eighteenth-century dwelling houses which were removed from their original sites in Connecticut and brought to Milton in the 1960's have settled comfortably into the rural environment of this village. In the order of their historical periods, they are:

The Deacon Peter Buell House — 1723, Litchfield
The Congregational Church Rectory — ca. 1750, East Haven
The Daniel Starr House — 1784, Litchfield
The Weigold House — 1785, Drakesville, West Torrington

Only two, the Deacon Peter Buell house and the Daniel Starr house, are within the confines of Milton proper.

1723
74 Saw Mill Road

In 1723 Captain John Buell, one of the two principal proprietors of Litchfield, raised a two-story, four-room, center-chimney dwelling on his second sixty-acre pitch on the "Third Chestnut Hill" near a place commonly called "Watch Hill." The dwelling was later conveyed to John's son Peter, who added the lean-to a few years after his marriage to Avis Collens in 1734. In the 1960's this dwelling was identified as "the old fort house."

By 1961 the house, which narrowly escaped demolition, was rescued and moved to Milton. Here it has been restored to reflect domestic life as it existed during Peter's fifty-year tenure and that of his heirs. The house stands on thirteen acres of the original Lot 6-East Tier, adjacent to the one-third interest in Lot 7, on the south, held by Peter's brother, Capt. Solomon Buell, in 1759.

1784
569 Milton Road

In 1784 Daniel Starr raised his one and one-half story center-chimney gambrel-roof dwelling house in Litchfield on the fifth lot from the corner of East Street. When the Congregational Church of Litchfield was in need of property for the Third Church, the Church Committee purchased the site from Starr. The dwelling was moved around the corner to the Torrington Road in the mid-1850's where it remained until 1964 when the church was once more in need of physical expansion. Arrangements were made for the removal of the dwelling from this site. It was later disassembled and moved to Milton in 1966, where it was re-erected on the Cornwall Road (now Milton Road) just south of the 4th Lot—East Tier, the land having been set to Jeremiah Griswold in 1759.

Basic subsistence farming was crucial to survival for all early inhabitants — regardless of occupation, position in the community or financial ability — as well as for those who followed, until late industrial development occurred within the village. We of the twentieth century should remember, with great respect for their creativity, stamina and accomplishments, all of those who paved the way for us.

Discovered on a wall panel in a Revolutionary War period dwelling house in Concord, Massachusetts:

> "He who loves an old house
> Will never love in vain—
> For how can any old house
> Used to sun and rain,
> To lilacs and to larkspur,
> To arching trees above,
> Fail to give its answer
> To the heart that gives it love?"

For all who have enduring love and appreciation of ancient dwellings, these thoughts are indeed meaningful.

Chapter V Part 2

NINETEENTH-CENTURY DWELLING HOUSES
— Where We Lived

❖

We have written about houses only where there is information available concerning them in the "Milton History Papers," or from personal knowledge. Other houses just as important have had to be omitted for lack of knowledge.

An anonymous pundit wrote, "Much of the history of any community is in its earliest buildings. Information about the builders and the original owners, data of the materials and methods employed because of the limitations of the materials and tools of the period, as well as the identity of those who used the buildings in later periods, would provide a unique story of the community. However, it can never be told, for most of it is lost in the vanished memories of those who have passed on into the mists of time." Agreeing that it can never be fully told, research through the records pertaining to dwelling places in Milton built in the 1800's reveals that there is adequate information on a number of them to merit their inclusion in this history of Milton.

Of special interest because it housed the Milton School for fifty years is the building at the south end of the Green, built in 1896 and now occupied by Barbara Todd, her daughter Mary Ellen and children. Although the building was renovated by the Todd family in the 1950's, its outer appearance is essentially unchanged. It is a frame building in the "rural Victorian architectural style," according to the Milton Historic District Study Committee report of 1975.

Front entryway, cupola and flagpole have remained intact, although the original bell is now in the belfry of the Milton Congregational Church.

Across from the former schoolhouse, at 10 Headquarters Road, is the house occupied until recently by G. Herbert Griffin, and before that by him and his wife Ethel and their two children, George H., Jr., and Caroline. It is now the home of Bradford and Lauren Richardson. Built close to the road before 1813 by William Gabriel, this is a small one and one-half story, shingled dwelling. The house is graced on the north side by a wide, open porch, enclosed at the west end during an illness in the Griffin family when it was used for sleeping quarters. A distinctive feature in front is the row of three unevenly spaced "eyebrow" windows, believed to have been added by Clarence Perkins who bought the property in 1912. Between Gabriel and Perkins the house was owned by Benjamin Griswold and son Lucius, who operated a tannery on the river bank. Besides many renters, some other recorded owners were Seth Beers in 1857, Erwin Bissell in 1873 and probably N. Downs. G. Herbert Griffin moved his family into the house in 1926 and remained there tending his beautiful garden, mowing his large lawn and rocking on the porch until his death in 1994.

On the east side of the Green stands the "Raymond Cottage," built prior to 1852 by Truman Leander Jennings and owned subsequently by Ithamer Page and Albert Birge. After Dr. Edward H. Raymond bought the property in 1921, the family moved into the cottage for the winter months as the big house across the road was difficult to heat. The cottage is a two-story dwelling with the front door on the gable end facing the Green. A special feature of the cottage was the large flowers painted on the walls by G. Isabel Raymond (Mrs. Edward H.). At present the house is occupied by John and Anne Winter.

Almost directly west of the cottage, across the Green and beyond the river and facing onto Milton Road, is the two-story house at 541 Milton Road now occupied by Paul and Patricia Deering. This house was built in the middle of the nineteenth century. Prominent features are the cellar in the lower story which was built into the bank, and the porch running the full width of the house on the front. As early as 1850 a store was established on this site by John Welch, followed by Herbert Register's store. Back of this dwelling on the pond formed by damming of the Marshepaug River was also the site of a wagon shop and tannery. Fred M. Seelye remembered coming barefooted into the store one evening, only to have Virgil Beach, who operated the store, accidentally step on his toe hard enough to take off the nail. Fred was placated with a stick of candy. Many present-day Miltonites fondly recall Jacob and Alice Ackerman's store in that "cellar" from about 1917 to 1932. Many of us grew up with that store in the center of Milton.

Continuing west on Milton Road, next door to the Milton Congregational Church on a prominent spot above the road, is the house begun by Almon James Beach in December 1885. It is a two and one-half story white clapboard edifice with a porch running the width of the front. Mary Beach Earle, Almon's daughter, resided in the house her entire life after it was built. Her husband

Beach/Earle/Wilson House

Frank, who was proprietor of a blacksmith shop in the Academy building on the school grounds, was also a storekeeper and "postmaster" for some years. After his death, Mary lived there alone until their son Charles and his wife Dorothy came to live with her. The post office was transferred to this house after the building which housed it burned in 1894 (on the spot where the Milton Public Hall now stands). Present day residents of the house at 552 Milton Road are David and Rosanne Wilson.

The Mansion House - Hugh Welch/Derby/Nesbitt

Just west of the Wilsons' home on an even more imposing site is the so-called "Mansion House" (556 Milton Road), raised about 1840 by the grandson of David Welch, Hugh P. Welch. It is approached through a break in an outstanding stonewall, in front of which myriad daffodils bloom in spring. The large frame dwelling has "Classical Revival architectural details...pilastered corners and a hip roof," according to the Milton Historic District Study Committee report. Unique are the horizontal floor level windows in the attic. Typical of that period are the large windows on the first and second floors. The original structure included four chimneys, but following two serious fires, the most recent in 1954 when the Thoma family lived there, the chimneys were dismantled. The ell on the north side, however, has its original chimney intact. As expected of a "Mansion House," there were originally carriage sheds and a barn which have since disappeared from the property. Anson Bradley Beach, brother of A. James Beach, bought the place and lived there until he died in 1885. After the 1954 fire, the Thoma family rebuilt the house with community help. Today the "Mansion" is occupied by Ingrid Nesbitt and family.

Jonathan Wright/Ackerman/Kizzia House

On the corner of Saw Mill and Blue Swamp Roads, at 115 Saw Mill Road, is the present home of Dewey and Elizabeth Kizzia. This house, built by Captain Jonathan Wright, is called a "half-house," because its chimney and front door are at one end instead of the center. A one and one-half story dwelling, it also has a lean-to on the west side. One distinguished owner was Captain Gross who manufactured nails in the southwest corner of the property, the last nailmaking operation in Milton. In the late 1870's Lewis Hutchinson owned the house and ran a cider mill nearby. In the first half of the twentieth century, Clarence and Edna Ackerman purchased the house and raised their four children there. Their daughter, Elizabeth (known as Betty) and her husband Dewey reside there now.

Traveling west from the Kizzia house down Blue Swamp Road, the first house on the left, number 15, is the present home of Richard and De'lis'ka Bates. The exact date of its construction is vague, but it was finished by 1852, and there is a record of an H. Griswold living there in 1870. Either before or after that date, Virgil Beach lived in the house and oversaw a cabinetmaking shop below the saw mill. One other inhabitant worthy of mention was William Ferris, who drove the hearse stored in a shed on the Green. The house itself is one and one-half stories and, like some others in Milton, the gable end faces the road. Windows on the ground floor are twelve-over-twelve quarrels. Because of its location close to the dam, it was an ideal home for those involved in industries like the aforementioned cabinet and carriage shops. A kitchen ell is to the east.

Immediately west of the Bates house at 23 Blue Swamp Road is the present residence of Evelyn Williamson. The earliest recorded owner was Mrs. William Woodin, who lived there when Walter Vaill was a boy in the late 1800's. Her son, Wolsey, succeeded her in the home. Subsequent owners or tenants of the house were Howard and Edna Sheldon, whose son, Walter, was born there. Following them at some point was the Jason Hallock family. Carl Kilbourn owned it later, and it is believed that Auguste A. Gray purchased the house from Kilbourn in the 1930's and moved in with her three children, Florence, Howard and Raymond. Although the house suffered through two major fires, its original frame is intact. Raymond Gray remembers it as having beams fastened together with wooden pegs. A one and one-half story building with an ell on the east and a recent addition on the west, its siding is of modern vintage. One interesting feature was the half-partition with columns separating the dining room from the living room.

Returning to the corner and continuing south on Saw Mill Road, we come to the house at number 99, presently owned by Frank and Anne Kerrigon. While it is most probable that the house was erected in the late eighteenth century, many nineteenth and early twentieth-century changes have been made to the interior. It is a grey clapboard, white-trimmed, one and one-half story cape, again with the gable end facing the road. The early barn northwest of the house is a distinct feature of the property. This house passed through numerous hands. Walter E. Vaill wrote that John Hall, Revolutionary War soldier, was one of its first owners, followed by Daniel O'Brien and George Seelye in the 1870's. John Sall (Small?) purchased the house from George Seelye's widow, Jenny, and ran a saw mill on the site. In the 1900's Judge John Hubbard owned the property, and Howard and Edna Sheldon rented from him for many years. Subsequent owners include J. Russell and Helen Ackerman, the Lans Christensen family and now the Kerrigons.

If one proceeds along Saw Mill Road one-half mile past the Anson Dickinson memorial stone, past several eighteenth-century houses built by the Dickinson family, and on past the infamous James Duggan place immortalized in *Arsenic and Old Lace*, one comes to the corner of Saw Mill and Headquarters Roads. We should mention the house built by Malcolm P. and M. Adaline Seymour in the 1940's on that corner because of its historical site as the old dwelling house of Julius Griswold, the eldest child of Lt. John Griswold who invented the first ironclad vessel after the Revolutionary War and tested it on Milton Pond. The old house had fallen in by the time the Seymours built, but they incorporated materials from the old building into the new, including a Dutch oven in the cellar and an unusual mantel above the shallow living room fireplace.

Turning left from Saw Mill Road onto Headquarters Road one observes off the right side of the dirt road the present day home of Barbara Birge Winn at number 81. The house was presumably built around 1830, on a parcel of seven acres, by Willard Parmalee, who died at Cold Harbor during the Civil War. Parmalee's heirs sold the house to Everett H. Wright, who sold it to William O'Brien in 1875. Mr. O'Brien purchased additional acreage from Julius Griswold increasing the property to fifty-seven acres. In 1908 Rev. Alfred H. Stock and his wife, Maria Augusta, acquired the property. Their daughter, Mercy I. Birge, and her husband, William, were later deeded the property and lived in the house, which was badly in need of repairs. William Birge, a carpenter, was able to make the necessary improvements. Here they raised their four daughters, and the house was passed to their youngest daughter, Barbara, and her husband, Fred T. Winn, Jr. This is a one and one-half story structure with a large, later addition on the south. The original six-over-six windows and the "eyebrow" windows under the eaves, as well as the offset front door, are reminders of its earlier days. The Winns removed the wood shingles to reveal the original narrow clapboards. A "saltbox" barn to the north above the house is also of nineteenth-century vintage.

About one-half mile up the dirt road towards Milton Center stands the present home of Janet (Mrs. Donald) Sibley at 32 Headquarters Road. The origin of the property goes back to the time when Headquarters Road was situated many feet west of its present location, on the high bank above the Sibley house. The building which developed into this dwelling place apparently was originally a farm shed. Though part of the house was built before 1852, one of the first owners of record was John Bissell who inherited the property and sold it in 1863 to Frederick and Clarissa Jennings. Lavinia Conklin owned it in the 1870's. She ran a "gin mill" there to the consternation of the neighbors. The next owner was a Beach who, in June 1874, sold to Mrs. Ambler. In 1885 she traded the house with Lucy Sharp for a house near the site of the present schoolhouse. That house burned down after her death with her brother, Wadham(s) Beach, in it. At some point Daniel Taylor, who is referred to in the "Schools" chapter of this book, resided there and supplied the school boys with "lunch boxes." The next two owners were Henrietta Griswold, 1891, and Homer Griswold, 1899. After them was Elizabeth J. Douglas in 1923. Mrs. Adella E. Lamb and daughter, Kate Louise, lived there for many years. Later owners were Lester and Myrtle Whitford, Emile and Rose Bouthillier, Helena and Leif Anderson and finally Donald D. and Janet A. Sibley. The main portion of the present house, probably built by farmhands because of its structural characteristics, was added to the shed, with the abutting corner posts bolted together. The large red barn/garage on the north side is of recent construction and sustained a great deal of damage in the 1989 tornado, but was rebuilt by Mr. Sibley, a respected artist and illustrator.

Having completed the circuit around the "Square" (as locals designate it) and reversing our route past several twentieth-century homes, we reach the southern end of Headquarters Road where it becomes Prospect Mountain Road, and two significant nineteenth-century houses. The first, often referred to by Miltonites as "Headquarters," straddles the corner of Litwin and Headquarters Roads. It was constructed in 1896 by James Monroe Birge, who was the great-grandfather of its present owner, Charles F. Birge, Jr., and his family. The house replaced an old one which was north of the present building, and has passed from Harvey Birge, probably the builder of the old house, to his son Cornelius, to his son, James, who built the new house and left it to his son, Frank S. Birge and his wife, Priscilla. From Priscilla it went to their grandson, Charles Birge, Jr. and his wife, Kelli. This two-story clapboard house sits atop a long drive leading up from Headquarters Road to the side door. The front of the house, with a full porch, faces south on what was Forge Hollow Road and is now Litwin Road. Several small outbuildings are reminders of the time when this was a small farm and a place where charcoal was made.

Prospect Mountain Road, with Prospect Mountain always in the distance, takes us due south to the second house on the right, number 321, originally known as the Granniss place. Probably built in the mid- or late nineteenth century by the Granniss family, it was subsequently owned by Morton Benson and later his daughter Lucy and her husband, Hobart DeLos Gilbert. Lucy died young, and DeLos married Mary Pepper. After their deaths, the house was owned by her son, Gordon Pepper, and his wife, Irene Benjamin Pepper. They had built a large addition to the south to make it a two-family house. According to their daughter, Helen Pepper Loomis, this was in the 1920's, about ten years before she was born. The one and one-half story cape has interesting post and beam construction. An unusual — and potentially dangerous — feature was the set of attic stairs which were only laid, never nailed, in place. There is the usual clapboard siding, and there are three dormers on the front. Here Philip and Helen Pepper grew up.

South on Prospect Mountain Road (also called Mount Prospect Road), close to what is considered to be the southern extremity of Milton, is the imposing Fremont Granniss-John Helding farm at number 252. The exact year that it was erected and confirmation of its original owner are vague, but it was known early on as the Asa Lyman Granniss Farm, in an area where granite was quarried in the 1700's. From Asa Granniss, succession passed to his son, Fremont M. Granniss, who lived on the property virtually all his life. John Helding, father of Mildred Helding Griffin, leased the property in 1922 and purchased it from the estate of Fremont Granniss in 1931. A large piece of property, it consisted of 175 acres surrounding a house with white clapboard siding set on a foundation of large fieldstones. Floors were all hardwood of random width boards; walls and ceilings were lath and plaster. Centered in the house was a large chimney with a second one in the kitchen. A long narrow front porch faced the road. Downstairs there was a large bright kitchen with one of its five doors leading to a woodshed and a carpenter's tool shed, the latter with a privy at one end, its window looking out at Mount Prospect. Outbuildings were an ice-house, carriage shed, corn crib, small barn, horse barn and a three-level cow barn. After the death of John Helding in 1953, his wife Augusta ran the farm with the help of John's nephew, Harris Hilding, until it was sold in 1955 to Lukas and Borghild Hilpert; and from them it went to Andrew Gagarin, who put the land in the Litchfield Land Preservation Trust. We learned much about a young person's life on a big working farm from reading Mildred Helding Griffin's detailed account of her early years.

Traveling north from the corner of Litwin Road and Maple Street we approach the Walker Farm at 439 Maple Street, where the focal point is the old, two-story house on a rise of ground and the large red barn. It is verifiable that Asahel Griswold built the house; a stone in the foundation bearing the initials "A.G." testifies to its builder. Verification of the exact date of its construction remains elusive. The house passed from him to his grandson, Lucius, son of Benjamin and Sally Wright Griswold. It was deeded to him by Asahel, based on his promise to care for his grandmother while she lived, and though he was blind, he apparently fulfilled his obligation. Later Zelim and Waldburga (called Burga) Richard and family rented it from Lucius. Close to the turn of the twentieth century John S. Walker purchased the farm from Lucius Griswold, and John and his son, Martin, who followed him, operated a large farm on the premises for many years. The house had no fireplaces, but it was unique in having two attics, one over the kitchen — perhaps for storing vegetables — and the other over the main house. Few changes were made to the original house except to combine two small rooms to make a larger one and to add an enclosed porch to the front. Mrs. Martin Walker (Catherine) still resides in the home.

Heading north on Maple Street past the old Shepherd Knapp Camp, a turn-of-the-nineteenth-century house deserves our attention. On the east side of the road beyond the old Catlin-Doyle-Stevens house, on part of the land of John Baldwin, 1731, east of the East Tier, is the Smith farm at 588 Maple Street. One of the early transactions on the property was its purchase by Anson C. Smith from Wallaston Wadhams who may have obtained it from Amos Bishop's children. Since Anson was born in 1812, this transfer probably took place in the mid- to late-1800's. A grandson of Ernest K. Smith has traced the house back to early Milton days, but we do not have that data and it is not mentioned in the early days of Milton (1740 and on). Ernest Kenney Smith, Anson's grandson, and his wife, Mary Benjamin

Smith, inherited the property, farmed the land and raised their three children there, Helen, Malcolm and Elinor. After the deaths of Ernest and Mary, the farm passed to Helen who sold it to her nephew, Gregory Smith, the present owner. It is a clapboard, one and one-half story cape, typical of other Milton farmhouses, with two dormers as a prominent feature on the front. A long addition on the back (east) side is also typical of houses of that era.

The final nineteenth-century house on our tour is the second house on the right on Hemlock Hill Road. A wooden plaque on the front identifies it as of 1820 vintage with the name Noble Wetmore. One of the earliest inhabitants was Ira Page (1852-1885), succeeded by his son, Austin, and wife, Kate Hinchliffe Page. Later residents were William and Laura Doty Woodington and family, and later still, Hubert Hubbell. The Woodingtons lived there in the early to mid-1900's, and the Hubbells after that. Described by a real estate agent as being in a "wonderful country location," the original farm is now situated on just over two acres. Although little is left of the original interior, wide-board floors still remain in the living room and dining room. The dining room's large hearthstone is of significance, though the fireplace was closed off when the Woodington family lived there. The shed which originally was attached to the kitchen has been modernized, and a detached barn/garage remains. The house is attractive with a fieldstone foundation, clapboard siding, an elaborate corner-hugging cornice and twelve-over-twelve windows.

Chapter VI

MILTON INDUSTRIES
— How We Made a Living

❖

The village of Milton once had at least twenty-six commercial enterprises, largely located along the present Marshepaug River (then known as the East Branch of the Shepaug) and served by some six dams.

The earliest appearance of industry seems to have been the Grist-Saw Mill Dam, built soon after Justus Seelye came in 1753. This was likely followed by additional industrial activity upstream.

Starting at or near the Goshen town line, along what is now Shear Shop Road, were several dams furnishing power for the "Marshepaug Saw Mill," which had many co-owners including Ambrose Collins, Abraham Wadhams, Jeremiah Griswold (1767), William Munson, Jonathan Frisbie and Christopher Wheeler.

There was also "Frisbie's Little Shop," a saw mill, as well as an elusive "Clark's Dam." Nearer the village was the Shear Shop Dam, Rowe Iron Works, Welch's Puddling Works, W.W. Bissell's Wagon Shop and lastly, Thomas Hinchliffe's Aetna Shear Company.

The Center Dam on the west side of the present Green served a great variety of enterprises — a woolen shop, a fulling mill, a feather bed rehabilitation shop, one of Alban Guild's cabinet shops (later owned by David D. Guild), a shoemaker's shop, a tannery, Seelye's blacksmith shop and a file-making operation.

Drawing by Walter E. Vaill

Blacksmith Shop, 1884

Across Milton Pond, at its southwest corner, was a grist mill, saw mill, cider mill and shingle mill, plus a blacksmith shop. South of these a short distance, on the east side of Saw Mill Road, was the second of Guild's cabinet shops, a blacksmith shop and perhaps earlier, a shoemaker's shop, also owned by the Griswolds. More or less north was a nail factory.

Heading north again, the river flowed into yet another dam, serving a carriage shop, with the predecessor Marsh Forge and an early saw mill. Farther up the East Branch of the Shepaug was Seelye & Holmes' "Edged Tools" works, and more than likely, earlier saw mills and dams.

To the west was a granite quarry, while to the east on Butternut Brook, near Milton Road, was Norman Barber's mill; potash manufacturing was carried on, with much of the product carted to New Haven Harbor for shipping.

The Carriage Shop

Located on the west side of Blue Swamp Road, the Carriage Shop, first operated by the Smiths (1851-1873) and next by Charles and Emma Clark, lasted some fifty years and was served by a very high dam located at the rear of the house now occupied by Mr. and Mrs. Richard Bates at 15 Blue Swamp Road.

According to Walter E. Vaill, Andrew Palmer Smith and Chester F. Smith ran this business very successfully. Chester was also president of the Farmers and Mechanics Mining Company, one of the many Prospect Mountain mining companies which eventually failed. The Carriage Shop, built in 1851 and painted red, was a three-story frame building with eyebrow windows on the top floor. There was also a large paint shop, and one large and one small outbuilding. A long stone raceway ran from the dam to the factory, according to Fred H. Seelye. Litchfield Land Records recorded the transaction in February 1851, when Clarissa Welch for $287.25 conveyed to Andrew Palmer Smith and Chester F. Smith nine acres, two roods and twelve rods of land "in said Litchfield Milton Society in Tamarack Swamp..."

A photograph shows a group of some forty-seven people at the shop. Since the building burned in 1891 and was rebuilt, the picture is not likely of the earlier structure. F. Kingsbury Bull remembers being told by Ralph Smith, son of Chester Smith and owner of the Old Curiosity Shop in Litchfield, about his experiences working for his father in the carriage shop before the Civil War. He recounted that as many as two hundred carriages and sleighs were made during a year. It was in that old shop that Smith perfected his expert knowledge of painting which enabled him to do such delicate work on old furniture.

Years later, Mrs. Chester Lee (Gertrude) Smith gave many interesting insights into this bygone chapter of Milton's infant industry:

"The photographs show the 'stucco building,' what

The Carriage Shop

remained of the carriage shop about 1910. The Smith homestead was directly across Blue Swamp Road from this stucco building. In the gable end at the right was the kitchen and on the second floor was sleeping quarters for workmen. Mrs. Smith prepared meals for everyone. Lodging and board was the greater part of the workmen's pay. This ell was an addition to the original house built purposely for workmen accommodation as the factory grew.

"There was a large garden across the river south of the shop which supplied vegetables for canning and for the table. It was equipped with a piping system for irrigation in dry weather, probably one of the first systems in commercial use. Water was supplied from the tail race from the wheel which supplied power. Water came from the Milton pond at the head of the ravine.

"The carriage business failed after the Civil War and the Smiths moved first to South Plains in Litchfield and then to Cotton Hollow (now West Torrington)."

When in March, 1862, Chester Smith sold his half of the business to his brother, trouble was already brewing. The next several years saw various people attempt to save the business. From the *Litchfield Sentinel*, dated October 2, 1874, came the Milton News:

"This place was formerly the location of quite an extensive sleigh manufactory but the business has nearly ceased for the last two or three years. There is something being done in that line this season by Horatio P. Griswold who is making a few sleighs of the Albany pattern, and David D. Guild who is engaged in the manufacture of Hartford jumpers." Since the Clarks had already bought the carriage shop, the Messrs. Griswold and Guild were undoubtedly using other premises, but this item points to the factory having ceased operations about 1871. About the same time that Thomas Hinchliffe was arriving in Milton with Aetna Shear, Charles and Emma Clark, also from Sheffield, England, were taking over what had been the Smith Carriage Shop, "across town." Litchfield Land Records noted the purchase of "ten acres more or less with two carriage shops and a barn and the water privileges belonging to said premises, also the machinery in said shop excepting the plaining and paint mills."

Perry D. Green, of New Milford, recalled that the Clark wagons and carriages were well constructed and executed by expert workmen. The Clarks manufactured their own paints, further maintaining the high quality of their products, which competed with vehicles made by Flynn & Doyle of Bantam, Guild of Bethlehem and Throop of Lakeside, to mention a few.

It appears that it all ended with Charles Clark's death in September 1907. Subsequently, as with all the mill properties in Milton, the City of Waterbury ended up owning what had once been valuable sites. The end of the carriage shop came one day in 1923/24, as Walter Sheldon, then about five years old, watched his father and other men use teams of horses and yokes of oxen to tear down the building, then only some thirty-three years old.

Marsh's Forge

Milton's second iron works, after Welch's, was Marsh's Forge, later called Simmons Forge, located on Blue Swamp Road and the West Branch of the Shepaug.

On October 6, 1781, "we Abner Landon & Ebenezer Marsh have this day taken a lease of Ezekiel Graves at a mill plain for the purpose of building an Iron Works at Blue Swamp in Litchfield and the lease gives Liberty to said Graves to build a sawmill and grist mill on the east side of said River and to use the water for said Grist Mill at his pleasure but not to use water for the sawmill when it is wanted for iron works on the same dam that the iron works stands on."

Both were given "full liberty to build an iron works and Dam the stream to pass and repass through 100 acres of land lying in Blue Swamp which had been purchased of Isaac Catlin, Jr, also to cut such timber on said land as shall be necessary for the purpose of building said dam and iron works and use and occupy and improve said stream for the term of 999 years."

Thus, it would appear that there was a mill complex at Blue Swamp on the West Branch of the Shepaug (above the Guild-Blake Mill) which would later become the Smith/Clark Carriage Factory, with the saw mill apparently continuing at least intermittently. This mill is mentioned in September 1804, when Guerdon Granniss sold to Solomon Simmons, "1/8 of the sawmill standing on the west branch of the Shipaug and 1/8 of all tools and implements."

The Litchfield Land Records record many transactions concerning the Iron Works. In November 1787, Ebenezer Marsh conveyed to John and Solomon Simmons for twelve tons of iron, "one iron works, dwelling house and two other houses..." In January 1790, Ebenezer Marsh again sold to the Simmonses, "one half of an iron works...together with dwelling house and one coal house." On the same day, Marsh sold to Elisha Forbes of Canaan, "the half of one iron works or forge...known by the name of Simmons Forge, the fire called Waterfire or fire N of the stream and coal house known by name of Landons coal house..."

Other similar transactions followed. In Eri Granniss' estate, March 1854, his administrator "reserved 8/9th of a forge privilege to the proprietors of the same being located on the west side of the Shipaug, near Hardscrabble-Milton Road." There was also a note against Albert Anson of $90 payable in iron. This would seem to indicate that the forge was still in active operation, but probably not for very much longer. A deed dated April 1873 from Henry Frisbie to William M. Wheeler mentions an ancient forge in the westerly part of town, referring to another deed dated 1859.

Aetna Shear Company

"A company of shear mfgrs from Hoadleyville have rented W.W. Bissell's Wagon Shop and intend bringing up their machinery and commencing work forthwith. Mr. Bissell is repairing 3 houses to accommodate their workmen. This increase of 7 families is a welcome addition to the population" (*Litchfield Enquirer*, September 18, 1873). Thus was announced the Aetna Shear Shop, which brought some thirty-seven years of prosperity to Milton along with its great "Golden Age." On September 21, 1873, Warren W. Bissell conveyed to Thomas Hinchliffe of Plymouth four parcels of land on the east side of what is now Shear Shop Road, being what was earlier the Welch Puddling Works and subsequently the Bissell Wagon Factory, for a total of two acres and two rods of land, along with water privileges and building, which included a dwelling house.

Aetna Shear Shop begun by Thomas Hinchliffe, 1873; photo ca. 1930

In 1877, Bissell loaned another $2,000, secured by prior mortgages on the building, land and machinery, including "two blowers...with running gear, and one foot press, 138 feet of shafting, twenty four iron hangars, thirty iron pulleys, six lathes with counter shafts and attachments complete, forty polishing wheels with spindles & pulleys, twelve bench vises, two anvils, one water gate."

In nine years, the $10,000 in notes and mortgages were paid off, surely indicating close attention to business. "The shear business is in prosperous condition, working overtime to fill orders. Within the past year, the business has added about twelve families to the place, and increased population to about sixty" (*Litchfield Sentinel*, December 4, 1874).

The *Litchfield Sentinel* also noted in January 1875, that, "The shear works are unable to run all of the time from scarcity of water." Subsequently, Mr. Hinchliffe acquired more water rights, according to grandson Fred H. Seelye, through the help of the Town of Goshen. Then during 1882-3, he bought four acres north of the Shear Shop, which may also have had some water rights, possibly in connection with an alleged earlier blacksmith shop.

At first, the Hinchliffes lived in one of the small factory houses, but in 1880 a splendid new two-story dwelling with full front porch along with two sets of front steps was erected on the west side of Shear Shop road on a quarter acre of land. Early pictures of the house included the happy family, even the carriage horse, while later pictures show large shade trees and a very greatly aged Thomas Hinchliffe.

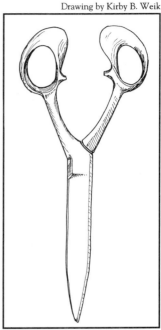

Drawing by Kirby B. Weik

Shears from Aetna Shear Shop

When the Milton Hall was built in 1900 by Jesse H. Derby on the site of the burned Granniss & Elmore branch store, Mr. Hinchliffe contributed $30, the largest donation. When Granniss and Elmore decided not to rebuild, Mr. Hinchliffe set up Herbert L. Register (also from Sheffield, England) in the store business, at the southwest corner of the "new" bridge, where Milton's first telephone would be located. Florence Hinchliffe and her husband, Walter E. Seelye, operated the business for several years, living above the store. They roasted their own peanuts, which became a Saturday night tradition in the village.

In July, 1909, Thomas Hinchliffe executed a warranty deed to William H. Doyle. Included was "the dwelling house, factory and other building, dam, flume and all appurtenances, excepting shears finished and unfinished which are excepted, reserving possession of said factory and machinery and use of water power for 6 months." Several years later, in 1912, Hinchliffe died in Milton after a short retirement.

Standing idle for some ten years, the Shear Shop became a huge wooden clapboard "pin cushion" for some village boys and other naughty summer camp boys to throw shear halves at. Eventually, in the late 1920's, the City of Waterbury tore down all the factory buildings, but the dam remained until around 1940.

The house came to be owned by Beatrice M. McKechnie. Later it was planned to move it to Warren. Unfortunately, a bold and enterprising thief stole the entire chimney for the bricks, which caused the structure to partly collapse. For a practice session, the local fire department (probably) set fire to it. Thus did that superbly constructed house with chestnut beams and boards come to a most undeserved ending, after having stood bravely for some one hundred years.

The Guild-Blake Grist and Saw Mill

The oldest, best known and longest operating mill in Milton had many owners and part owners during nearly two centuries, beginning with Justus Seelye (d. 1795). Seelye doubtless constructed both a grist mill and saw mill along with the necessary dam — apparently on part of the fifth lot in the West Hundred Tier — purchased by him in November 1753, for £750 from Joseph Tuttle and Thomas Robinson of New Haven. Shortly afterwards, Seelye sold half his acquisition for £375 to David Welch.

Saw Mill, corner of Saw Mill and Blue Swamp Roads

Next the mill became "Landons Mill." In September 1788, Seelye for £30 conveyed to Daniel, Abner and John Landon, "one equal half of one certain Piece of Land...Together with the whole of a Grist or Corn Mill the same standing with all the Privileges & appurtenances belonging and appurtaining to said Mill together with the one half of a Saw Mill..." In 1796, Abraham Norton acquired portions of "said Grist Mill standing on the Same Dam with a Saw Mill: the Grist Mill is to have the whole of the water when there is not enough for both..." Moore Gibbs purchased a portion of the mill in 1798, "together with the Privileges & Appurtenances...sd Mill has two Pair of Stones & said Grist Mill has the privilege of Daming & raising the water as high as may be wanted." Additional transactions, including David Welch's, occurred frequently, both before and after Gibbs.

In September 1815, William Tuttle sold to Rufus Pickett for $1500 "the sixth part of a certain Grist Mill with Two run of stones in said Mill situate in said Litchfield in Milton Society on the east branch of Shippaug River..." In October 1831, Isaac Wadhams of Goshen and Jeremiah Guild of Litchfield purchased from Arvil Morris, "one certain

Gristmill with two run of stones in said mill situated in said Litchfield in Milton Society on the east branch of Shippaug river together with all the tools belonging thereto sd Gristmill also the mill house & garden and all the building called the bark house situated on the south side of the dam, together with about half an acre of land..."

Subsequent transactions occurred as divided shares in the mill properties were traded frequently. Anson Beach sold to Lyman Carter land which was "the mill privilege on which a Saw Mill now standing & I hereby release to sd Carter all my right title & interest in & to sd mill & to the appurtenances thereto belonging."

Ellen Doyle noted that, "Mill privilege was granted to the town by the government. Certain conditions had to be fulfilled, though title was not rigid." Doubtless this applied more during the colonial period than to later times.

In April 1847, Daniel and Norman Hall conveyed to Frederick F. Guild of Goshen one-half of a parcel of land containing the saw mill and "one equal half the shingle and cider mill situate on the south side of the river opposite sd Saw mill..." Walter Vaill reported that during Guild's ownership, there was an up and down saw, a cider mill and a grist mill. "Children used to visit it (the cider mill) and drink out of an awful dipper," he said.

More buying and selling shares occurred, including Nathan Bassett, Buel Blake, Samuel F. Bassett, Gad Guild and Henry Guild. In November 1863, Henry Guild deeded to Lewis Hutchinson a "certain piece of land...with a Grist Mill, Saw mill & shingle mill, cider mill, dam & water privilege & old factory building thereon containing about three acres more or less..."

"Lewis Hutchinson came from New York; just beginning to use the circular saw and he made this improvement. It didn't prove practical. It took 15 minutes to stop the mill to adjust the logs. Overshot wheel had been used. These were replaced by turbine wheels. It was customary to take toll out of the grist for pay," remembered Walter E. Vaill. "Mr. Hutchinson has remodeled his cider mill and is preparing for the making of a few barrels 'for vinegar' by those anxious of so doing. The apple crop promises a sufficiency..." (*Litchfield Sentinel*). A later report from Milton states: "It is said that more than a thousand barrels of cider have been made at Mr. Hutchinson's mill this fall" ("Milton History Papers"). "On Saturday, Mr. James Hutchinson raised a new grist mill in Milton, on the site of the old mill lately owned by Henry Guild" (*Litchfield Enquirer*, July 21, 1864).

"Bradley Beach finally acquired the mills. Samuel Bennett was thrown out of work in Providence in 1873 during hard times and came to Milton to run the mills for Beach. He was an exact accountant and balanced his books every night. Bennett ran the mills for eight years and saved $2400 during that time" ("Milton History Papers").

In 1890, after intervening years of property transfers, Charles S. Blake of Cornwall acquired the mill property. "Charley Blake enjoyed the mill a great deal. He used to get his chores done up hurriedly in the morning and walk to Milton" ("Milton History Papers"). Blake surely put his stamp on the Mill's history, as had the several Guilds— Jeremiah, Frederick F., Henry H., Laura Clark, Julia F., and Alfred T.— and quite successfully brought the 1753 mill (even though rebuilt) right into the great twentieth century. But this was not to last; Charlie died in 1913, leaving no will.

In 1919, John T. Hubbard conveyed seven and one-half acres to William H. Doyle, thus completing "control of the flow of water along the whole course of said River to Tyler Pond." But all too soon the "plug" was to be pulled. In

December of that year, Doyle deeded to the H.S. Chase Co. of Waterbury, "the right, privilege and franchise of interrupting, diminishing and entirely withholding from time to time and at all times the flow of water...[on the] Shepaug River or Marshepaug River..."

This legal maneuvering put control of all the water in the hands of the City of Waterbury, through the Chase Co. Now with Waterbury controlling all the water on both rivers and their many rivulets, Judge Hubbard could continue "his" mill, which was apparently confined to sawing logs, with Harry Haviland as operator. Harold Bunnell, as a lad of ten, went there with his father around 1932, and well recalled the sawmill operation.

Eventually, in 1947, the buildings were taken down. The flood of 1955 washed out the dam and with it the mill pond. Milton had reverted back to its quiet, pre-industrial days.

The Marshepaug Saw Mill

This early saw mill was mentioned in Jeremiah Griswold's "Love & Affection" deed to his son Asahel in May 1767: "And also one tenth Part of four acres of land in said Litchfield near Goshen Line and is the East bounds of Shippaug River together with one eighth Part of a Saw Mill thereon standing."

In May 1796, Abraham Wadhams of Goshen sold for £12 to Jonathan Frisbie "the one eighth part of a certain Saw Mill situate in the Society of Milton in said Litchfield on the East Branch of Shippaug river about half a mile Northward of the Iron Works belonging to said Welch, Esqr..." At the same time Jonathan Frisbie bought from Ambrose Collins "one twelfth part of a certain sawmill..." Later that year another twelfth part of this mill, "about half a mile Northward of the Iron works..." was conveyed to William Munson by William James, both men being from Goshen. In 1811, Munson sold this twelfth share to Levi Frisbie of Litchfield.

The last mention of the sawmill came in 1870 when a transaction in the Litchfield Land Records mentioned property bounded by "sd River & Saw Mill privilege..."

Horace Seelye/Martin Kubish House

Iron, Nails, Seelye & Holmes, Clark's Saw Mill

Salisbury iron had a great deal to do with the early settlement of Milton. In the early days iron was the principal industry here, and nail making was carried on all along the stream.

The nail makers used charcoal as fuel and had undershot water wheels to furnish power for their blowers and forges. Salisbury had virtually the finest quality iron to be found anywhere in this country — equal to Swedish iron — and it was being mined as early as 1730. In 1762, General Ethan Allen purchased property and built a blast furnace in

Salisbury, supposedly the first in Connecticut. David Welch brought iron from Salisbury and had a forge on the Shear Shop site. Iron nail bars — made into small strips for nail making at a slitting mill — were made at the Welch Puddling Works and sold to the nail makers.

One of Milton's nail factories was located west of the Guild-Blake Grist Mill, proximal to the Jonathan Wright house at the corner of Saw Mill and Blue Swamp Roads. Stephen Ranney advertised in the *Monitor* in 1795 for three nailors, "steady and faithful hands who are thorough workmen in the business," by the twenty-eighth of December to "whom the highest wages will be given." Another was located behind the Reuben Dickinson house, now 65 Saw Mill Road.

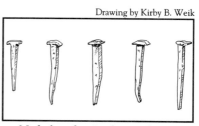

Drawing by Kirby B. Weik

Nails forged at Reuben Dickinson/William Hall place

H.L. Seelye & Son (later Seelye & Holmes) was located "up river" on Kubish Road. The partners, Horace L. Seelye, his brother, Harmon Seelye, and Andrew S. Holmes were all blacksmiths. The 1860 Census lists them as manufacturing "Edge Tools," with annual production of five hundred axes valued at $500, chisels and other articles at $400, requiring two tons of iron at $400, one-half ton of steel at $200, two thousand bushels of charcoal at $160 and three smith's fires. The firm was still in business in 1870. Fred H. Seelye said that iron was hauled from Lime Rock and the stagecoach used to bring axes and tools to be headed and sharpened. Seelye had the only trip hammer in the county and had a wonderful reputation for treating steel and making edged tools.

North of Seelye & Holmes was another dam, with a saw mill, built about 1845-46 by Sheldon Clark on a seventy-five acre farm. This dam — mentioned by Walter Vaill as Clark's Dam — was described as being "up the river where the Indians made pottery." Subsequent owners were George O. Clark, 1851; James I. Newton, 1858; Lyman Richards, 1864; and Elbert Richards, 1866.

Tannery, Woolen Mill and Guild's Cabinet Shop

Seymour Stevens, a short, stout man who died of apoplexy, ran the tannery. For $400 he acquired a large tract of land in March 1863, from Lucius Griswold. It was "bounded...North by Ada Blake, Milton Green and Shipaug River ... containing Twenty acres be the same more or less." Earlier, in 1819, John M. West is recorded as selling an established business to Benjamin Griswold, mentioning "...a constant supply of Water for all the Vatts of a Tanyard together with a Supply of the water through the year for grinding Bark..." The business continued for forty-four years under Griswold ownership.

Benjamin Griswold & Co. executed a lease with John M. West in 1828, which refers to still another tanner: "one certain building with water privileges...(it being the same building & water privileges that Elizur B. Smith has occupied for a number of years past as a tannery works)..." The mill stones in front of the Milton Hall and the old Academy building on the Green came from there. They were used to grind bark used in the tanning of leather.

The Tannery was comprised of quite a few buildings which stood across the stream, west of the Green, from a large two and one-half story woolen mill, which blew down about 1874. The Tannery building also blew down, possibly around the same time. The woolen mill, thought to be operated by the Fervers, is said to have been on the east side of the river, the old cellar wall still showing the location.

Just below the woolen mill was a cabinet shop which blew down in 1872. Walter E. Vaill thought some of the Guilds had run it. Another said the cabinet shop, run by Virgil Beach and the Guilds, was located on the river below the sawmill, "about where Edmund Switzer's cottage is located [now 107 Saw Mill Road]." Still another claimed the shop was below the bridge and that David Guild had a carpenter's shop there at one time.

The *Litchfield Enquirer*, on November 20, 1874, stated that, "The Seelye Brothers are about moving their blacksmith business from the old Smith shop to the shop of David Guild in the centre to make room for the file cutting business."

The Clothing and Carding Mill

A Clothing and Carding Mill probably began to develop near the older Fulling Mill after a separate parcel was obtained in 1813 for relocating the latter to the east side of the river from the west. The Fulling Mill was mentioned in a 1799 transaction, and again in 1801, when Abraham Norton sold to Oliver Gibbs and Thomas and Truman Grove one-third part of a Grist or Corn Mill, one-eighth part of a Saw Mill, while reserving his "right of raising the water at my Fulling Mill Dam as specified in a lease given by me to Lyman Norton."

In 1817, Solon Bishop sold his "Clothing works thereon" to Zelah North of Goshen and William North of Amenia, New York. In 1819, the Norths sold to Hubbel West of

Colebrook property containing "one half acre with a Clothing and Carding Shop thereon Standing together with all the Tools and Machinery belonging to said shop..."

In 1822, Hubbel West, Asahal H. Bolles and Ithamer Ferris, now owners of the Clothing and Carding Shop, sold the business to Rufus Pickett. Several transactions later, in 1827, West sold for $750 the half-acre Clothing and Carding Shop to Stephen, Jr., Gerardus and Robert Ferris, "including one stove and pipe in the possession of Mr. Birdsey Gibbs, one loom in the possession of Seth Prince Jr., and one pr of clothing shears in my own possession not in sd shop..." More transactions followed, and in 1841 Alban Guild quit claimed to Fenn Mallet of sd Litchfield, "...about one half acre with a clothing and carding shop thereon standing together with all the Tools and implements and machinery belonging to the shop."

"For a sum of money" on May 10, 1848, Fenn Mallett of Litchfield gave a mortgage to Alban Guild, covering a $300 Note of Hand, on the Carding Shop "...to wit one double carding machine, one spinning jenny, one cleaning machine being the same which I bought of Ezra Ferris...one hand loom, one Picker, one copper dye kettle and two iron dye kettles, one condenser, one shearing machine which I bought of the Sharon Manufacturing company."

In 1852, probate allowed sale of all real estate at public auction with 50 cents paid on the dollar by Robert Ferriss of New Milford, the highest bidder for the Clothing and Carding Shop.

The Guild Tavern

Over two dozen owners, covering over two hundred years and at least sixteen families, have combined to make Milton's Guild (pronounced as in child) Tavern a venerable landmark and once an important cog in the week-long Hartford-Poughkeepsie stage route. The great stagecoach era, which brought contact with the outside world ever closer, was well under way when Alban Guild and his family opened their hostelry around 1862. Mail contracts had by then brought greater stability to "staging" and the need for lodging.

According to Walter Vaill, "Alban Guild had a tavern where Peter Ackerman lives. This was all made over in 1876 and verandas put on. The barn was moved where it now stands north of the house. It used to be across the river where the bridge now is. The old bridge was further south.

"Alban Guild owned back of Jacob Ackerman's (across the road). There was a dam there and woodworking shop on the west side of the stream, while on the other side was a big wooden water wheel and woolen shop. This blew down about 1875."

When Alban died on May 2, 1874, Horatio N. Griswold who operated the Milton Cabinet Shop on the west side of the village, found a "retirement job" operating the inn. It was he who greatly improved the structure, but shortly after his death in 1892 the tavern apparently closed. Thus Horatio was the "last innkeeper of Milton."

Standing on land laid out to Thomas Lee, the Guild Tavern was probably built in 1788, shortly after Samuel Sheldon, Litchfield's famous tavern keeper, had purchased the land for £60 from Ashbel Catlin. Sheldon probably started construction of his house sometime in 1788; it was then sold to Isaac Baldwin who sold it to Jonathan Frisbie in 1791.

Frisbie lived there for some twenty-three years, and after several transfers the property went to Alban Guild who lived there for fifty-four years. His niece, Augusta R. Griswold, lived there afterwards for thirty years. With Horatio Griswold's death in 1892, an already diminishing business turned into financial ruin for Augusta. The stage had been reduced to a local mail route between Litchfield and Cornwall Bridge, and few, if any, stayed at the tavern. William J. Hall appeared, loaning the poor widow $800. Two years later, in 1898, Hall took over the place via Quit Claim Deed, and in 1904 sold it to Lucius D. Leonard who sold it five years later to Willis O. Perkins.

A long line of twentieth-century owners followed. Peter Ackerman, with a number of children, including his very pretty daughters, was selling his farm to Martin Kubish, so Perkins gladly sold him his roomy house in 1920. After twenty-four years, Ackerman sold the property to Thomas and Alice Lindsay and Mary and Otto Deering of Torrington.

Then followed Helen D. Gage of Augusta, Maine, the Smiths, the Loyds, Ficks, Dooleys, Prentices, and Janssens.

The Milton Store

Again, here is a tale of many owners, many names, at least four locations and considerable lore. David Welch, from New Milford, started things off in his new residence in 1756. Prior to 1790, an east wing was added including space on the first floor exclusively for the store. It was reached by climbing five or six granite steps through a separate doorway. David had married Irene Marsh, granddaughter of founder John Marsh. This Irene Welch is credited with giving Milton its name, derived from the English poet, John Milton, per descendant Walter E. Vaill.

According to Col. Edward A. Raymond's *History of the David Welch House, 1756-1976*, the store operations doubtless began as an outgrowth of the iron business, expanded by returning Revolutionary War officer John Welch, the owner from 1784-1844.

Hugh P. and Garritt P. (also spelled Gerret/Gerrit) Welch appear next, but in February 1845, their co-partnership was dissolved, "with the business being conducted at the old stand by H.P. Welch where the favors of our old customers will be thankfully received."

Shortly thereafter it was Garritt P. Welch and Harold Kilbourn who ran the store and kept it stocked with an astonishing array of goods for that era and location. Following Welch's death in 1847, new management transferred the business to a separate structure, near the site of the present Milton Hall.

On January 21, 1854, for $800, Hugh P. Welch conveyed to Walstein C. Wadhams, "...the building occupied by the sd H P Welch as a Store situated near the Episcopal Church in Milton, also the building occupied by said Welch as a store house or shop...also the platform scales in front of sd store on the highway."

By 1861, Wadhams had moved on to Cornwall, selling for $800 to E. Smith Hubbell of Bridgeport, "one store" situated in Milton, which was shortly quit claimed to David T. Welch. In 1864, Welch sold to Warren W. Bissell.

Frank M. Barton ran the store for several years, buying calves and produce over a wide geographic area. Seymour Johnson, who lived at the foot of Bunker Hill in Cornwall, brought his calves over one day and returned with $200, as an example. The store team even went over to Waterbury twice a week. In 1885, Barton sold out, and in November 1885, Barton Bros. left Milton, having done $60,000 business in his final year in Milton.

Immediately, in December 1885, Elmira Beach of Litchfield executed a Warranty deed to "Weston G. Granniss and George S. Elmore, partners in business under the firm name of Granniss & Elmore." Business appears to have been good, the Shear Shop just up the road to the north being in full operation. Yet, while it had been most prestigious for Weston Granniss to have had a branch at Milton, when the store burned in the winter of 1894, he did some "close figuring" and decided not to rebuild. Thomas Hinchliffe then set up Herbert Register in business, with the store relocated in the walk-out basement of what had been Seymour Stevens' house, southwest of the present bridge. The house (541 Milton Road) is now owned by Paul and Patricia Deering. Before moving to Bantam, Register installed Milton's first telephone in his store and collected $20 from AT&T for a right of way north of the village which crossed his ninety-four acres on Shear Shop Road.

Probably next came Florence Hinchliffe and her husband, Walter E. Seelye, to operate the business. Cleveland Landon followed, and then came Jacob "Jake" Ackerman, who surely left his name and mark, along with his wife, Alice. "Jake Ackerman's Store" became widely known, and despite its closing around 1935, its memory has managed to linger on amazingly well. "I remember the Ackermans sitting on the second-story porch over the store entrance on those long summer evenings. They would wave to my parents as we drove past on our return from East Cornwall. Father would toot his horn in reply — all part of those quickly vanishing 'good old days'," remembers Andrew Pikosky.

The Great Hill Iron Ore Manufacturing Company

While Milton had several mining companies located in the Prospect Mountain area, at the far western fringe of town, the Great Hill Iron Ore Manufacturing Company was located within the Town of Cornwall, near the top of Great Hill, in the general triangle of College Street and East Cornwall Road.

The company could engage in mining activities throughout the entire state, but confined its activities to clearing and leveling an area in front of what was to be the mine portal. This entrance was still visible years later, as recalled by longtime East Cornwall residents, Harriet L. Clark and George Bouteiller. Iron is most certainly in the ground there, for lightning is regularly attracted thereto with sometimes unhappy results for the neighbors.

The company's Certificate of Organization was dated January 20, 1865, with Capital Stock of $125,000. The company was to pursue the business of "searching for, digging, smelting, refining, vending and converting into metals, substances and conducting mining and quarrying operations of any description within the State of Connecticut..." The list of stockholders was most impressive, including Elizabeth Benedict, Christian Reinhart, Chester F. Smith, Riverius Marsh, Geo. H. Baldwin,

President, Chas. B. Bishop, Frederick D. McNeil, and David C. Bulkley.

Despite the great potential for a flourishing mining operation with a vast deposit of iron ore beneath Great Hill, the company quietly disappeared, along with so many other attempts to find "gold in them thar hills" of New England.

AT&T Through Milton

During the summer of 1902, Edward J. Hall, vice president of the American Telephone and Telegraph Company acquired line rights for a long distance (toll) line, which ran west from Torrington out Highland Avenue, crossing Norfolk Road in Litchfield, thence along Brooks road and Newcomb Road, crossing Upper Maple Street and thence north of Milton village, crossing East Cornwall Road just north of the Welch-Vaill House and proceeding westward up and down the hills of Warren, crossing the great Housatonic River to connect with the north-south line on the west side, which alledgedly ran all the way to Toronto, Canada. A two-cross-arm pole line was constructed and became a landmark for nearly eighty years.

The sums paid for line rights varied greatly. William J. Hall was paid $25 and Herbert Register, proprietor of the Milton store, was paid $20 for the right of the company to "construct, operate and maintain its lines over and along the property which I own or in which I have any interest in."

In August 1981, AT&T released all the easements by Quit Claim to the original grantors, none of whom was still alive!

Miscellaneous Enterprises

From the *Litchfield Enquirer*, December 3, 1863: "A patent was issued last week to James B. Lyon of Milton for improvements of a butter worker." (A butter worker was a roller used to force any remaining water and buttermilk out of the newly churned butter before further processing. One style ran on metal tracks.)

Old-time peddler, Mr. Squires, and Egbert Sheldon at Page/Skidmore House

On November 1, 1853, the New Haven Shirt Manufactory instituted "a new scale of prices" for shirt making done at home. "Persons wishing work can have it by calling on the Agent," H. Kilbourn at Milton.

There was a button mill opposite the grist mill (E. B. Buel — "Milton History Papers").

"Mr. Hoffman, a German shoemaker, has opened a shop in this place, and is busy making boots and shoes for those who in purchasing prefer getting their money's worth" (*The Litchfield Sentinel*, September 25, 1874).

"Austin Page said that the Indians used to make pottery up by the dam on the brook west of the O'Brien place. This was the site of the saw mill run by Sam Bassett" ("Milton History Papers").

Milton had a granite quarry located north of the present Comstock Reservoir (in Warren). Dorothy Wagstaff Ripley has described how her horseback riding groups were able to wind down through the scenic, grassy area around the abandoned quarry in the late 1940's and early 1950's before it was flooded by the new Comstock Dam (City of Waterbury). Granite was also found on the Granniss property on Prospect Mountain, and at the William Hall (now Harris Hilding) place.

There was also a cheese factory south of the Comstock Reservoir, on Old Forge Hollow Road.

Frederick Fenton Guild invented a tooth-pulling device, a turn-key which operated on the principle of a cant hook. Neighbors went to his house to have teeth pulled. He made a fitted case for the turn-key. He also made a low boy and top for it, also a writing desk of butternut, the lumber being sawed at the Milton sawmill (the grist mill) which he owned (Fred H. Seelye).

Potash making once was an important industry, with much of the output being taken down to New Haven Harbor and loaded onto ships. Still stored in Hubbard's Mill in the 1930's were potash pots along with a splendid carriage, probably from the nearby Clark Carriage Shop.

On Potash Hill Road was located the Milton Flower Farm, Alice G. Phillips, proprietor, which had an extensive mail order business. Sadly, it became a victim of the 1929 depression.

The several area iron works created a large market for charcoal; charcoal manufacturing was carried on by many, including James Birge and Sheldon Clark. An experienced charcoal burner being absolutely essential, Benjamin Taylor was frequently engaged. Despite more than one hundred years having passed, a very special site on the west side of Mohawk Mountain is still called "Ben's Cabin."

Chapter VII

SCHOOLS — Where We Studied

Ellen Doyle with horse and buggy

The Early Years

As was typical of most newly established communities in the "New World," organizing a school held a high priority, and Milton was no exception. As far back as 1718, when a company was formed for the settlement of the Town of Litchfield with proprietors as shareholders, one portion was reserved for the support of schools. Milton Society, as the Third Society of Litchfield, was made up of parts of Litchfield, Cornwall, Warren and Goshen. It was organized in 1795 and steps were soon taken to provide for the administration of school matters. According to the General Court of the State of Connecticut, "school must be kept in every society, the length of the sessions to be governed by the number of families, none being less than six months."

Records in the history of Morris reveal that Connecticut's first permanent school fund was created in 1795 from the proceeds of the sale of western lands in Ohio, which belonged to the State of Connecticut. The income, called an enumeration grant, was to be distributed annually to the towns, prorated according to the number of children between four and sixteen years of age. For twenty-five years, from 1824-1849, Seth Beers was commissioner of the School Fund for all of Connecticut. As commissioner, Mr. Beers visited the Western Reserve Lands, travelling mainly by canal. His successful administration of the funds saw them increase from their original $1,200,000 to over $2 million through sale of the land, and the revenue of the fund from $72,000 to $133,000. A Town Deposit Fund was established in 1836 when President Jackson closed the Bank of the United States. This money was distributed to the states on the basis of population to be used for schools.

Certainly in those early years children were taught in private homes, notably "Aunt Hannah" Seelye's house (the present Walter C. Sheldon house at 557 Milton Road), the Benedict place on the East Cornwall road (615 Milton Road), and the present Raymond cottage (529 Milton Road). One wonders what constituted the curriculum, but undoubtedly the New England Primer was used. It is described in Clifton Johnson's *Old-Time Schools and Schoolbooks* as, "...originally a book of private devotions...typewriting reduced the cost of books so materially that they were available for people to have in their homes, and it at once became desirable that the rudiments of language should be put within reach of the many who now wished to learn to read. In consequence an alphabet was often included in the little devotional primers, and this led presently to giving the name 'primer' to all elementary books for the use of children. The contents of the old-time primers changed, but for hundreds of years the teaching of religion and reading continued united in them."

We know that letters were being taught using the hornbook, or battledore, the latter described in Johnson's words as "...a folded card of 2 or 3 leaves with a little flap like an old-time pocket book...essentially little illustrated primers; the price was from a penny to 4 pence."

Little emphasis was put on spelling but much time given over to penmanship and reading of the Bible. Specific needs of older male students were emphasized according to their planned profession — mathematics for those going into farming or foreign trade, and "learned languages" and grammar for potential doctors, lawyers and ministers. Pen and ink were the exclusive tools of the master and scholars; slates came into use about 1820 and lead pencils not until a good many years later. Little copy and sum books could be made by folding foolscap paper into fourths and folding several together, a cover being made of coarse wrapping paper or wallpaper sewed into shape. It was decreed that, "Two hours in the Day be Devoted to the instruction of Females as they are a tender and interesting Branch of the Community."

In their first schools children were expected to "read in such books as they bring to school." Locked drawers or cupboards would protect these and such writing materials as the committee procured.

The earliest recorded meeting of the First School District in Milton Society was November 27, 1797, and it dealt with a new schoolhouse. Judging from the word "new" we know that there was already some kind of school in the district; moreover, the records note that "the place to set the School House shall be on the ground where the old School House stood." The dimensions of the new school were advised to be thirty-four feet long and eighteen feet wide. Ebenezer Pickett and Jonathan Wright, the committee appointed to see the project through, were instructed to "build a school house by subscription," presumably of materials or money. By 1799 the building was up but not finished, and though it had been hoped that £60 would cover its cost, twice that amount was needed to finish it and was "assessed upon the Poll and rateable estate of the inhabitants in the 1st district in Milton School Society."

Old Milton School on Cornwall Road and schoolchildren, before 1896

The Nineteenth Century

Many people were involved in overseeing the schools in 1800 — a clerk, a moderator, a treasurer, a three-member School Society Committee, five inspectors and a six-member district committee (representing the other districts). By 1803 the district committee had increased to seven members and the inspectors to seven. At the 1804 meeting, described as a "more than usual meeting," the 4th district in East Cornwall was divided into two districts, so in 1805 the number of committee members was increased to eight.

According to the Warranty Deed of November 25, 1820, Chauncey Dennison of Warren for "a valuable consideration" deeded to Thomas Granniss as spokesman for the 3rd School District in the Society of Milton a "certain parcel of land...being 26' long by 20' wide bounded S on highway, W on Solomon Moulthrop's land, N and E on my own land for the Purpose of Erecting a ... School House thereon for the up (sic) and benefit of said district." It was often the custom to acquire a deed to land for a school after it was built. By late 1825, according to the "Records of the 1st School District in Milton Society," the motion was passed to move the meeting house to the place where the school "now stands" (which is believed to be West of the present Trinity Church) as per the Dennison deed, and "secure the Ground for the purpose of a public green." This swapping of sites did not materialize, as the Church Society in 1828 agreed to move the church across the river to where it now stands.

The first clerk of the Milton School Society was Judge John Welch. Reference is made to his working with a committee of three regarding a spot of ground at the southeast corner of the green for the purpose of setting a school there — a move which did not take place until the late 1890's. Quoting from Clifton Johnson's aforementioned book, "To settle the question of where one of the little frame schoolhouses should stand has been known to require 10 district meetings scattered over a period of two years. The one point on which all could agree was that the schoolhouse should be built where the land was as nearly valueless as possible." Milton was not alone in its dilemma over the school site.

There is an abundance of information about conditions in the first school from records of the Milton School Society. Teachers lived "here and there" as provided for in the Society's meetings. In 1825 it was voted "that the board of the man teacher be 88¢ a week." He started out that year in the home of Dr. Partridge Parsons. Asa Morris was to board the woman teacher at 75¢ a week (she undoubtedly having a lighter appetite!). A few years later the Society announced that no one was to be allowed to bid for the privilege of boarding the teacher if that person lived more than one-half mile from the school.

At one time wood for heating the school house was furnished by the lowest bidder, "a half cord at a time, to be delivered at a specific time, cut up and ready for the stove." Later reference was made to citizens being individually responsible, and if they were delinquent, the wood would be delivered and they would be held liable for all expenses. Johnson in his book relates that "...sometimes they (children whose parents didn't contribute to the woodpile) were refused 'the benefit of fire' and the master saw to it that they sat in the schoolroom's bleakest corner." Hopefully this method of punishing the child for the parent's shortcomings was not practiced in Milton. A cord of wood was selling for 88¢ in 1836. This manner of assuring a supply of wood remained the one used for about twenty years until the District voted to procure its own wood.

The original intent of the Society was to make the school house available for other functions when not in session, but "carelessness and destructiveness" required "firm measures," and finally came the pronouncement that the "School House be Locked up to be opened for no other purpose only for Schools and School Business."

Two years after the 1825 meeting, in March 1827, Birdsey Gibbs, son of Deacon and Mrs. Moore Gibbs, and his wife proposed to the School Society that they teach the school in Milton for one year at the rate of $30 per month. At the next meeting it was voted to employ Mrs. Gibbs to teach summer school for six months and furnish her own board. At a meeting on December 31, 1828, this notation appeared, "Schollars (sic) that attend Mrs. Gibbs school constantly and nowhere else should be entitled to take their school money from the District." Apparently by that time Birdsey Gibbs was conducting a private school as witnessed by this advertisement in the *Litchfield County Post*:

The Fall and Winter term of the B. Gibbs Select School in Milton will commence on the 6th day of October next.
Tuition for English Studies $4
$3 per quarter
for Greek and Latin $4
Board $1 per week

In 1832 a vote was taken to make Birdsey Gibbs' school a branch of the district school. At some point his school was conducted in the upper room of the church according to the notes of the Ecclesiastical Society of the Congregational Church of Milton for 1834, where he was listed as the teacher of record.

From the first establishment of school districts until the 1850's there were eight schools within the Milton School District: 1) Milton, 2) Gilbert, 3) Headquarters, 4) Prospect, 5) Mt. Tom, 6) Newcomb, 7) College Street in East

Cornwall and 8) Goshen (Nichols). There were as many committeemen as there were schools, one from each district. In this history, when reference is made to "the school," unless otherwise specified, the school that served the center of what we think of now as Milton is the one intended.

In 1835 there was again talk of moving the school house but it was voted to repair the existing school. In late October 1836, the district committee was authorized to receive a deed from Hugh Welch for the land where the school house was then located. This site was on the Cornwall road near the present home of Reeves Hart, a grandnephew of Walter E. Vaill. Ten days later the district was empowered "to convey to the town of Litchfield for a publick (sic) highway the ground upon which the school formerly stood and to receive for the use of the district the Welch property." The story behind the deeding of this land started in the early days of the school when Garrett Welch, Walter Vaill's grandfather, ran a store on a site near the original school. Having a school so close became an annoyance to him so he offered land to the Town opposite his house on the corner where the road turns north to East Cornwall. The school house was moved there in 1836, although the deed may not have been forthcoming until 1845.

The length of the winter school terms varied from year to year but was usually four to five months. One item of interest gleaned from the records of 1836 was the decision that no scholar over ten years of age would attend a school with a female teacher. In November 1839, it was voted to hold winter school for four months headed by a male teacher. Ezra Ferris' bid to supply board for $1.75 per week was accepted, an improvement over the 88¢ per week in 1825. By that year the school enumeration showed fifty-one pupils with eight more in the Town of Goshen, making fifty-nine in the whole district.

Insight into what those early schools were like comes from the Rev. Mr. Hibbard's *History of Goshen*: "But the old school house we were speaking of was not exactly airtight. The stove pipe, which was a quarter of a century of age, passed through the planking and out the E side of the room and whenever the E wind blew the contents of the old pipe went downward instead of upward, and the coals and ashes of a green beech fire were strewed over the floor. But, notwithstanding all this, we worried through four months and again through the next winter." A stovepipe also figures in Walter Vaill's well written memoirs of the Milton schools. Although he was a student in the 1870's, many of the things he writes about undoubtedly were true earlier. His story of the big boys climbing up through a trapdoor and stuffing the end of the stovepipe so that the stove would smoke and a holiday would be declared has been repeated by others. Those occasions when a "licking" was meted out to a miscreant created a diversion, especially when another student was sent out to cut the whip. It was quite a challenge to see who could "play hooky" and get away with it. Mr. Vaill recounted the hardships the miller, Mr. Hutchinson, suffered at the hands of the school boys. In his own words, "I remember one day when, with the help of another bright party, I let the water down on Hutchinson and old Bill Parmalee, when they were working on the flume down under the dam. Some of the quaint English words they used, I can remember yet."

In 1839, the same year that the responsibility for naming the school committee passed to the districts, a vote authorized the committee to build a "Back House" (toilet) with a partition and two doors. The December school census (apparently) showed a declining enrollment because the committee was given permission to reduce the summer school term from four to three months if at the end of three months there were fewer than twenty-five scholars, "provided Mr. Doolittle (the teacher) is willing to relinquish his claims." At this time the committee also rescinded the former vote to build the Back House. By April 4, 1840, the committee had decided to increase the school term to five months and to commence on April 20. They agreed not to pay over $1.50 per week for board and from a list of candidates selected Nancy Bissell to be teacher. However, records show that a later meeting settled on five and one-half months for the school term and chose Henrietta Griswold to teach the summer school. It is unclear whether both teachers were employed or whether Nancy Bissell disdained the $1.50 per week.

By November 12, 1840, the "Back House" had been upgraded to a "Necessary," but the motion was defeated to lay a tax to defray the cost of building it. However, by 1841 we again note that exacting plans were in the works for building a Back House or Necessary. It was to be "7 ft. by 5 covered with pine boards, roof also of pine boards, notched, with one door, seat to be on an inclined plane."

Records of 1848 suggest that the teachers, usually male for winter term and female for summer, were boarded for four to five weeks at a time in different homes for an approved sum (at this time $1.25 per week). Whereas the register of 1840 showed twenty-one students, by 1848 only fourteen were enrolled. At this time the board "took pleasure in commending the general work of our teachers, but if they were to find any fault it would be the lack of order, the beginners in particular." Apparently the district committee wasn't always prompt in paying its teachers; in 1841 Alice Wright held a claim against the district which the committee hoped to resolve by "selling certain stovepipe and if that didn't suffice to add it to the winter school bill."

On March 29, 1849, a document entitled "Establishing Boundary Line Between Milton and Litchfield School Societies" very carefully laid out the boundaries. In the next year, 1850, Edwin Dickinson deeded a piece of land about eighteen feet by twenty feet square to the Second School District for the sum of $2. The land, abutting his property, was already being occupied by the school and according to the deed was to be used for no other purpose.

The following table shows the number of pupils per district and the condition of the schools in the First Society of Litchfield around 1850:

District	Pupils	Condition of School
(1)	144	Good
(2) and (12)	40	Good
(3) and (15)	43	Bad
(4)	21	Very Bad
(5)	32	Bad
(6)	38	Very Good
(7)	35	Do (Ditto)
(8)	40	Bad
(9)	34	Very Bad
(10)	26	Do
(13)	58	Do
(14)	42	Good

By 1850 the physical condition of the school was of such great concern that a decision was made to repair the old one thoroughly at a sum of not more than $300 and to employ a constable, if need be, to collect the tax levied to cover expenses. May 15, 1851, was the target date for the completion of repairs. Seemingly minor matters took up much of the committee's time — by 1851 the subject of building a privy and woodhouse took up parts of several meetings. Eventually it was voted "to appropriate so much of the money in the treasury as is necessary for building Woodhouse & Backhouse," with Willy Gibbs to be Committee and Builder of the Woodhouse. Building Committee members received 75¢ per day.

There were as many as twenty-eight school districts in the Town of Litchfield by 1855. Originally these were in the hands of the First School Society, until management was taken over directly by the Town in that year, and Milton lost districts 4 and 8.

There were also a number of private schools, notably the Milton Academy, later a blacksmith shop and still standing on the southeast side of the Green. The Academy was organized in 1856 by the Rev. George J. Harrison, pastor of the Congregational Church for nearly forty years; it was considered a success financially and academically. From *Litchfield in Three Centuries* comes more information about the Academy. The interior was divided into two rooms, the back one having a large closet with glass doors for storing materials. In the beginning, three teachers handled courses

The Milton Academy

in Latin, Greek, classical literature, mathematics, natural science, "Belles Lettres," music and French. Three departments were later added, one to teach bookkeeping and business practices, another to prepare teachers, and the third a "Primary Department" stressing English. The school prided itself on its advanced equipment. According to the 1857 Catalogue, there were "24 gentlemen and 21 ladies" enrolled. The discipline was described as "moral and parental" with no "disgraceful punishment inflicted"; the "moral sense will be appealed to."

The school year comprised two terms of twenty and twenty-two weeks, each followed by a vacation of four weeks. There was also a vacation of one week in the middle of each term. Tuition per quarter ranged from $2.50 for the Primary Department to $15.00 for the Commercial. Pupils could find board at private houses for $2.00 per week or $1.25 for five days. The first roster listed most of the pupils coming from Milton, Goshen, Cornwall or Litchfield, but at least one family was from Brooklyn, New York. Kate Bogert, who lived across from the school, wrote of her experiences at the district school and the Academy. Her parents sent her to the Academy in the winter because the district school was "too crowded and rough." She attended the district summer school, as the Academy was open only in the winter. She told a charming story of the children spreading out their lunches on a rock (though she lived so close she said, "I had to take my lunch — it would not be going to school any other way"). After displaying their lunches, and politely offering and politely refusing the offers of the other students, each one tackled his or her own lunch.

During the years Miss Bogert attended the Academy the old district school system was changed and the Town government took charge of the schools. Following that, a petition requesting that scholars from the upper grades transfer to the Academy and scholars from the lower grades remain in the district school was honored. Miss Bogert recounted the exciting spelling matches between Academy students and East Cornwall students. Transportation was supplied by an enjoyable sleigh ride. She spoke very fondly of her years at the Academy and her regret at its closing. "Many felt that it should have been made into a public hall, but there was no one to start the project," she said.

In the mid-1850's the localities and number of pupils in the district schools were as follows: Marsh (18), Fluteville (19), Milton (20), Headquarters (21), Prospect (23), Newcomb (24), and Wolcottville (25).

In 1856 a decision was made to appropriate 1¢ on the dollar of the taxes collected by the Town to the several school districts for the "benefit, support, and encouragement of common schools." Prior to this time, it was the responsibility of the individual districts to collect all the money needed to operate the schools.

These items of interest were gleaned from the "Acting Visitors Report of the schools in the Milton School Society for the year ending October 1855," the visitor being Mr. E. H. Wright (Everett). His assessment of District 1 follows: "This school has been considered in many respects, of the lowest standing of any in the Society. From the experience and skill of Mr. Guild (Truman Guild, teacher) your committee were led to expect a marked improvement and we are happy to state that we were not disappointed." In that year, Truman Guild received $80 for the winter term and Lucy Goslee's pay for the summer term was $32. Mr. Wright judged the success of this, and all schools in the district, to a great extent, on the discipline which the teacher maintained. Contrary to modern beliefs, he spoke of the variety of textbooks being used as an "evil," and not according to the guidelines of the list of books recommended by the Board of Visitors. Teachers who made good use of the blackboard were complimented. In District 3 (Headquarters) there had been no winter term and an average of only eight pupils in the summer. Districts 4, 5 and 6 pupils were showing good improvement. In a summarizing statement Mr. Wright commented, "The schools of the Society are lessening as to numbers, and where this is the case, the consequent diminution of wages and less experienced teachers operate against the general advancement." He criticized reliance on rote learning, where the students do not understand fully what they're repeating, and his conclusion was that, "the *real teacher* must do something besides turning the crank of well-regulated machinery." Mr. Wright spoke of the school houses being in good condition but lacking outbuildings.

In 1860 changing the names of the different school districts was discussed, as well as designating them by their localities, not, as formerly, by number. By 1862 school seemed to have been in session for nine months — winter session mainly for the older students from October through March, and summer session mainly for younger students from April through June. In that same year, to settle the difference between the amount in the School Fund and the school's expenses, a tax was levied on parents according to the number of children in each household and the number of days each attended! Also in 1862, notice was given to the school districts that each district must make a written report to Board of Visitors by the fifteenth of September to be eligible for public money from the State Treasury. Outline maps were being bought for the schools. The Gilbert School, so called because it was built on land owned by Truman Gilbert at the corner of Maple Street and Brush Hill Road, was a respected school, being second in size in the Town of Litchfield. It was painted red and boasted a small library. This school employed some prominent teachers: Desire Griswold, with a college degree from Mount Holyoke; Deacon Samuel Dudley who invented the diagonal road scraper; and L. J. Nickerson who was also studying law, became one of the first criminal lawyers in the state and also a Judge of the Superior Court. Deacon Dudley returned often to read to the scholars, a favorite piece being "The Deacon's One-Hoss Shay."

Ellen Doyle spoke proudly of her father, Terrence Doyle, then twenty-five years of age, attending the winter session of the Academy in 1870-71. Prior to that he had attended the Goshen Academy but he wrote, "I wasn't doing anything that winter so I thought I'd take advantage of the chance to go to school."

The following chart is a sampling of five schools showing the costs incurred for the year ending August 30, 1871, as taken from "Report of the Selectmen of the Town of Litchfield, 1871":

School	No. of Scholars	Wks. of School	Recd. from State & Town	Total Expenses
Milton (#1)	58	34	$240.00	$280.00
Prospect (#6)	19	30	$175.00	$175.00
Gilbert (#2)	20	30	$159.20	$159.20
Head Qtrs. (#3)	18	28	$151.30	$151.30
Mt. Tom (#5)	16	30	$149.90	$228.00

In 1877, the District Committee paid $250 for a chimney pot and thirteen new desk tops plus $30 for repair of the outbuildings. Again the following year more repairs were needed, particularly "shingling, silling and covering" the outbuildings and applying two coats of paint (one whiting and one lead) to the school house. Following the decision to have the work done was always the problem of how to pay for it, usually by laying a tax.

An 1878 receipt from George E. Taft confirmed that he was paid $120.00, probably for a four to five month period. At approximately that same time, Mrs. Northrup received $63 for winter school and $33 for summer school. School teaching was considered a worthwhile vocation as it is noted that, in March of 1880, forty-four persons in the Town of Litchfield took a written exam for teaching credentials, of which seventeen were selected to teach in the various schools. The statistics on the Milton School in 1880 were as follows:

No. Rooms	No. Registered	Over 16	Ave. Att.	No. Wks.	Value	Total Expenses	Cost per Ave. Att.
2	51	7	34.5	30	$350	$368.75	$10.69

By 1882 there were forty-six pupils in the "Old Center School," only two over the age of sixteen. Since this caused excessive crowding, Mr. Fillmore Brown taught part of the class in the school building and Miss Ellen Page taught the advanced scholars in the Academy building which was apparently closed by that time. An 1882 article on "Moral Control" emphasized that primary students should not have less than four reading lessons per day, "not necessarily long but interesting," and it was noted that teachers should try to have their pupils become "reasonable thinking men and women."

A Town Teachers' Association, organized in early 1880, was well attended by teachers — and parents — with high expectations of improving the caliber of schools in the district. By this date, parents were being urged to inform themselves of what was going on in the schools. Complaints were being heard of the poor physical condition of some schools, notably Prospect, Mount Tom and Gilbert. Moreover, in 1883 it was noted that Milton School "suffers for want of a better home," and in 1884 Mount Tom's condition was so bad that it "forbids the holding of a winter school in this locality."

A Town meeting in 1886 at which the school committee strove for uniformity, authorized the providing of free textbooks under the provisions of a state statute. Books provided were: Harper's Geographies, Franklin Readers, Harper's Writing Books and a few history and physics books. Lippincott Readers were used as supplementary sources. Also the length of the term was increased to thirty-eight weeks. In that same year within the Town of Litchfield there were seven men and twenty-three women employed as teachers, the former earning an average of $30 per month and the latter $28; the reason for the difference is speculation. Teachers were commended in the report, but a remedy for lack of control was stated as follows: "The power to look with calmness upon every event and every individual; to avoid excitement from any cause, but with judicial serenity and official promptness to act in such a wise way that without saying so, it will be shown who is in authority there." Wise words!

Dr. William Deming was Chairman and Dwight Kilbourn secretary of the School Committee for several years and both are often quoted in reports. Dwight Kilbourn complimented most of the teachers upon the progress of their students, but had some scathing criticism of others, "...some of them, however, seem to care more for pay day than anything else... For this class we shall have but little use hereafter. We are certainly paying wages enough now ($30 per month!) to claim from the teachers their full measure of energy and faithfulness." He regretted the fact that some exhibited ignorance on the yearly examination of geographical facts, like the location of Iceland, the names of the Circles and the year of Lincoln's death.

Despite their reported poor condition early in the 1880's, Mount Tom and Headquarters remained open though enrollment had dropped to ten students by 1891. It was noted that Milton had a good program and was well supplied with blackboards and outline maps, and twenty-six pupils were listed as in regular attendance in 1892.

At the beginning of the 1890's the custom of sending boys to school until they were fully grown was discontinued, thus making discipline easier. Complaints were often received of mischief by students who roamed away during noon time. By that date some of the older students were attending Litchfield High School — in 1895 there were forty-two pupils and two instructors in the High School. Most members of the Visitor's Committee expressed great interest in the progress of the students. The Rev. Hiram Stone stressed the use of good English, objecting to "drawed" instead of "drew" and the overuse of the word "awful." Mr. T. Leander Jennings always wanted to see evidence of the children's progress in mathematics, both oral and written. One writer states, "It (the one-room school) had its deficiencies but certain fundamentals, a few tools, were thoroughly taught by the better teachers."

Dwight Kilbourn had some perceptive remarks to make on the instruction, or lack of same, being given by some teachers. He bemoaned the fact that one teacher didn't explain the rules governing solution of math problems, only teaching more or less by "machine." He claimed that this "machine teaching" was a hobby in graded schools rather than teaching "how to study, how to master difficulties, and rules and definitions of the text."

It was about this time that the grading of school was becoming more generalized, and Mr. Kilbourn disliked some of the results. He felt that brighter pupils were often held back by laggards, so instead of mastering the material and moving on, they were forced to repeat skills they had already achieved. One hundred years have passed without resolving the argument of teaching to the average student vs. teaching to the individual.

It is interesting to note that 1893 laws of consequence passed by the General Assembly included allowing women to register and vote on school matters, and mandating the teaching of physiology and the dangers of the use of intoxicants. Schools who failed to comply were threatened with the loss of their entire public money.

A résumé of the schools and the boundaries of some before the closing of Headquarters and Marsh schools reads as follows:

1) #1 - Milton - W to Wm. J. Hall & N to Terry Doyle and Duggans
2) #2 - Gilbert - former Shephard Knapp Fresh Air Home
3) #3 - Headquarters - between Bensons' and Granniss'
4) #4 - Prospect (known as the "school on the hill") - near the C. J. Landon Mining Co.
5) #5 - Mt. Tom - West Bantam, S from Ravenscrofts'
6) #6 - Newcomb - over the line in Goshen
7) #12 - Nichols - in Goshen (then part of Milton District)
8) #16 & #17 - East Cornwall

Finally, in May 1896, plans for a new schoolhouse had advanced to the stage of hiring a contractor — it was ready for use in October of that year, so the contents of the East Cornwall Road school were moved to its present site at the South end of the "Green." The actual cost for the new school was given as $1211.93 plus the cost of a new teacher's desk, forty-eight student's desks ($145 total), an arm chair ($2.85), a door mat ($1.30), clock ($6.50) and a second-hand furnace ($119). Before these items were moved in, the residents dedicated the new building with a dance. A live orchestra from Warren played on an improvised platform at the south end of the room. When the day to move arrived, Mr. George Smith, Board of Education member, brought a horse and wagon to transport much of the equipment. The forty-six pupils with their teacher, Miss Jennie Coe, whose salary at that time was $10 per week, followed carrying armloads of books, etc. Edna Birge Sheldon, a lifelong resident of Milton who was about ten years old at the time, had a vivid memory of that day. With the opening of the school, Headquarters School was closed and children transported to the new school. Marsh School was also closed and children from both schools transported to Milton or Northfield. In 1899 Miss Julia Peacock had fifty five pupils in Milton — too many to put into grades so she taught by grouping according to ability.

The Twentieth Century

In 1901, only five years after the new school was opened with registration of over fifty students, it was deemed necessary to build an addition — the "little room," as it was still called in the 1930's and '40's. Completion of the room — used mainly for recitation — came in January 1902 at a cost of $250.

Milton School children, about 1900

The caliber of teachers in the larger one-room schools like Milton was higher than those in the smaller schools — described by a critic as often "the first girl who came along and was willing to teach for $5.00 a week so as to get enough money to buy a bicycle or something of that kind."

In 1903, under Miss Peacock's tutelage, some of the children at the Milton School "published" their own newspaper entitled the *Milton Chronicle (See "Appendix")*. Included was an editorial by William C. Birge giving vital statistics about Milton, stating that there were two churches, two stores, three blacksmith shops, one school, a hall, a Post Office, a shear shop and a grist and saw mill. Under the heading of Industry, Allan Page explained the operation of the shear shop, claiming that the shears were "as good as any made in the country." Charles Birge, as Editor for Local News, found the following items of interest:

"Mr. Arthur Somerse's hors (sic) had the colic Sunday night and is very weak."

"Mr. Walter Seelye's horse got down in the stable and they had to kill it."

"Next Friday night there will be a dance in the Milton Hall."

"School News" was written by Oscar Tompkins and

showed what pride the pupils had in their new school with such statements as "The school has a fine library of between 70 and 80 books. They were obtained by the students giving Entertainments;" and of a more general nature, "The examination has been going on for the last week for 6th, 7th and 8th grades." Also, "The boys had great fun coasting on Potash and Tollgate hills. There are several double rippers as well as some single sleds belonging to the scholars." Under "Household Dept." with Irene Snyder, Editor, were found recipes for Baked Indian Pudding, Poor Man's Pie (a deep dish apple pie), Washington Pie Filling, Johnny Cake and Cold (sic) Slaw, the recipe for which was as follows:

"Slice cabbage fine. Mash with potato masher and mix with salt and pepper — not very much. Throw over this 1/2 cup of cream."

Finally Ernest Smith contributed some items of general interest such as, "Engineers are working on plans to utilize the Grand Canon (sic) of the Colorado to make electric power. The plan is to gain the power by diverting the water into tunnels."

Miss Ellen Doyle had proven herself to be an excellent teacher in North Farms School in Litchfield, so the Milton School was pleased to welcome her in 1907. Attendance improved and her methods were highly praised. In 1908 the building was said to be clean, sanitary and attractive. Music had been made a feature of instruction in response to parents' wishes. Soon the request for a piano was responded to by Lucius Leonard who bought a piano for the school. It still sits in the schoolhouse/home of Mrs. Barbara Todd and family. The understanding was that the community would pay for it as soon as the money could be raised. Miss Doyle recounted that "King Winter's Carnival," an operetta, was given at Christmas time to raise money. Despite a blizzard, everyone came, "going over fences and through fields with their woodshod sleds and the affair was a grand success."

Ability to brave the elements was demonstrated by Miss Doyle herself when she would don her raccoon coat, a warm hat, and come to school across the fields on snowshoes while some of the early comers to school, as told by Walter Sheldon, watched her progress from the schoolhouse window. Seldom, if ever, was school called off.

In 1910, under the first Superintendent of all Town schools, Mr. Horace Hovey, the necessity was seen for a

Ellen Doyle - ready to start for school with racoon coat and Dodge

uniform grading system in anticipation of preparing children from all districts for High School. Miss Doyle was required to prepare a complete outline of what and how much should be taught in each grade, a monstrous job which she accomplished by adapting the syllabus for New York State schools to fit her small school. This quote from a school report of 1912 shows in what high esteem she was held: "This school (Milton) has constantly improved in discipline and scholarship. The attendance has increased so much that this school overranks all of the one-room schools of the town and the work is really too heavy for one teacher to do well." Although frequent visits by "Howling Horace" (Hovey), as he was dubbed by Fred Bunnell and friends, were dreaded by pupils and teachers, Miss Doyle accepted his criticisms as kindly and constructive. In 1913 the new Superintendent, Mr. Ira Allen, was instrumental in obtaining an additional teacher to handle the primary department.

Perhaps Miss Doyle's most affectionate memories were of Mr. Earle Childs who succeeded Mr. Allen. She praised him as "an indefatigable worker himself and clever at keeping everyone else on the run." When visiting he often brought his lunch, staying nearly all day. He instituted a novel practice of giving tests in the Milton School, and then exchanging them with like tests in Northfield School, to be corrected by pupils and teacher. All teachers were obliged to spend one Saturday per month at an all-day meeting in the Center School. One time Mr. Childs entertained the teachers at his home where they discussed educational topics and ended with a social hour.

Based on Town reports for 1915-1916, we have more information about the second teacher hired for the Milton School. Ellen (Nellie) Doyle taught the grammar grades 4-8, and Léonie Thompson was employed for the primary grades 1-3. Adding to the need for an extra teacher was the closing of the Headquarters School, making it necessary for the Town to supply transportation for children from that area as evidenced by payments of $215 to Charles Birge for transportation for the four months from January to May.

School reports published for 1917 list the average number of pupils as 28.9 and the cost per pupil as $43.97. Evelyn Connor and Nellie Doyle taught the grammar grades and Léonie Thompson and Mary Weir the primary. The school year was scheduled to start on August 13, close for the hard winter months, and resume later. Although Superintendent Childs praised most of the teachers in the Litchfield system, he issued this stern criticism: "Our work was slightly disturbed by the unprofessional attitude of some (teachers). A school system demands loyalty and support for those making it. Cheap gossiping about their business is no more in place on the part of teachers than on the part of other professional people."

In 1918-1919 Milton's problems echoed those of the nation — school had to be closed for three weeks because of the influenza epidemic. The effects of World War I were reflected in the collection of $3.35 for French war orphans by the children of Milton. In the same year, the Superintendent proudly announced that all schools in the system now had Victrolas purchased with money earned by school entertainments and community contributions. Schools were visited every other week by the Health Officer for inspection of the room and students, the giving of exercises and teaching of hygiene. By this date the practice of offering inoculations against diphtheria and smallpox for a voluntary contribution had been started. Teachers of record were: Mary Sheehan (who also doubled as janitor) and Mrs. Clarence Blake for grammar grades and Ellen Doyle and Gladys Perkins for primary grades.

Ruth (Richard) Gray Peck, who attended from 1914-1922, remembers piling up leaves (from the beautiful maples destroyed in the 1989 tornado) on the Griffins' lawn across from the school and paddling in the brook during recess in hot weather. She also recalls dancing and singing around the Maypole on the Green, holding onto ribbons fastened to the top. J. Russell Ackerman, who started school in 1917 and went on to become Valedictorian at Litchfield High School, reminds us that in addition to reciting the Pledge of Allegiance each morning, the Lord's Prayer was also repeated. Usually following the opening exercises, Miss Doyle led a discussion of famous quotations, especially appealing to Barbara Birge Winn who loved to study them during the day in Miss Doyle's "beautiful handwriting" on the blackboard. However, she regretted that they weren't changed often enough.

Russell Ackerman and others recount indoor group activities in singing and reciting poems in unison like "Charge of the Light Brigade," "Hiawatha," "Barbara Fritchie," "I Shot an Arrow into the Air" and "Abou Ben Adhem." Outdoor games were the ever popular baseball — which was mentioned by almost every former pupil for the next thirty years — as well as Crack-the-Whip, One Ole Gat, Hide-and-Seek, Red Rover, Blind Man's Bluff, Wolf, Giant Steps, Jump Rope, Snow Fort making and others. Marjorie Woodington Starr declares that Miss Doyle taught the rules of baseball and sportsmanship while keeping an eye on those too young to play. Her pupils knew that one of her rules was: "Don't tattle!" The tattler got punished along with the wrong-doer. Baseball spilled over into competitive community games on Sundays which lasted until "milking time" called a halt.

Some of the highlights of the school games were having a board substituted for a bat, and the times Alford Fretts or one of the Litwin "boys" hit the steeple of the Episcopal Church, or when Harold (Bud) Bunnell was knocked unconscious by a stray ball, or when Betty Ackerman Kizzia, who could hold her own in baseball with any boy, lost her front tooth in a game. Howard Gray still has a distorted finger from being hit by a ball which was thrown at him at third base. The hour-long noontime was usually exciting, and Russell Ackerman remembers running over the bridge to his home (where his father Jacob (Jake) ran the Milton store), eating lunch quickly and returning to play.

The 1920 Town Report identified two teachers for the Milton School — Mary Derby for Primary Grades and Ellen Doyle for the twenty-five pupils registered for Grammar Grades. Salaries for teachers were between $700 and $1000 per year, but with board and room in Litchfield listed at $624 per year, many teachers were understandably dissatisfied. Records show that of the twenty-four teachers in the system, eleven had no training beyond High School.

Paul Dillingham, the Superintendent, made some comments pertinent to schools of Milton's size. He wrote, "The rural schools should have as good teachers as the graded schools. We hear a great deal these days about equal educational opportunity. Just so long as we continue to put our weakest teachers into the rural schools, just so long will equal educational opportunity continue to be a farce. Is there any reason why the country boy or girl should not have the advantage of just as good a teacher as the city boy or girl? If there is to be any discrimination, let it be in favor of the country children who do not have the benefit of many of the other educational advantages which the city children enjoy."

Certainly the children attending Milton School during those years felt no such discrimination as testified to by their memories of group singing, reciting poems, learning the

Milton School children, 1908

Palmer Method of Handwriting and putting on dramatic productions like Dickens' *Christmas Carol* with Miss Doyle directing — and often even making the costumes, according to Frances Doyle Barrett, her niece. Mrs. Barrett is quoted in the Litchfield Oral History Project as saying that Nellie Doyle was a poor sewer but achieved a good effect. School was not all fun and games, however, as Russell Ackerman said, "Nellie Doyle was a very strict disciplinarian of the old school type." Theodore (Ted) Litwin spoke of her as his "second mother to this day." Again quoting from Frances Barrett, "Miss Doyle...placed the children at the proper grade levels. However, this schedule was never allowed to be hampering and was always extended by real-life experiences in games, acting and public speaking."

The 1921 Town Report was the last time that two teachers were reported as being assigned to Milton: Nellie Doyle and Mabel Strattman. Although there were thirty-three children registered as being of school-age, only twenty-eight registered for the Milton School. The average daily attendance was only 22.5, prompting the Superintendent in his report to urge parents to get children to school each day and on time, to visit the schools and talk with the teachers.

During these years a music teacher came out from Litchfield every other week to teach music appreciation and two- and three-part singing. The same teacher taught drawing, cut-paper projects, free-hand drawing and "study of color." A total of $3,144.71 was spent that year in Milton under the new School Buildings and Endowment Association, although there wasn't much left for supplies, textbooks and equipment after salaries and fuel were paid.

Dr. Dillingham urged the formation of PTA's in his 1922 report as he said the school house is the logical "social center of any community," and nowhere was this truer than in

Milton. In that year, separate teachers had been hired for music and drawing, but as they were usually teaching at the same time, the drawing teacher found it advantageous to compliment the children for learning the "art of concentration." The number of students remained fairly constant. During that year a recommendation was made "in connection with the development of a Planned Program for the Improvement of the School Plant," to consolidate the Milton School with the Bantam School or effectively remodel the Milton School into a modern building sufficient for Grades 1 to 6. Obviously the recommendation was ignored.

Milton School children, 1923

Starting in 1923 there were several concerns voiced about the physical health of rural school children. Complete physical examinations were made by Dr. Childs, the Health Officer; regular visits were also made by a nurse whose duties might include home visits where necessary and taking children to a dentist. Net registration in 1923 was thirty-two, but the average daily attendance was only 22.7. A major item in the budget was $115 per month for Walton Morehead to transport students to Litchfield High School.

In 1924 work was done on upgrading courses of study from Kindergarten through High School. It was concluded that each year the pupils must have the following: 1) English, including language, reading, literature, composition and spelling; 2) Social Studies — history, geography and civics; and 3) Physical Education. Mathematics was to be taught in grades 1-9, Nature Study and Natural Science in grades 1-8, Handwriting in grades 1-6, Music in grades 1-9, Drawing and Art Appreciation in grades 1-7 and Household Arts for 7th and 8th grade girls and Industrial Arts for 7th and 8th grade boys. Concern for the health of the children extended to the creation of an All-Day Dental Clinic in the school.

According to the Town Report for 1925, only twenty-one students were registered in the Milton School and the per capita cost rose to $112.33, the highest in the Town except for the High School. A scarlet fever epidemic and mention of the poor nutrition and general poor health of the students were noteworthy.

Although Nature Study was a required subject, it was augmented by personal observation, especially during the long walks to school.

Oscar Richard remembers tending a trap line on the way to and from school to catch muskrats whose pelts could be sold; and a catch in the morning could mean a day off from school for him!

During those years the outdoor toilets — "necessaries" or "privies" — remained a fact of life, with separate ones for boys and girls. Even though permission was given for only one student at a time, one former student remembers the boys trying to peek through a hole into the girls' privy.

Since all the children brought cold lunches, where and what one ate was of prime importance. Many remember eating on the old millstone, the same one still in front of the Academy building, which was called the "shop." First ones there got to put their feet in the hole in the center. Willard Vaill recalls the boys going downcellar to eat their lunches in the bad weather, where they sat on a bench over the intake pipe which kept them warm. While there, their job was to stoke the furnace. In addition to lunches of peanut butter sandwiches, jelly sandwiches, cucumber and tomato sandwiches in season, occasionally a meat loaf, or a Sunday dinner leftover meat sandwich, there was usually a homemade goody and perhaps an apple.

What to use for a lunch box was solved for some of the boys in the 1920's by Dan Taylor who lived below the school on Headquarters Road. If the boys stood around outside long enough, Dan might invite them in and hand out tobacco boxes which had "Wiener Cut Plug" emblazoned on them. As Dan Taylor was getting on in years he often talked to himself. Oscar Richard remembers the amusement of the boys hearing him struggle to get his shoes laced. Though sixty years have passed Oscar still recalls Dan saying, "Used to lace them two holes from the top and now can only lace them three holes from the top — must be getting old!"

Again quoting from Frances Barrett, "...some children walked three to four miles to get to school. The poorest walked barefoot and put on shoes when they got to school. Sometimes two boys or a brother and sister would ride a horse which they would tie up in the church carriage shed on the Green." The Litwin children remember walking, running, skiing, biking and riding in a horse-drawn cart. Walking was the mode of transportation for most. In 1926 plans for a new school were based upon a calculation of the total number of miles walked by the children to different sites. It was hoped to choose a site where no child would have to walk over one and one-half miles, which was being accepted as a reasonable walking distance. In the late 1930's and early '40's some transportation was provided for those living at the greatest distance, notably by Ruth (Richard) Gray Peck who drove the children from the lower end of Headquarters Road, Litwin Road (then Forge Hollow Road) and a few from Cat Hole Road. Alford Fretts and Charles Birge both complained that if the Headquarters car was too full, the boys had to walk while the girls rode. When the roads — especially upper Headquarters Road — flooded in the spring, some of the younger children had to cross a sluiceway West of the Herbert Griffins' house or journey to school on the shoulders of the bigger boys. Nettie Sheldon Huften has memories of Jake Ackerman carrying children across the river during spring floods.

The school bell could be heard in all the corners of the village, sounding the beginning of school and the ending of recesses. Many a tardy, or reluctant, student was prompted to start running when the bell was heard "sharply reprimanding," according to Marjorie Woodington Starr. The Birge girls knew if they had gotten as far as the 2-4-6-8 telephone pole by Louise Lamb's they could make it. Pupils usually managed to be in their seats before the last peal was sounded, perhaps by William (Billy) Ackerman, Martin Kubish, Kenneth (Kenny) Richard, Raymond Gray or some of the other boys who were allowed to ring it — an enviable job! Another task besides ringing the bell was raising and lowering the flag, a solemn ritual.

Quoting from the Town Report for 1926, the building in Milton was in "very good condition." Ellen Doyle temporarily resigned in 1926 to care for her aging mother and was replaced by Anne Shanley. In commenting on the difficulty of scheduling and attending to the needs of individual pupils in one-room schools, Superintendent S. B. Butler said, "...With pupils of so many grades most of any single pupil's time in a rural school must be devoted to individual work." Former pupils spoke often of working alone with a background drone of lessons being "heard" in the front desk-less seats. A great deal of learning rubbed off that way. The older ones were also called upon to help those less capable or younger — a great forum for teaching self-reliance, concentration and consideration for others. However, the teacher somehow found time to encourage her students when she detected a special talent. Orcelia Birge Winn recalls her "taking time to help me understand rhythm, rhyme, meter and encouraging my early efforts at poetry." Audrey Raymond McMahon reminisces about helping in the "Little Room" with the "preschoolers and sandbox crowd." She also remembers how Miss Doyle would call to her desk those students who had failed assignments and needed individual help. She was "incredibly patient, always even-handed and kind to each and all of us."

A measles epidemic occurred in 1926. It was also noted that only a few rural students were having dental work done because of lack of facilities in the community. Enumeration figures showed nineteen students attending Milton School, four in private schools and three paying tuition in Litchfield School. The toilets and cupola on the school were shingled that year and a window put in the "supply" room. Per-capita cost for Milton students had risen to $67.79, but in 1928 it was $74.23, the lowest of all area schools even though the enrollment had risen to twenty-three.

An elementary sewing period for the upper-grade girls once a week was added to the schedule. The music teacher visited every other week, stating in her report that her "chief aim has been to make children love music." Many former students speak of retaining that enthusiasm for music, remembering fondly Miss Doyle's relying on her pitchpipe to get everyone started on approximately the same note of the scale.

Rural schoolchildren were sometimes included in regular assemblies at the High School, usually as observers. One of the students from the 1930's has memories of going to the *Mikado*. Admission was ten cents, but she didn't have that much, so Miss Doyle let her earn it by sweeping the floor. Mary Fox Marsh speaks of competing in a program at the Center School.

Annual school reports from the years 1930-1935 are sketchy, speaking only of minor repairs to the building and of the physical plant being in excellent shape because "the caretakers... evidently take great pride in the appearance of their buildings." For some years Herb Griffin filled in as custodian, and former students recall how neat and clean the building was under his care. Although there were no momentous events to record, erstwhile students have a great deal to say about those years. By 1935 Dr. Orwin B. Griffin, superintendent, reported that, "...at Milton School more sanitary provisions for toilet facilities will have to be made"; and finally in 1937 the grand occasion arose where inside toilets and drinking fountains were installed — no more pumping water into folding paper cups or rushing to the privy in cold weather (perhaps some regretted the chance to procrastinate along the way in good weather).

The 1939 Town Report gave the assessed value of the Milton School as $2500 and the lot on which it stood as $150. In his 1940 report, Dr. Griffin is quoted as saying, "Additional painting and carpentry work at the Milton School has put the building in excellent shape."

We have much first-hand information about the way holidays were celebrated during these years:

Valentine's Day was special in that talking out loud was acceptable; usually some simple refreshments, perhaps popcorn, found their way to the celebration by way of Miss Doyle; and as usual, dancing to the Victrola was allowed. Popular dances were the Virginia Reel, Highland Fling, square dances and improvised dances. Those who hadn't purchased Valentines — most of the pupils — had the great fun of competing for the prettiest ones with wallpaper, magazine pictures, ribbons, colored paper and doilies. Then appropriate messages were added and they were put in the "mail box" to be delivered.

Filling May Baskets was a challenge, but usually the bloodroot on Potash Road could be depended upon as well as Adder's Tongues and others. Pursuing the bloodroot gave one an opportunity to sit in the "King's and Queen's Chairs" — natural seats in the ledges on the north side of Potash Road — always a delight.

Memorial Day was a highlight of spring. The afternoon before was a busy one collecting lilacs, iris and beautiful, aromatic honeysuckle and azalea. Edward Litwin names also Wild Geraniums, Buttercups, Violets, Adder's Tongues, Bellwort, Trillium, Hepatica, Columbine, Fleabane and Windflowers as being added to our bouquets. In the morning the flowers were put in the wellroom to keep fresh. They were later fashioned into sprays by the older children, and transported in wagons or in Miss Doyle's green Chevrolet as students marched two-by-two to the cemetery on Blue Swamp Road. In later years Alice Walker DeCosa and Grace Fisher Litke led the way with their flutes. Members of households along the way were expecting the parade and came outside to watch and listen as the children breathlessly sang "The Battle Hymn of the Republic" or "John Brown's Body." Then the graves of veterans had to be decorated, including those from the Revolutionary War which were especially fascinating because of their antiquity. Willard Vaill recalled that some bouquets were thrown in the water of the nearby river to pay homage to those lost at sea.

Other holidays like Halloween were also observed in the school, though most of that fun came in the evening. Caroline Griffin Jefferies remembered a ghost ascending from the cellar (it could have been her mother!), and helping to dress the younger children in their costumes. Costumes were paraded, neighbors invited in, refreshment served and games played like bobbing for apples. Always the Victrola would be called into use.

Field Day came on perhaps the last day of school. Besides baseball, Howard Gray cites Three-Legged Races, Sack Races and 50 Yard (or lesser) sprints. Just a fun time to end school.

In 1940 and 1941 there were thirty-five pupils attending Milton School and the building had risen in value to $6000.

Milton School children, 1939

Reports for 1943 and 1944 declared the interior to be in excellent shape. Probably not foreseeing that the building would be closed in two years, the roof was reshingled and two coats of paint put on the exterior. Attendance in 1944 and 1945 was down to nineteen.

The Victrola, so often mentioned, was *the* audio aid, but the visual aid that most remember was the stereoptican with the slides of far away places in miraculous 3D that could transport one to foreign realms. Magazines, especially the *National Geographic*, were a relief from textbooks, as were books in the library at school and at the Parsonage, and later the Congregational Church, and the World Book Encyclopedia. The walls were unadorned by modern standards — no bright bulletin boards — and just the stern countenance of George Washington, Sir Galahad and others looking down at the students. Pull-down maps appeared during the later years and the globe was always on the piano.

The large piano was used by the music teacher and sometimes by Miss Doyle. The students yearned to use it but were usually forbidden to do so. On one occasion the writer recalls climbing in through a window at noontime, when Miss Doyle was next door at Griffins', to play the piano. Of course, the prank was discovered, the perpetrator(s) hiding their heads under their lift-top desks to let tears flow undetected.

Although the Green was the focal point at recess time, there were also many wonderful places discovered during Hide-and-Seek. Barbara Gray Gill remembers that the swamp was "off limits" but hard to resist. Every stone, tree and bush was familiar and suited for some purpose while playing Horn-A-Way, Fox and Geese, Ducky-on-a-Rock, Hop Scotch or some other game. The brush was a great spot to play "Doctor and Nurse" or "House." Frozen puddles were perfect for foot-skating, and Willard Vaill recalls that the boys dammed up the brook near the Trinity Church and it became a hockey rink.

Childhood diseases ran rampant in those days with fewer preventive inoculations. Orcelia Birge Winn reported in her diary that there were so many mumps and measles cases in 1935 that at one time only fourteen pupils were present, and the April 1936 vacation was cut short because so many days had been lost due to scarlet fever. Contracting one of these diseases usually meant a twenty-one day quarantine at home with a posted notice on the door. It must have been a monumental task for the teacher to send home books and assignments and check to make sure students were keeping up with the class.

Certain routines never varied at the old Milton School. Besides the aforementioned opening exercises, who can forget "Sit, stand, turn, pass" for each recess and the end of the day? Also, "Good night, Miss Doyle" was so ingrained that students often bid their mother good-night that way. Raising fingers: one for whispering, two for a drink of water, and three for the outhouse responded to by a nod from the teacher saved a lot of verbal interchange. A frantic hand-waving could mean that one needed to come to the front for help — a welcome chance to stand on the register and enjoy the warmth in winter.

Maintaining order was no small task especially for substitute teachers. Frank Fisher has a story of Miss Doyle handing out paper to make airplanes and allowing the flying to go on for a while so the children could get it out of their systems. Miss Doyle's mere presence or ringing her little bell for order — or if things were really getting out of hand, a hard rap on her desk with the bronze Plymouth Rock — brought the classes to order. Charles (Chuck) Birge claims she cracked a desk top with it one time when a recalcitrant student had really tried her patience!

The two coat rooms, or cloak rooms, in the front of the school hold poignant memories. Relative neatness was demanded — coats had to be hung up and lunch boxes or bags placed on the floor beneath. In wet weather, water pooled on the floors and the smell of damp clothing was overpowering.

One historic event that touched Milton was associated with the coat rooms. It was the kidnapping of the Charles A. Lindbergh baby in the early 1930's, a time — pre-TV — when one's imagination ran wild. The girls, especially, were emotional as the search went on for the child. To escape the teasing of the boys over possible tears, the girls retreated to the coat room and hung coats over the lower window sash to mourn undetected.

So many events, like Fourth of July picnics, though not specifically school functions, are remembered as quasi-school affairs. Likewise, the Honey Bee Club organized by Miss Frances S. Walkley at the Congregational Church involved all Milton children, who came directly from school to the meetings. The hidden bag of lollipops, with the finder getting first choice of flavors, made a lasting impression.

In the 1940's the school was often visited by Laurel, the pet fawn of Dorothy Wagstaff's on Potash Road. The fawn would appear at the door around 3:00 P.M. and seemed to wait for the Smith children who walked up that way, or if it were recess time, waited to chase stray balls. Though a diversion for the students, he could get to be a pest — the "final straw" coming when he lurched through the open East window and slid across the floor one day. Miss Doyle "put her foot down" and requested that the Wagstaffs restrain the deer at that time of day.

Raymond Gray reported that school was let out so the children could watch as the Harry Haviland house, fronting Saw Mill Road alongside Saw Mill Pond, was moved across the road via Clarence Ackerman's yard and onto Blue Swamp Road.

An example of Miss Doyle's ambition to widen the horizons of her students was a trip in which she drove the class of 1939 into Hartford, probably on a Saturday, to visit the Capitol and other spots of interest. This event culminated a study of our State and the making of scrapbooks, for which Janette Birge Winn remembers receiving a copy of *Connecticut Beautiful* by Wallace Nutting from Miss Doyle as a gift.

Each year the children were asked to sell Christmas Seals for the Red Cross, the only reward being a red metal cross on a straight pin, but one highly prized.

One year when the tent caterpillars were predicted to be a particularly bad menace, the schoolchildren were called into service to gather the eggs before they could hatch. Receiving the enormous sum of five cents per one hundred eggs, paid by the Milton Woman's Club, was enough incentive to send everyone scurrying far and wide. Counting one's collected trophies and calculating potential earnings left a lasting memory.

In the 1930's and 1940's most people relied on ice boxes for refrigeration, and harvesting ice from Shear Shop and Milton Ponds was a thriving industry. This writer recalls a representative of the ice-cutting business coming to the school before the machines or men with saws went to work. He explained to the children how a small stone thrown on the ice could damage valuable equipment. He asked the children to refrain from that practice and offered compensation. True to his word, a few months later a large box of candy and candied fruit was brought by him to the school.

The end of World War II produced two memorable events: President Franklin D. Roosevelt died a month before victory was declared in Europe, and some older classmates of those years remember Miss Doyle allowing them to sit in her car and listen to the news on her car radio; on VE-Day, Mary Walker Curtiss and her sister Alice Walker DeCosa, recounted that Mrs. Edward H. Raymond supplied all the girls with hats so everyone could attend celebratory services at the Trinity Church that day.

Finally in 1946, with enrollment dropping, the decision was made to close the school and bus the children to the Center School in Litchfield. Barbara Gray Gill was the lone graduate of that last 1946 class. An abortive attempt was made several years later to reopen the school by those who cherished the community school. Thus an era ended, an era of the kind of school where the school body was more one unit than separate classes. This is evident when one asks, "Who was in your class?" More often than not the person questioned, like Cecile Richard Jacquemin, can give you a long list of names, but can't separate them into classes. Miss Doyle went on to Center School where she taught several more years in the eighth grade. The school building was offered to the community, but there were no funds for upkeep, and it was eventually sold to the Hugh Todd family who resides there today.

Information comes from "Milton History Papers," Litchfield Town Reports and records and recollections of many former pupils, as well as Litchfield in Three Centuries by Edward A. Raymond, Rev. A.G. Hibbard's History of the Town of Goshen, Connecticut, and Clifton Johnson's Old-Time Schools and Schoolbooks.

Chapter VIII

THE CHURCHES — Where We Worshipped

❖

Drawing by Don Sibley

Milton Congregational Church, 1791

Milton Congregational Church

Foursquare and enduring, Milton Congregational Church, the oldest church in continuous service in the Town of Litchfield and one of the oldest in the State of Connecticut, sits on a rise of ground on the west bank of the Marshepaug River just across the bridge in Milton Center. It dates its beginning to 1768.

Established in that year as the Third Society of Litchfield by petition to the Legislature, the Milton Society was incorporated in May 1795 by an act of the General Assembly. Boundaries included the southwest part of Goshen, southeast section of Cornwall and east part of Kent (now part of

Warren). It was a full ecclesiastical society until 1818 when the Hartford Convention defined the separation of church and state.

The church building was raised on the Green — at that time called the Common and which the church still owns — and roofed in 1791. A year later the congregation voted to paint the exterior, lay a floor and put in windows. The expense was paid by members in cash, bar iron, wheat, rye, oil, flax seed and lumber.

The establishment as a separate society was welcomed by the people, who previously had to attend services in Litchfield each Sunday. Winters in particular could be difficult. There is a notation in *The Litchfield Book of Days*, in regard to Milton winters and the stamina of its people: "William Norton came to church on runners for 20 consecutive Sundays during the winter of 1872/73."

On August 19, 1798, "a small band of 28 persons gathered in the meetinghouse on the Green and organized the Milton Congregational Presbyterian Church." The twenty-four charter members were: David Welch, Irene Welch, Samuel Beard, Elihu Stone, Thomas Stone, Israel Potter, Thankful Potter, Benajah Smith, Daniel Beach, Jonathan Wright, Moore Gibbs, Patience Gibbs, Dr. Elijah Lyman, Mrs. Elijah Lyman, Dr. Partridge Thatcher, Mrs. Partridge Thatcher, Prudence Buell, Mary Spencer, Tabitha Gibbs, Sarah Parson(s), Anna Bishop, Sybbill Bradley, Avis Munson and Mehitable Deming. The first deacons were Israel Potter and John Munson.

Rev. Wesley E. Page described the meetinghouse thusly: "The building then stood near the center of the Green, and was painted yellow on the outside. The inside was in the rough, no paint, no plaster, no pews. The people sat on planks, raised from the floor by putting sticks in the ends." The land on which the church stood was formerly that of David Catlin.

Benjamin Judd was called as the first pastor, installed May 19, 1802. His salary, as voted by the Society, was "the sum of Seventy Pounds, and fifteen cords of wood annually." Raising money by direct taxation proved difficult, so the new Society formed a Committee of Donations to collect the money. Mr. Judd apparently was too greatly influenced by the sectarian spirit of the day and was rather outspoken, causing some dissension within the church. In 1804 he was dismissed, the reason given being that the Society could not pay his salary, perhaps because earlier funds were lost through "imprudent conduct." During his pastorate several members were dismissed for non-attendance, and they transferred to Trinity Episcopal Church.

Mr. Judd was followed by a peacemaker, Rev. Abraham Fowler, who was dismissed in 1813. The evangelist, Asahel Nettleton, came to the church for a short time and brought twenty-seven converts into membership. Rev. Levi Smith, also an evangelist, was sent to Milton in 1825 by Rev. Lyman Beecher of Litchfield. While he served, the church membership increased to seventy-five.

Because of the objection to the yellow church being on the Green ("Old Yellar," it was called), the church building was moved across the river on rollers with oxen in November, 1828, and placed on land donated by Asa Morris, where it stands today.

After the move the church was repaired and renovated. Six years later the gallery was finished off to provide room for a select school. There was no settled pastor until 1841, and the church floundered. Through the efforts of Rev. Ralph

Smith, minister from 1841 to 1844, the church began to rebuild. The belfry was added in 1843. The next minister was Rev. John F. Norton, 1844-1849, followed by Rev. Herman Landon Vaill, 1849 to 1851. Rev. Francis Williams, 1851-1853, was next to serve the church, then Rev. James Noyes, 1853-1854.

For nearly forty years thereafter, 1854-1893, the Milton church was fortunate in having the services of Rev. George J. Harrison. He and the rector of Trinity Episcopal Church, Rev. Hiram Stone, worked together "faithfully and well to bring into the hearts of Episcopalians and Congregationalists the spirit of brotherly love." Mr. Harrison also founded the Milton Academy on Milton Green in 1856.

To provide housing for the Harrisons, the Ecclesiastical Society bought the Moore Gibbs house (563 Milton Road) as a parsonage. During these years a bell was hung in the belfry, an organ purchased (for $110) and a new communion set, still in use, was presented by Miss Lucretia Deming of Litchfield (for list of gifts to church, see "Appendix").

In 1882 the church was completely repaired. On August 18, 1882, a large gathering was present to appreciate the results. Eighty-three members joined the church during Mr. Harrison's tenure. In 1876 it was "resolved that female members have a right to vote upon matters pertaining to the welfare of the Church." Mr. Harrison died on Christmas Eve, 1893.

Two ministers, Rev. Hugh S. Dougall and Rev. Aurelian Post, followed during the next three years until the coming of Rev. Wesley E. Page, a graduate of Yale Divinity School, who was ordained in Milton on June 15, 1897. He married Mary Page, daughter of Deacon Samuel D. Page, on May 31, 1899.

The church celebrated its one-hundredth anniversary in August 1898 with many people in attendance. On

February 11, 1899, the church was incorporated by Public Act of the State of Connecticut, becoming the Milton Congregational Church — the Milton Ecclesiastical Society renouncing all right to church property in favor of the incorporated church. First trustees after incorporation were: Rev. Wesley E. Page, Fremont Granniss and Orlando Perkins. Charles S. Blake was elected treasurer and Miss Bertha Register, clerk. Mr. Page resigned in 1903.

On January 10, 1904, Rev. Joseph D. Prigmore, after graduating from Yale Divinity School, became pastor. In June, he married Miss Amy Davis of Missouri. The young couple endeared themselves to the church and community. Mr. Prigmore organized a Boys' Club, using the gallery which was shut off from the church proper at that time. Mr. Prigmore left on May 23, 1906, and was followed by Rev. Frank H. Patterson and Rev. Pearl Mathias for the next eighteen months.

In April 1908, Rev. Thomas A. Williams came to the church. He was ordained June 17, 1908, at a large convocation. Mr. Williams married Miss Bertha Register in 1909. Three years later he resigned to be succeeded by Miss Martha E. Millen of St. Johns, New Brunswick, who was missionary-in-charge for two years. Subsequently she married Fremont Granniss, senior deacon.

The man who next came to the pulpit, in February 1915, was Rev. Eugene L. Richards, a native of Cornwall who was married to Elizabeth Stock, daughter of Rev. Alfred H. Stock, Milton, pastor of the East Cornwall Baptist Church from 1902 to 1904. The social life of the community became active during the next four years while the Richards' were here. Monthly sociables were held at various homes, the Social Committee in 1918 being James (Jay) Gilbert, Ellen M. Doyle, Mercy I. Stock, Bertha Brown and Mr. (Jacob?)

Ackerman. The Ladies Aid Society was reorganized during this time.

Following the resignation of Mr. Richards in 1919 the church had no settled pastor for five years. Church members, under the direction of Sunday School Superintendent Wilbur A. Haviland, kept the Sunday School alive. Mr. Haviland was Superintendent for over thirty years.

The two churches in the community — the Congregational Church and Trinity Episcopal Church — worked and worshipped together for several months, meeting alternate Sundays at one church and then the other. There was a combined Sunday School and joint choir. Rev. Arthur B. Crichton, rector of St. Paul's, Bantam, and priest-in-charge at Trinity, conducted this "noble experiment" which was eventually forced to end.

Rev. Donald McGavran, a student at Yale Divinity School, preached Sundays, 1920-1922, during the college year and was entertained by parishioners in turn over the weekends. Summers he gave his full time to pastoral duties, including leading the Boy Scouts and organizing church members into committees for social service, missionary study and work. After his resignation, he married and went to India as a missionary.

"In June 1924 there came to the church one who served for over fourteen years with marked ability and success, Miss Frances S. Walkley," so wrote Mercy I. Birge in her history of the church presented at the 150th anniversary program in 1948. "All of us who knew Miss Walkley loved her dearly. She was vitally involved in the church and community and left it a better place through her efforts. She not only taught Christianity, she lived it. She preached fine sermons as well as played the organ, going from organ to pulpit and back.

Some of the activities she initiated were the Camp Fire Girls, the Honey Bee Club for all the youngsters in Milton, the Blue Bird Club, a Boys' Club, Sewing Club, 'Cootie parties,' splendid and original Children's Day programs, along with a wealth of flowers raised in the parsonage gardens. The library which she began was housed in the parsonage and open to everyone. Picnics were held around the outdoor fireplace at the parsonage. Miss Walkley had a unique understanding of and empathy with the problems of everyday living; she listened, she cared, she counseled."

The church was completely renovated soon after Miss Walkley came. It was reopened on Sunday, August 2, 1925, with a large congregation; thirteen new members were welcomed. The church records of this memorable day end with these words: "After the service, people from out of town gathered on Mrs. Earle's (Mrs. Mary P. Earle) lawn for lunch and a reunion. The day marked a golden milestone in the annals of this venerable and historic church."

Five years later the exterior of the church was painted, the entire expense being paid for by the Ladies Aid Society which for all the years of its existence raised funds for upkeep of the church.

In 1938 Miss Walkley retired and Rev. Irving J. Enslin, who was retired himself from the First Baptist Church in Derry, New Hampshire, came to supply the pulpit for December and stayed for twenty-three years, until the end of 1961. He bicycled constantly between Litchfield, where he lived, and Milton in the performance of his pastoral duties. He, like Miss Walkley, provided exceptional sermons and spiritual guidance for the congregation in Milton.

After Miss Walkley's retirement, the parsonage was rented for a number of years. Then the expense of keeping it up proved too much for the church, and it was sold to Donald K. Peck in 1953. A number of men followed Mr. Enslin during the next several years — in April 1962, Otto Reuman; then Eben Chapman, June 1962; Rev. Norman Farnum for most of 1963; Harry King filling the pulpit until the end of 1964; three pastors in 1965: Rev. Earl Abel, Rev. John Billings and Rev. Bruce Rigdon. In August 1965, Rev. Thomas Campbell of North Haven came to the church and stayed until July 1969, to be followed by Rev. Thorpe Bauer until 1974. During his pastorate the library, which had been moved to the church gallery, was disposed of and, with the help of the Ladies Aid Society, three Sunday School classrooms were installed there.

Dr. Harry L. Peatt, Jr. of Roxbury, came to Milton to preach in March 1975 and remained until the end of 1978. A series of ministers preached at the church through October 1979, when Rev. George A. Smith of Woodbury was called and remained until the spring of 1987. The two Milton churches once again combined services in the winter of 1980/1981 when Trinity supplied the warm church and the Congregational Church supplied George Smith and his excellent sermons. In August 1981, services were held in the Congregational Church for both churches.

Mr. Smith was ill in 1980, and the church again had a succession of preachers including the deacon, David R. Wilson, a layman, who presented the congregation with inspiring sermons. Mr. Smith returned in August 1980.

Dr. Peatt came again to preach in April 1987 and stayed until the end of 1990. He also preached at the First Congregational Church in West Torrington during that time. A shared minister. Rev. Bradford Harmon, a fine minister, came to the Milton church in March 1991. Ill health forced him to leave in May 1992, and brought back David Wilson for several months. Rev. Gordon Vought of Beacon Falls was called as interim pastor on August 2, 1992, and left the summer of 1994 when Mr. Harmon returned. Like Dr. Peatt and Mr. Harmon, Mr. Vought also preached at the West Torrington church. In all of its nearly two-hundred years, the Milton Congregational Church has, for the most part, been very fortunate in its spiritual leaders.

Financial aid from the State Missionary Society had been requested and granted continuously for over a century until October 1944, when the church membership voted to discontinue seeking this aid and support the church itself.

Milton Congregational Church is on the National Register of Historic Places, as well as being in the Milton Historic District.

At present the church faces extensive repairs to the church house, repairs which have been deferred for many years and must now be addressed. Attendance has fallen off, and, like many small churches, the Milton church is seeking to rebuild both physically and spiritually.

Information comes from "Milton History Papers"; Milton Congregational Church Papers; Rev. Wesley E. Page, "Centennial Address," 1898; Mercy I. Birge, 150th Anniversary speech, 1948; Litchfield Land Records, Vol. 15, p. 229; Vol. 30, p. 118; Vol. 62, p. 13; Vol. 75, pp. 509-510.

Trinity Episcopal Church

Drawing by Don Sibley

Trinity Episcopal Church, 1802

As you enter the village of Milton you are greeted by Trinity Episcopal Church across the road from Milton Green, with its tall spire, its jewel-like stained glass windows, its doors open to the worshipper. Trinity is a beautiful small church — one of the oldest in the state — patterned by its builder, Oliver Dickinson, Jr., after the second Trinity Church in New York City. It contains a unique Thomas Hall tracker organ, the oldest such organ in use in the state, presented to the parish by St. Michael's Episcopal Church, Litchfield, in 1866.

There is another treasure in Trinity Church — the stained glass window over the altar, one of the oldest in the country — also a gift from St. Michael's. In 1976 the church was placed on the National Register of Historic Places.

Erected in 1802, the church was completed in 1826 and consecrated in 1837 by the Right Reverend Thomas C. Brownell. Land was donated by David Welch, recorded after the foundation was put in during the summer of 1802. Prior to this, until 1792, the Episcopalians in Milton traveled to St. Michael's in Litchfield for formal services (in Milton, informal meetings were held in homes). In 1791, the Episcopalians were granted permission to meet in the schoolhouse, near the site of the present Milton Hall. That year, the rector of St. Michael's, Ashbel Baldwin, who was made deacon at the first ordination held by Bishop Samuel Seabury after his return from Scotland, began holding periodic services in Milton.

Original subscribers of the Episcopal Society in Milton, as appeared on a Certificate filed with the First Episcopal Society of Litchfield, December 13, 1834, were: Hugh P. Welch, Gerrit P. Welch, Alva Sharp, Phineas Cook, Augustus Morey, Frederick Griswold, Harmon Seelye, John Carter, Jarvis Griswold, Moses Smith, William Bissell, Lucius Carter, Samuel Kilborn, Benjamin Griswold, Jr., Hiram Bissell, Algernon S. Lewis, Joseph Birge, Jr., and Sam Addis. The first rector to serve the church was Rev. Truman Marsh, 1799-1810, followed by Rev. Isaac Jones, Jr., assistant to Mr. Marsh, 1811-1826. See "Appendix" for complete list of rectors.

Around 1812, St. Michael's Church presented Trinity with pews, a "tulip" (or goblet) pulpit, reading desk and railings. During the years 1858-1860, an effort was made to remake the church in the Gothic style. The pulpit was cut down and moved to the floor, and the benches were replaced with new pews. Probably about this time the steeple was removed and a balcony added to the belfry. Before this, in 1843, Gerrit P. Welch and his brother, Hugh P. Welch, gave the church a thirty-inch bell to hang in the belfry.

Like most churches, Trinity has had its misfortunes. On July 23, 1897, lightning stuck the belfry, setting it afire. Fortunately, heavy rain quenched the fire, but the belfry was damaged and had to be rebuilt.

The church was "in feeble condition" in 1902, the year of its centennial, according to the Rev. Hiram Stone, who added, "...the Church has witnessed the passing away of three generations who have worshipped here." By 1929 there was the possibility that the church might not survive without financial help from an endowment made in 1863 by the Honorable Seth F. Beers.

Again, in 1938, just prior to the coming of Rev. H. Waldo Manley, the church needed so much repair work that there was talk of tearing it down. However, when Senior Warden Dr. Edward H. Raymond, Jr. and Vestrymen G. Herbert Griffin and H. Ernest Axford met with Bishop Walter H. Gray, the Bishop felt that the Milton parish should be preserved — it was also too expensive to build another church. That spring repairs were begun, including restoration of the steeple which had been absent since the mid-1800's. A service of dedication was held in November 1938.

While Mr. Manley was at Trinity (1938-1954), the church was revitalized for a time. This included the sharing of activities with Milton Congregational Church, including membership in the Women's Guild which had been reactivated by Mrs. Henry E. (Edith) Axford and Mrs. Allen G.(Carrie) Peck and which gave aid to the church in many ways.

In June 1949, extensive repairs were again required when a crowd of people attending the wedding of Caroline Griffin and Robert Jefferies nearly caused the floor to collapse. The space beneath the floor under the nave was filled with gravel and a reinforced concrete slab was laid. Repairs were made to the sills and joists and the church was reroofed. Forty years later it was discovered that the concrete floor had rotted the sills to a point where only the interior columns under the balconies were supporting the building. Repairs were effected through the fund raising efforts of Rev. Gordon

Duggins and extensive alterations took place which changed the interior of the church. Much needed additions included a parish hall and bathroom facilities, along with a vestry room. Unlike many churches, Trinity has retained its galleries around three sides of the church proper, which are supported by four hewn pillars.

The stained glass windows, installed in 1910, stand as memorials to the following people: Erwin and Susan Birge Bissell, Charlotte Page Clarke and Janette Birge Page, Charles D. and Elizabeth Wheeler, Lucius and Desire Granniss Griswold, William and Amanda Bissell, Truman and Lamira Guild, Oliver Dickinson, Alban Guild and Everett Wright. These windows were dedicated by Bishop William J. Brewster on April 23 of that year.

Trinity has been fortunate in the rectors who have served the church through the years. One in particular who should be mentioned is the Rev. Hiram Stone, who was with the parish for thirty years, 1873-1903. Rev. Stone was presented with a silver cup at the one-hundredth anniversary celebration of Trinity Church in 1902. The cup bore the following inscription: "...in token from his brethren of the Litchfield Archdeaconry, on the centenary of Trinity Church, Milton, on the 25th anniversary of his rectorate, Sept. 2, A.D. 1903." It was also noted that day that the Milton, Bantam and Litchfield parishes were unique because they constituted one parish as far as Civil Law was concerned, yet in Canon Law they were three separate parishes.

Other notable leaders of the Milton church include, in later years, the Venerable Joseph T. Urban, who took charge of the sacrament of Holy Communion himself when he was needed, and the Very Reverend Dr. Girard Carroon who was active in the discovery of the antiquity of both the Thomas Hall organ and the altar window. While he was at the church, a service of rededication of the old organ, which had been repaired, was held by the Bishop of Connecticut on December 15, 1985. Several fine organ recitals have been held in the church on this organ, and other musical offerings include musicals and singers of note, and Scottish bagpipes on the annual Fourth of July celebration, which includes cannon salutes by the Litchfield Artillery.

As with many small rural churches nowadays, venerable Trinity Episcopal Church is experiencing low attendance and is endeavoring to maintain the life of the church and bring new members into its fold.

Information comes from "Milton History Papers"; Litchfield Land Records, Vol. 19, p. 400; Edward A. Raymond, Trinity Church Milton; Grace Isabel Raymond, The Episcopal Church at Milton, 1939; Arthur Goodenough, The Clergy of Litchfield County, 1909; Milton Congregational Church Records.

The Methodist Church

There is little on record about the Methodist Church in Milton and, as far as is known, there is no picture of the building when it was a church. Most of the information available comes from the record of the Milton Congre-

Methodist Church, Milton, after removal to Prospect Mt.

gational Church and the "Milton History Papers."

The church building was erected in 1824 on the east side of Headquarters Road, a few rods south of the present schoolhouse building. It preceded the Methodist Church in Litchfield by some twelve years. Methodism came to Milton years before the church was built, and it is presumed that Milton was included on the Litchfield circuit of itinerant ministers, or "Exhorters," who journeyed from New York to Boston beginning in 1790.

It is believed that the Methodists met at the old Guild house at 122 Saw Mill Road (now the home of Craig and Suzanne Litwin). Services were undoubtably held in other houses as well, but the Guild house has been known as the old Methodist church building. The circuit preacher "would find his way hither and hold a service."

The journey of the circuit rider was made on horseback, for the most part. The three hundred mile trip was undertaken every four weeks, and it is supposed that Milton was included in the circuit.

These traveling preachers had the energy and appeal of most Methodist ministers which drew converts — the uneducated, as well as the educated, could relate to them on such matters as choices on baptism, opposition to taxation to support ministers. The ministers would also hold classes in private homes, gathering members. These pastors, who changed every year, often had no formal education or training and learned on the job, becoming well versed in theology.

From the "Milton History Papers" comes a description of the church on Headquarters Road: "The Milton meetinghouse, never painted, was built in accordance with early Methodist style — no spire or other architectural embellishment, only a cupola at the west gable end over the two front doors. The high pulpit was between the two front doors, with altar rail and kneeling stool beneath. There were no pews, only benches of split logs, with four sticks driven into augur-holes in the corners for legs. A row of such seats was arranged around the outside of the room, where 'weaklings' who were unable to sit bolt upright in the centre of the room during services could rest their backs against the unplastered outside walls. This primitive furnishing was not unlike that of many other churches." Comfort was never a primary consideration in early churches.

Circuit preaching continued for twenty-five years; for a time services were held every two weeks at the Milton Congregational Church, drawing a large crowd. There were thirty-five members in Milton at one time. This number dwindled to fourteen by 1841, then to six in 1863. That year, after having had no preaching for fifteen years, the church building was sold to a mining company for $50, taken apart and carried down Prospect Mountain Road to be used as a boarding house for workers at the nickel mines on the mountain. It is still standing on Prospect Mountain Road — across the road and just before the corner where the Joseph Kubish farm is located — and was the home of the Banks family for years. When it was sold, four signatures were required on the deed. Only two adult male Methodists remained in Milton — Isaac Baldwin and Abraham Wadhams — both of whom had been instrumental in the building of the Milton church. The deed had to be sent to California where Clark Baldwin lived, for his signature.

During the years that the Methodist Church was in existence there was concern about the village becoming "the headquarters of drunkards and dealers in ardent spirits from the neighboring towns," and concern also because the "quantity sold here at two stores and one tavern is immense." This information, included in the "Milton History Papers" along with information on the Methodist Church, was provided as illustrative of contemporary problems faced by the church.

The following is also included because it is found in the address by Miss Esther Thompson and lends a bit of humor to this account: "Early one Sunday morning some boys hid a litter of young pigs in the high pulpit of the Milton Methodist Church. When the Circuit-rider climbed the stairs and opened the pulpit door, there was a stampede of pigs like that of Bible times — to the astonishment and disconcertion of the assembled congregation."

Today most Milton Methodists attend church in Litchfield, including those who used to go to the Methodist Church in Bantam until it was destroyed by the 1989 tornado.

Information comes from "Milton History Papers"; Litchfield Book of Days, George C. Boswell, ed., 1900; Litchfield, Connecticut, 250th Anniversary booklet, 1969; Arthur Goodenough, Clergy of Litchfield County, 1909.

The East Cornwall Baptist Church

Situated almost at the junction of Milton, East Cornwall and Warren, the area where the East Cornwall Baptist Church later was located was included in the Third Society of Litchfield when it was established in 1769, making it part of the village of Milton. The church was built on a rise of ground where College Street, Flat Rocks Road and South Road come together. First known as the Warren Baptist Church and located in Warren, it was organized on November 15, 1787. Earlier, on September 27, thirteen persons were baptized by immersion. They requested, on October 29, that they become a church. After "individual examination," twenty-two members were accepted, ten men and twelve women: Anna Beeman, Rachel Beeman, Truman Beeman, Jemima Cogswell, Ely Datun, Benning Dunning, Isaac Dunning, Mercy Dunning, John Lord, Sarah Merriman, Abigail Pratt, Hannah Raynold, Abigail Spooner, Anner Sturdivant, Samuel Sturdivant, Samuel Sturdivant, Jr., Sarah Sturdivant, Jerusha Thomson, Asahel Wedge, Hannah Wedge, Ira Wedge and Salmon Wedge.

They voted, on November 28, to hold covenant meetings on the second Saturday of each month. Most of the meetings were held at the home of Asahel Wedge, elected deacon on March 4, 1788. Rev. Isaac Root was the first pastor on May 23 and was ordained on September 25. The following year there was some discord with problems of discipline and exclusion. In 1790, the church joined the Danbury Association. It was at this time closely tied to the Bantam Falls Baptist Church with whom it shared preachers on alternate Sundays until 1881. After 1881, the minister preached every Sunday in Bantam in the morning, East Cornwall in the afternoon and Cornwall Hollow in the evening — a rigorous schedule. In 1793, Elder Isaac Root and nineteen members left to join the church in Sharon, which separated that year to form its own church. This action and poor ministry led to a decline in the Warren Baptist Church which existed for nearly twenty-five years, during which time they were without a pastor. Little or nothing is left on record of those years.

Rev. Ananias Derthick came as minister in 1817 and stayed until 1828. He persuaded the Baptists to move their meeting place from Warren to the nearby schoolhouse in East Cornwall. The church was transferred to the Hartford Baptist Association. In 1847, it became a member of the Litchfield County Association with the name of the College Street Church, Milton.

Building of the church house was begun in 1850 after Rev. James Avery came to East Cornwall the previous year in 1849 and helped raise $1000. When the church was finished, Rev. Luther B. Hart came as pastor. On May 21, 1851, the church was named the College Street Baptist Church. A month later, June 19, the church was dedicated, and Mr. Hart was ordained. He preached until January 10, 1853, and taught school at the same time. Through the years the Baptist Church conducted baptisms in the pond above the dam where Flat Rocks Road and Crooked Esses Road meet. Over the years the church raised up four men: James D. Avery, Henry Alling, William G. Fennell and Ralph H. Tibbals. For list of ministers, see "Appendix."

One of the church's most famous members was William George Fennell, D.D. Born just over the line in Goshen, he was educated in local schools and taught in Hardscrabble before becoming a minister. He began to preach in the East Cornwall church at least once a year, a practice which continued each summer for thirty-nine years until he died in 1917. He was one of the foremost ministers of his denomination. The Sundays when he came to East Cornwall were known as "Fennell Sundays," an old-home day which was attended by a large crowd of about two-hundred. It is said that the Milton Congregational Church closed that day so that parishioners could go to the service in East Cornwall. Following the service the people gathered on the lawn of the James Blake house across the road for lunch and a reunion. The summer of 1917, after Mr. Fennell's death — which would have been his fortieth annual sermon — members held a memorial service.

On December 24, 1900, the church was incorporated under the name East Cornwall Baptist Church. Two years later, in January 1903, Rev. Alfred Holmes Stock of Hamilton, New York, came to preach, bringing his wife and three youngest children to the Fennell house on College Street (given to the church for a parsonage). Mr. Stock also preached at the Cornwall Hollow Baptist Church. His three daughters remembered with pleasure the socials, parties, outings each season, the companionships, the arrival of evangelists, quiet evenings at home together.

The church is described by Adaline (Stock) Seymour as a rather plain white building with a belfry and tall windows along the sides. There were large stone steps at the entrance and church sheds, built around 1862, off to one side. The interior of the church was varnished tongue-and-groove boards. Rows of folding wooden chairs filled the body of the church, with long pews at the rear next to the stove where people could warm themselves. There were some fine old chairs on the platform, with a small square organ on the left.

Mr. Stock left after two years and was followed several years later by his son-in-law, Rev. Eugene L. Richards, a Cornwall native who was supply minister from 1915 until 1917. After that, the Milton Congregational Church had charge of the Baptists in East Cornwall and vicinity, and there were occasional services held in the East Cornwall church.

For many years there were no settled pastors and few records of the church. In 1922, the recommendation was made that the church be disbanded; in 1929, it was officially closed. Periodically — usually each summer — there was a reunion for all interested people on Fennell Sunday. Then, in 1949, at a meeting at the home of Warren and Annabelle Welch, the surviving members of the church society agreed to dissolve the East Cornwall Baptist Church and dispose of the property. According to a letter from Mrs. Warren (Annabelle) Welch to the Connecticut Convention of American Baptist Churches in November 1949, the building was sold for $90 and taken down. Later Louis R. Ripley built a house on the site.

As one travels today along College Street, Flat Rocks Road and South Road, near the place where the East Cornwall Baptist Church stood, one still half expects to see the old church building there, even after some four and a half decades. The hills remain, and the trees, and some of the fields and open meadows where deer play, and the dark woods; but the little church is gone.

Information comes from "Milton History Papers"; Edward C. Starr, History of Cornwall, 1926; Dwight C. Kilbourn, History of Litchfield County, 1881; Recollections of M. Adaline Stock Seymour.

The Russian Orthodox Chapel

Proposed Russian Orthodox Chapel, 1958

A dream which never reached fruition was played out here in Milton in the late 1950's. A Russian Orthodox chapel named the Convent of the Holy Virgin Protection was to be constructed on Blue Swamp Road with a cloister for Russian refugees coming to this country. There were to be Russian Orthodox priests, nuns, teachers and laymen in residence. The chapel would be erected on property formerly owned by Charles R. Vose at the site of the small house then locally known as "Miss Carberry's" beside a man-made pond across the bridge and southeast of Milton Cemetery. The house (53 Blue Swamp Road) is now owned by Paul and Eleanor Goss. For awhile there was a large cross near the house where the chapel was to be built.

The designer of the chapel was Vladimir Morozov, himself a refugee from the former Soviet Union, and a prominent architect in New York. A rather beautiful sketch of the proposed chapel appeared in *The Litchfield Enquirer*. The design was in the traditional Russian style with a steeple and several "onion" domes. The chapel would "unify memories and traditions of Russian people in exile..," according to Mr. Morozov. It was to conform to building requirements of the day while also conforming to the countryside where it would stand. There would be room not only for religious and teaching staff but for visitors, where they could find rest and enjoyment. The two houses on the fifty-odd acres were to provide "living accomodations."

A ceremony of dedication was planned for the morning of July 5 at which some seven hundred members of the Russian Orthodox Greek Churches in America would participate. Although a number of people came from all over the area for the ceremony, the crowd was far less than anticipated. The ceremony was led by Metropolitan (referring to an archbishop who heads other bishops of a locality) Leonty, Archbishop of New York and Metropolitan of the Russian Orthodox Greek Catholic Church in America. Work was to begin immediately on the raising of the chapel. That afternoon Serge Jaroff led a concert by the world famous Don Cossack Chorus at Litchfield High School.

The property on Blue Swamp Road was given by Charles R. Vose to the St. Nicholas Foundation, Inc. of New York, a charitable organization which assisted displaced persons arriving in this country. Unfortunately, Mr. Vose had signed only one of the four deeds to the property when he and his heiress, Elizabeth Carberry, were killed in a private airplane crash in Alaska. The land and buildings were inherited by Miss Carberry's brothers who did not share their sister's and Mr. Vose's altruistic leanings. The Russian Foundation could not continue with the plans for a chapel. Several of the people from the Church spent at least one winter in one of the houses on the property in Milton with little food or fuel or money. Neighbors helped out where they could. Eventually the people had to leave, and the beautiful chapel and humanitarian effort never materialized.

Information comes from "Milton History Papers"; World's Great Religions, Staff of Life, ed., 1963; Recollections of Walter C. Sheldon.

Catholicism in Milton

There has never been a Roman Catholic church in Milton, although there have long been Catholic families here. In the early days, as now, these families attended services in Litchfield, first at the old St. Anthony's Church on South Street, built in 1888, and then at the new St. Anthony's of Padua on the same site, erected October 1948, four years after the tragic fire of October 1944.

Before 1858, Milton children of Catholic families probably had to travel to the Court House in Litchfield on Saturdays to attend catechism classes. Later, in the 1930's and 1940's, a priest came from the Litchfield church to Milton School on Wednesday afternoons after school to teach catechism.

Milton Catholics were closely tied to the Litchfield church. In the days before the first St. Anthony's was built, there were occasional visitations to the Litchfield community in which the Milton Catholics undoubtedly took part.

Litchfield was a mission area of the St. Joseph's Catholic Church in Winsted until 1882 when Litchfield was recognized as a parish. The Catholics then came under the patronage of St. Anthony's of Padua. Nowadays Milton's Catholic population has the choice of attending services in Litchfield or at the chapel in Bantam, Our Lady of Grace Chapel, built in 1949.

In later years there has been some ecumenism and assimilation by Catholics and Protestants, a sharing even of holy rituals, which has brought those in small villages like Milton closer together. The divisiveness of the old days is disappearing, and this is applaudable.

Information from "Milton History Papers"; Litchfield, Connecticut, 250th Anniversary booklet, 1969.

Chapter IX

ROADS — How We Got from Here to There

❖

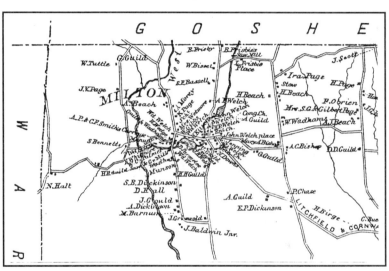

Map of Milton Center (from Seth Beers map, 1856)

In his fine history of Connecticut written during the 1930's, and titled *Connecticut, Past and Present*, Odell Shepherd observed that the early roads of Connecticut were a combination of the practical and the poetic; to retrace these roads today is to appreciate the truth of his words. They were practical in that they brought (eventually) travellers from one place to another, poetic in that they led through all the variations of picturesque beauty and grandeur that constitute the New England landscape — up to the highlands along hog-back rocky hills, in and out of swampy lowlands, through grassy valleys, down steep banks, beside still lake waters or turbulent, rushing streams. Today they are guides to the directions and courses of history and national character. Indeed, together with rivers, roads have become a common metaphor for the human journey in general — the open road, the road to happiness, the Via Dolorosa, the road not taken, the yellow brick road; the list goes on like a road itself.

The local roads of early Connecticut settlements were of course more evident of practical affairs than of universal concerns — they served a purpose, with convenience and expediency certainly of foremost importance. The early roads of Milton reflect the common interests of everyday life of a small village. The intricate network of Milton's roads may resemble the web of a demented spider, but it indicates clearly the pathways necessary for commerce, schools, churches, and social activities during the past two hundred years. Churches, burial grounds, schools — wherever these were to be found, there also would be roads — although it is far from clear which appeared first. In all likelihood, "roads" long preceded settlements or settlers. Indian trails formed the basis for many of the early roads.

These early trails followed, literally, the paths of least resistance, turning aside for boulders and fallen trees, avoiding swampy areas, going around steep hills or cliffs. Later, the "Indian File" narrow routes were widened somewhat, but only enough to accommodate carriages and wagons, and many of the obstructions remained, along with the turns and curves which add to today's charm of these back roads — they were suitable for walking or horseback riding, but did not make for comfortable or swift journeys. Undoubtedly they were typical of the highways of the time, giving Connecticut the reputation of having "the worst roads in the world." One traveller, a Count Castelux of France, complained in a letter of his visit to Litchfield in 1780: "The roads through Litchfield are more for the roe buck than for horses and conveyances — you mount for 4 or 5 miles, continually bounding from one large stone to another which cross the road, and give it a resemblance of stairs."

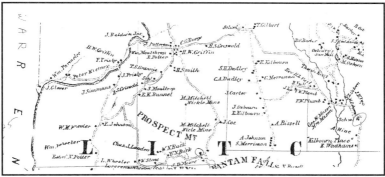

Map of Lower Milton (from Seth Beers map, 1856)

The Old Litchfield-Cornwall Road

It is not known what part of Litchfield the Count had been traveling through. He could well have been speaking of the road from Litchfield to Cornwall, which was laid out in 1741 through the northwesterly part of Litchfield known as Blue Swamp. Town records show that Messrs. Samuel Culver, Joseph Bird, Ebenezer and Moses Stoddard were appointed to "view and lay out a suitable highway," and were voted the power to pay "an equivalent in money for such lands as they shall find needful to take out of any man's land — and to draw the money out of the town treasury for the use aforesaid."

Blue Swamp at that time comprised a large area from Beach Street on the East to the Warren line on the West, and North to Goshen and Cornwall; the road to Cornwall, however, probably encompassed only the immediate environs of Milton village, passing through the swamps west before turning north to Cornwall. Where this road originated in Litchfield is not clear, but old maps and early Town records indicate that one of the earliest roads came up from what is now Brush Hill Road to meet Forge Hollow Road (now Litwin Road), then at the westerly end turning north to become Headquarters Road and thence into Milton village center.

In any case, the road through Blue Swamp (earlier called Tamarack Swamp) would have presented many difficulties in its construction. It probably resembled a roller coaster because of the hilly terrain which gave way to extensive wetlands. There were no trails or paths, nor for some distance any high ground which would allow for a road to go around the swamp. Years later, the area was described as being "a very singular place — a bottomless pit"; nevertheless, the Milton residents delegated to lay out a suitable highway found a way to do so. Long logs were laid in close parallel rows over other logs or "stringers" until there was a rude but serviceable passage or bridge over the swamp. "Corduroy" was the term used to describe this type of road because of the series of ridges and the resulting undulating ride; "washboard" would be more accurate, and even today anyone travelling on such roads if they are still unpaved can detect the underlying "ribs."

The deceptive simplicity of the road's original log substructure made Blue Swamp Road usable and enduring — facts recalled with praise and envy nearly one-hundred fifty years later, when attempts to build and maintain roads on this site met with continual failure. An article in the May 3, 1877, edition of *The Litchfield Enquirer* notes some of the problems: "For the last 10 or 12 years, the town has been trying to 'touch bottom' (in this area) — by filling in — sometimes with stone or gravel, and then gravel and stone again; every effort supposed to be the last — last year it was decided to try large rocks or boulders as large as a team could draw down the hill, and thus the road bed was raised 3 feet above high water mark. But all to no purpose. Down it has all gone again, and the road declared to be two feet lower than ever, so that the water touches the buggy box when passing. The road, though an important one, has been fenced in most of the spring. The plan most talked of now for the next trial seems to be a 'corduroy' or log road — it is said to have been built so at first and to have lasted a long time. Draining or a different route are both said to be impracticable."

Blue Swamp Road today remains "a singular place" because of its scenic nature. Called Blue Swamp for the blue-green needles on the Tamarack trees which once were abundant there, as well as for the blue gentians in the fall and blue flag in the spring, the road affords a ride through scenes of great beauty, particularly at the southwestern end; here the view opens up to a pastoral setting of farmhouse, buildings cattle grazing in sloping meadows against a background of distant blue hills. Blue Swamp is a lovely name for a lovely area.

1814: The Litchfield-Cornwall Turnpike

As the main route from Litchfield to Cornwall, Blue Swamp Road was superseded in 1814 by the new Litchfield-Cornwall Turnpike, which went from Milton roughly parallel to it and was connected by several side roads, such as

Seelye and Page Roads. Blue Swamp continued to be an important road, however, because it provided a route to Warren and Kent by way of the Dugway Road at its southwest end, and Flat Rocks Road at the northern end where it also met the new road to Cornwall. "Dugway" was a fairly common name for roads throughout Connecticut, and may still be found on old sign posts and records. Letters in the Litchfield Historical Society archives suggest that the term may have derived from a feature of these early roads: a central ditch or depression, the evidence of much foot travel on the early Indian trails. This contrasted to roads with a center crown which would have been the result of wagon routes.

The Litchfield-Cornwall Turnpike originated in Litchfield at what is the beginning of Milton Road, but probably did not proceed into Milton along the same route as the present road. Early maps and reports indicate that the road to Milton from the Litchfield site went north along Beach Street as far as Newcomb Road, where it continued west over to Hemlock Hill at the northern end of what is now Goodhouse Road. From Hemlock Hill Road, the route crossed over East Street (now called Maple Street) and entered the road known as the Dan O'Brien Road. This road was discontinued in 1919, but was used by local residents as a convenient short-cut to Maple Street until the flood of 1955 destroyed the bridge at the Shear Shop end. The road emerged onto Shear Shop Road at the corner where Frisbie's Grist Mill once stood. Thence, the road went south, crossing at the foot of the hill the east branch of the Shepaug River (known locally as the Marshepaug), and so into the center of Milton. Portions of this old road are still discernible today in some areas.

The "new" route to Cornwall from Litchfield was a commercial venture undertaken by the Litchfield and Cornwall Turnpike Company, incorporated in 1814 by the private laws of Connecticut. The company was empowered to construct and maintain a toll road from Litchfield to Cornwall, with a capital stock of one-thousand shares. Further provisions entitled the company to sell shares, to make and maintain the roads and to "erect and establish a toll-gate" to collect tolls. Rates would be collected according to a well-defined schedule until such time as all expenses incurred by the company had been reimbursed, unless further financing was required for on-going maintenance.

This responsibility of maintaining roads by a private corporation was a departure from earlier customs, whereby as specified in the Blue Laws of Connecticut (the 1650 Code of Connecticut) every person able to do so was required to work at least two days a year on the roads, to keep them in a "fit posture for passage — for the comfort and safety of man and beast." Refusal or neglect to comply with the law would result in fines of substantial amounts. Even as late as the early 1800's failure to meet assessments for road building and maintenance could result in confiscation of property or imprisonment in "the gaol in Litchfield" for the delinquents.

Today, around the corner on Milton-Cornwall Road, still stands a vestige of this early toll road — a toll house at number 598 Milton Road. This is a large house with ell to the south, owned lately by Carroll Fischer and others. One turnpike gate, now long gone, was located at the corner of Saw Mill and Blue Swamp Roads; another was at the top of Milton hill by the Dickinson-Goldring farm.

Working on the roads and being paid for doing so was doubtless considered as progress, but the wages were never enough to sustain a man's family, even if conditions warranted more than a few weeks work in a year. Men were paid from $.75 per day, or $3.50 per day with a team. Augustus Morey in 1838 contracted to receive $11.00 for working on the road for one year. In any case, volunteers continued to turn out to keep the roads passable, particularly in winter storms or during spring "mud-time." The selectmen of the town were considered responsible for the condition of the roads, and some took it upon themselves to beautify the roadsides; Maple Street may well owe its name, for example, to the many young maple trees set out by selectmen years ago.

The "Lost" Roads

If it were possible to enter Dugway Road at the southwestern end of Blue Swamp Road (near the farmhouse at #181 owned today by the Harris Hilding family), and to follow its course south roughly parallel to the Warren boundary, the traveller would come to what is now the Lower Shepaug reservoir. Here, the road turns up to the east to meet Old Forge Hollow Road, now erroneously marked Old Hollow Road, in an area known as "Hardscrabble." Old Forge Hollow Road, itself a continuation of Forge Hollow Road (see below), made its way southeasterly towards Prospect Mt. Road, which it crossed before turning south to Washington, Warren and Kent.

Traces of these old roads can still be found. Old Forge Hollow was at one time, as can be deduced from old maps and remains of cellar holes, fairly well-populated. Both Old Forge Hollow Road and the Dugway Road had ceased to be well-travelled long before they were officially discontinued in 1965. A special Town meeting held in October of that year ceded the right of way to these two roads through the Marshepaug Forest to the City of Waterbury as part of its water supply development program. They are now the "lost roads" of Milton, their paths not open to public access, their names almost as obscure as their origins.

Other Local Roads

Shear Shop Road was laid out in 1768 and was an important road, extending north towards Goshen from Milton Center. It was the way not only to the grist mill but also to Welch's Puddling Furnace and later the Shear Shop for which it was named. Still unpaved today, Shear Shop Road probably looks much as it did in its beginnings, progressing roughly parallel to the course of the Shepaug along wooded hills and occasional farm houses — quiet beauty still relatively unspoiled by development.

Mention should be made here of Potash Road, which connects Milton Center with East (or Maple) Street, which may have been the route taken by the Litchfield-Cornwall Turnpike once the road came out onto East Street from Hemlock Hill. Certainly, it appears a likely route, and with the potash works located along its border would have been well-traveled. It, like Shear Shop Road, remains a dirt road and gives today's travellers the experience of the rough but scenic rides common to the early settlers. Since the present Milton Road as it enters Milton is located in an area once wetlands, the earliest passage from Maple Street would have been on the site of higher, drier grounds — Potash Road. Early travellers preferred climbing to wallowing!

"Almost impassable" was the complaint used for Prospect Mountain Road when, in 1846, the Honorable Selectmen of the Town of Litchfield were presented with a petition: "Whereas the highway between the dwelling houses of Willis

Stone and Thomas Granniss to Milton is almost impassable in consequence of the hill leading over Prospect Mountain — the undersigned pray your honors to examine the said road immediately and make such alterations as may be considered practicable."

Signed the twentieth day of May, 1846, by thirty-one petitioners, the plea was promptly and favorably acted upon; Town Records for September 7, 1846, show that the troublesome section of the road was discontinued and a better route laid out. It is not clear what part of the road had been changed as boundaries in the old records are described in terms such as "stakes," "stones," "tree stumps," so that exact locations are today obliterated. Clearly stated, however, is the provision for paying land owners for damage or for use of land, amounts varying from $14.00 to $28.00. Since Prospect Mountain Road is today still a winding, hilly, largely unpaved "highway" not affording the most comfortable of journeys, it can be assumed that the earlier route was indeed barely passable.

It was a road well-used, however, serving a number of residents from the Bradleyville section of Bantam to the Headquarters area in Milton, passing also by a school. The Bradleyville-Headquarters area connection appears to have been important also for other reasons: the men of these two districts combined their num-

Headquarters Road

bers to perform military practices and drills, the men from Bantam coming up to Milton Green. As the distance to the Green seemed disproportionate to the Bantam group, a compromise located their meeting at the Headquarters area. Since the Bradleyville contingent still had the greater as well as the more difficult way to travel, they must have been an affable lot.

The Headquarters area on early maps appears to be somewhat south of the present juncture of Prospect Mountain Road with Headquarters and Litwin Roads, but was close enough to give the road its name. Headquarters Road is also said to have derived its name from having been the site of military planning during the American Revolution. General Washington reportedly stayed at a house in the area, now unfortunately no longer standing, and it is said that the initials "GW" had been carved into one of the beams. However that may be, Headquarters was from the earliest days a main road to Milton Center, leading straight past the cemetery for a mile or so until coming to Milton Road, once called Main Street. The approach to Milton presents a calendar scene of a New England village: churches, school house, fine old houses and picket fences grouped around an attractive green or common. Nearly one-third of Headquarters Road is still unpaved, chiefly the section where it passes through wetlands, and the surface is recognizable as being an old "corduroy" passage. It was probably because of the swampy nature of the terrain here that the first Headquarters Road from Milton Center began at a point nearly across from where the Meeting House (Congregational Church) on the Green would have been originally located. From there it ran south over hills and dry, rocky ground, and emerged just north of the now paved lower section, across from the old Stock-Birge-Winn house before continuing south and up the hill to Prospect Mt. Road.

Branching off from Headquarters Road between the cemetery on the hill to the south and Milton Village to the north is Saw Mill Road, named for the early saw mill once located at its juncture with Blue Swamp Road. At this corner also stood a grist mill and cider mill, as well as a pond widely prized for skating and the dam which powered all three mills — evidence of the once active commerce centered in Milton. The flood of 1955 destroyed the dam and with it the pond, and allowed the waters of the Shepaug to once again flow unimpeded under the bridge and into the deep ravine known locally as "the Gorge." After heavy rains, or during spring run-off, small cascades and pools make this area a treasured place of great charm.

Saw Mill Road together with Milton and Headquarters Roads forms a two-mile rectangle that is much favored by walkers and joggers. Along its perimeter grow a wide variety of wildflowers, grasses, ferns and shrubs; these with the lawns, gardens, small ponds and trees of the neighborhood provide unending pleasure and interest. Few who use Saw Mill Road today, however, are aware that they are not traveling along the original route: at one time, when the road was still unpaved, its course ran very close to the front door of what was known as the Reuben Dickinson house — so close, indeed, that anyone standing at the front door could shake hands with a passerby. A later resident, W.W. Thompson, had the road "moved" in 1923, thus providing for more privacy, if less hospitality.

The Shepaug, or Marshepaug, River passes through Milton on its way to the City of Waterbury's Lower Shepaug Reservoir, which is west of the village towards Warren. As

Twin Bridges on Milton-Cornwall Road

the river courses through many twists and turns, it presents a classic example of the term "meandering," and requires four bridges — two in Milton Village, and the other two on Shear Shop Road and Blue Swamp Road. There is a smaller bridge on Headquarters, but it passes over the peripheral wetland rather than the river itself. Modern bridges currently span the Marshepaug in Milton, having replaced long ago the earliest structures of logs, stringers and outside trusses. Such wooden bridges were serviceable for many years, bearing the weight and jolting of travelers and wagons well into the nineteenth century — indeed, the Milton Center bridge also provided support for what Town documents describe as a "horse shed." Erected in 1829 by Alban Guild, the shed enclosed parts of the highway encroaching on the rights of travelers. Complaints to the County Commissioners finally resulted nearly fifty years later in the dismantling of the shed, but not before the owner, Mrs. Emeline Stevens, received "sufficient recompense" from the Town coffers.

The removal of the horse shed was followed some eight or nine years later by the removal of the old bridge itself, when in 1885 a fine wrought-iron truss bridge was completed. This bridge in turn bore up well for more than a hundred years, giving way only in 1992 to the present sturdy wooden structure buttressed by fine masonry work. Suggestive of changing economics is the price tag of $150,000 for this modern bridge compared with the $900 figure for the wrought-iron bridge.

Milton Road has long been the main route from Litchfield to Milton Center, but there are two other well-used roads: Maple Street which beginning at its south end in the Bantam area and continuing north to Goshen gives access to Milton via three routes, Litwin Road near Brush Hill, Milton Road itself and Potash Road; and Cat Hole Road, connecting the Bantam area and State Route 202 to Milton by way of Litwin and Headquarters Roads. Both Maple Street and Cat Hole Road are scenic, with fine old houses and excellent views, particularly to the west.

Of the two, Cat Hole Road is judged to be the older, partly because of its winding ways which recall the philosophy of early travelers, "the easiest way is the most sensible way," but largely because of an early Town agreement reached in 1785. In this agreement, the Town Committee laid out a highway on Ashbel Catlin's land with Catlin's approval that "said highway" was to be used by the inhabitants of Litchfield and others forever.

The name, Cat Hole Road, has an interesting genesis: the road was known as North Road for many years, but was officially named Cat Hole Road by the selectmen in 1950, and so registered with the State of Connecticut. According to accounts of early residents and as reported in the *Litchfield Enquirer* in an article by Barbara O'Shea Rodenbach (Feb. 26, 1976) "...a man from Milton used to carry his scythe with him when he walked to Bantam to work for a farmer during haying season. After a few too many glasses of cider, the man would relate how wild cats would come down out of the ledges and he would 'mow' them down with his scythe.

These ledges are located about a quarter of a mile south of Litwin Road, and the people in this area dubbed it the 'cat hole'."

Not everyone was pleased with the official name, as a letter in the Bantam Historical Society's archives indicates; writing in October 1971, First Selectman George C. Dudley explains to a complaining resident that it is "impracticable to have two names on one road" (i.e. North and Cat Hole), and that he along with the Bantam Borough Warden decided to continue the one-hundred-year-old name of Cat Hole Road. "I suggest," he goes on to say, "if you find this name distasteful, that you pronounce it 'Ca-thole Road'." It is not recorded how this suggestion was received; in any event, the complaining resident subsequently moved from the area.

Whatever the pronunciation, Cat Hole Road is today one of the more heavily used routes to Milton, and, running parallel as it does to Prospect Mountain Road, certainly one of the most colorful. The mountain is clearly visible through all the curves and bends of the road, and in addition there is a natural area for wildlife observation. About half-way between Bantam and Milton a large swampy section has become a small pond, thanks to the efforts of beavers, resulting in the population of a variety of birds — great blue herons, egrets, mallards and other waterfowl enjoy this habitat. Further along the road on the way to Milton, there are access routes to the Mattatuck Trail, one leading to Prospect Mountain, and the other going over east to Maple Street. There is a connecting road over to Prospect Mountain Road as well, although now discontinued and known only as Donahue Road. Ruby Mattson, a former resident, preferred the name "Old Mining Road." "It is good to use the old names for the Town roads," she wrote, and it is hard to disagree.

Cat Hole Road, Maple Street, and by extension, Brush Hill Road, all enter upon Litwin Road, which itself then serves to connect with Headquarters Road, and thence to Milton Center. But Litwin Road is more than a connector between the other, longer roads; a ride along Litwin Road lifts the spirit and informs the mind of the limitless beauties of nature.

"Forge Hollow Road" was the early name for this mile-long stretch, important at the time for leading to one of Milton's thriving industries. Now called Litwin Road for the family who have for many years owned and maintained the farm and adjoining farmlands, the road is still important and justly famed for the views and scenes of the encompassing landscape. To the north and west, wooded hills rise and recede into the distance; wondrous cloud formations are borne above them and the sunsets are often spectacular. To the south, fields reach out to the distant hills. Close by, the roadsides, pastures, small ponds, stone walls and apple trees form the background for grazing cattle and horses; occasionally deer pass through, as do wild turkeys foraging, and always in season there are Canada geese. It is not unusual to see artists and photographers trying to capture the scene. Litwin Road is a beautiful introduction to Milton, and a memorable way to leave it.

"The worst roads in the world"— so went the early characterization of Connecticut's long-ago highways; from this modern perspective it is not possible to judge either the accuracy or the justice of these words. Doubtless many roads were quite deplorable. Far more welcome is the description given by Odell Shepherd, "practical and poetic." The accuracy and truth of these words can be well determined by following the old roads which Milton is fortunate in having preserved. Some, as described here, have been more practical than others, but all of them, even the discontinued "roads not taken," have proven to be poetic, and beautiful.

All are interesting. All make for fine drives or walks, and all lead to Milton — a happy conclusion.

Information comes from "Milton History Papers," Town Records, Maps, Odell Shepherd's Connecticut, Past and Present, Bantam Historical Society Records, Litchfield Historical Society, Letters re: Indian Trails, 1918, Oct. 21 and 25.

Chapter X

THE BURYING GROUNDS
— Where We Were Laid to Rest

❖

The history of local cemeteries begins, properly, with some knowledge of the first graveyards in Litchfield. Charles Thomas Payne states in his invaluable *Litchfield and Morris Inscriptions*, published in 1905, that the West Burying Ground, "is the earliest of the burial places in Litchfield, and its establishment was nearly contemporaneous with the founding of the Town — Here were interred nearly all of the pioneers of Litchfield, and the yard remained the principal burial ground of the Town until the Revolution."

People in the outlying sections endured great hardship when death came because of the distance to the graveyard. Occasionally, burials took place in a plot which had been set aside on family property.

In general, the northwest part of Litchfield, Milton Society, was served in the early days by the graveyards in West Goshen, Milton and Headquarters. Milton and Headquarters cemeteries are now owned by the Town of Litchfield.

Many East Cornwall families, most of whom came to Milton to church, are buried in the Milton graveyard. Doubtless, some in that section of the Town were buried in the South East Cemetery in Cornwall — at the Crooked Esses off Flat Rocks Road — which is no longer in use.

Milton Society residents buried in West Goshen are those of the families of Ambrose Collins, James Newcomb, Lyman Richards, James Scott, Wallace Wadhams and Christopher Wheeler. For the most part, this cemetery is now unused.

Milton Cemetery

Milton Cemetery on Blue Swamp Road

The Milton Cemetery, located on Blue Swamp Road, is, as Charles Payne says, undated. Payne wrote, "A thorough search of land and town records reveals no definite clew toward determining when this burying ground was first consecrated to the dead, but the dates on the oldest stones would indicate that it was near the Revolutionary period.

"On July fifth, 1813, the selectmen of Litchfield bought half an acre of David Welch from the south part of his farm for a burying ground, but this was very clearly an addition to one already in existence. It is spoken of in a deed of 1791 to Justus Seelye.

"In 1872, Mrs. Clarissa Seymour Welch [should read Clarissa Marsh Welch] sold to the Town over three acres to be used as an addition to the Milton yard, excepting the family burial place therein.

"The ground lies nearly a mile west of the village of Milton, in a sheltered valley, and is now enclosed by a substantial wall of quarried stone."

The setting aside of land for this burying ground goes back to the pioneers, and although to date no record of its beginning has been found, it was probably in use before 1768 when the Third Society was established. It seems likely that a piece of land was donated and used without the formality of record. The oldest stones would indicate that it was before the Revolutionary War. The possibility remains that a record of the origins of both Milton and Headquarters Cemeteries may yet be found.

The first reference that has so far been found relative to Town ownership of the Milton Cemetery is that of a Town meeting held in Litchfield on November 4, 1805, at which it was "Voted, that the Selectmen be directed to pay to the Society of Milton the money that they Paid for their Burying Ground." This action was taken to clear accounts. If there is any connection between this transaction and the original plot, the information has not been discovered.

At an adjourned Town meeting held January 9, 1812, it was "Voted that the selectmen be directed to Purchase and lay out a Suitable Piece of land for a Burial Ground in the Society of Milton." The follow-up to this action is that of July 5, 1813, which is quoted at the beginning of this chapter from Charles T. Payne's book.

The earliest markers were of native fieldstone and slate. The lettering on the fieldstones did not hold up well against the extremes of weather, and most are nearly illegible. Those on the slate, however, are remarkably clear. Marble was used after 1842 when Simeon S. Batterson came to Litchfield from New Preston and, with his eldest son James G. Batterson, established and maintained for some years a marble yard on the East side of Meadow Street. A tall stone beside the grave of Capt. Samuel Wright, 1875, is the first one made of granite. Within the Cemetery there are about forty traces of old broken stones and about as many more traces of unmarked graves.

A fieldstone at the grave of Lieut. Jehiel Parmele, who died of smallpox, is the earliest marked stone in the Cemetery extant. The inscription reads, "In memory of Lieu^{nt} Jehiel Parmele, he died Jan^{ry} ye 15th 1776 in ye 58th year of his Age."

The following interesting narrative of the Old Section of Milton Cemetery was published in the March 1, 1877, edition of *The Litchfield Enquirer*: "In the northwestern part of the town of Litchfield, between the East Branch of the Shepaug river and a tributary called the Tamarack, is situated the old Milton burial ground. It contains about one acre of land and is of triangular shape, having its base toward the North, its Eastern side by the highway and its Westward by the Tamarack river. Its oldest gravestones (common grey and blue stones) date back about a century. For many years it was open to the Common, and had never been enclosed until about 1820 when a board fence was erected on the side by the highway, a rail fence having been previously maintained on the other two sides to keep cattle off from adjoining lands. Near the north corner stands a marble gravestone, probably the first of its kind erected here, bearing the following inscription:

'Roger Kirby
June 12th, 1793, aged 95 yrs.
    When undissembled Piety, inflexible Probity, and universal Benevolence have crowned a Long Life full of good Works, let it be recorded in Marble, and faithfully transmitted to Posterity'."

This stone is located near the north corner of the Old Section.

When the wall of "quarried stone" was built in 1872, children's bones were found outside the fence. It was concluded at the time that they were those of unbaptized children, who in accordance with some beliefs could not be buried in "consecrated ground."

There is a sad story about "Little Caroline" Clark, daughter of Jaleel and Susan Clark of East Cornwall. Caroline died of scarlet fever on January 25, 1831, at age five years and eight months. The snow was so very deep at that time that the men of the family had to guess where the Clark lot was. When spring came, the grave could not be found and never has been. On the back of the stone placed for her brother Henry is the inscription, "We shall find her in Heaven." Henry and his sister Lydia, being unable to locate Caroline's grave one day in May 1831, planted the two rose bushes they had brought from home on either side of the cemetery entrance where they grew and blossomed for many years.

In the private walled Welch lot, the only privately owned lot in the cemetery, the tombstones bear no epitaphs, just name and date and age. According to Walter E. Vaill, whose mother was Rosa Welch Vaill, the story has come down that Major David Welch banned epitaphs after the headstone erected for a relative buried in another town stressed the ability of the deceased to lay up worldly goods; the reaction by those who knew the family was, "And his son, Paul, spent it all." Upon hearing this the family gave orders that no words of praise should appear on their tombstones.

An interesting statement of one way money was raised to provide for some landscaping in front of the cemetery is found among Milton Cemetery records:

"We, the undersigned, agree to pay the sum affixed to our several names to pay towards an Evergreen Hedge to put in front of the Grave Yard in Milton Society.

"The sum to be raised is not less than Forty-five Dollars. $45.00 Milton, Conn. Jan. 18th 1881.

"B. M. Woodward $5.00; Wm. J. Hall 3.00; E. H. Wright 3.00; W. C. Ferriss 2.00; H. L. Seelye 2.00; Heman Beach 2.00; H. P. Griswold 2.00; Clarissa Welch 2.00; Geo. B. Parmalee 1.00; A. T. Guild 1.00; Truman Guild 1.00; T. Leander Jennings 1.00; Charles Lorber 1.00; Jacob Baker 1.00; R. F. Tompkins .50; Perkins 2.00; Wm. Bissell 1.00; Samuel Bennett 1.00; Geo. J. Harrison 1.00; E. Beach 1.00; B. Beach 1.00; E. P. Dickinson 1.00; Geo. A. Smith 1.00; Abner Gilbert 2.00; Charles I. Page 2.00; Charles B. Page 1.00; Ethan Kilbourn 1.00; Horace Nichols 1.00; Sylvester Griswold .50."

All are marked paid.

Whether they planted a hedge and were not satisfied with it or changed their minds and planted trees instead is not known. In any case, there are evergreen trees at the front of the graveyard.

The Milton Woman's Club raised and contributed a great deal of money towards the restoration and upkeep of the Milton Cemetery. Through their influence a cemetery association was established, it being their belief that "...the neglected burying ground speaks of itself. It dishonors the dead and discredits the community." The Milton Cemetery was indifferently cared for over the years, mowed once or twice a year, and stones had deteriorated badly, especially those in the Old Section.

One of the most important actions in local history was the organization of the Milton Cemetery Association on

October 21, 1940, and "Recorded in the office of the Secretary of State on November 25, 1940." The first officers were: Mrs. Ernest Axford, President; Miss Marian Blake, Secretary: Mrs. Willis O. Perkins, Treasurer.

Much-needed restoration, the construction of a circular driveway through the Cemetery and the building of a storage shed are notable accomplishments of the Association. Of special significance was the placing of a Memorial stone in the Old Section honoring all those in unmarked graves. Its inscription bears witness to the objectives of the Association:

In Memory Of The Unknown
Who Were Laid
To Rest Here
Previous to 1790
Erected By The
MILTON CEMETERY
ASSOCIATION INC.
A Group Of Interested
Descendants Of The
Early Inhabitants
Of Milton Formed
This Association On
November 25, 1940,
For The Purpose Of
Restoration And
Maintenance Of
Milton Cemetery.

Information on the six trust funds for both the Milton and Headquarters Cemeteries is included in the Annual Reports of the Town. Listed as restricted funds, these include the Granniss Fund, Headquarters Fund, Harriet Lorber Fund, Belle G. Russell Fund and Welch Fund. Unrestricted funds are the Blake Fund, established by Marian Blake, and the Julia Frances Guild Seelye Fund established by Fred H. Seelye.

In September 1974, Milton Cemetery was extensively damaged by vandals. A great deal of money and countless hours were required by men of the community and nearby towns to restore the cemetery. Many donations helped with this repair of over one hundred broken stones. A number of stones will forever show the evidence of this maliciousness. But the spirit of cooperation and ingenuity, so typical of Milton and its neighbors, was a fine example of the best of the Yankee in small towns.

Following this vandalism, the Association realized the need to catalogue all of the gravestones in both cemeteries and, at its request, Orcelia Birge Winn compiled this catalogue which is kept up to date. Copies are deposited at the Oliver Wolcott Library and the Litchfield Historical Society, and a copy is included in the records of the Association.

On July 10, 1989, the Milton and Headquarters Cemeteries, along with the entire village, suffered greatly from a series of devastating tornados. All except four of the majestic spruce trees along the front wall of Milton Cemetery were blown down across Blue Swamp Road, pulling loose the stones of the wall. Some trees inside the grounds fell onto gravestones — the damage could have been worse than it was. Volunteers from all over the area, as well as the National Guard, assisted in restoring much of the two cemeteries. A local Boy Scout troop donated and planted spruce seedlings to replace those along the front wall.

Among the many interesting inscriptions in Milton Cemetery are the following:

John M. West, M.D.
"Let the dead rest"

In memory of MR Jonathan Wright, 2ND,
who died Dec. 14, 1799, Aged 34 years
"Reader behold as you pass by
As you are now, so once was I.
As I am now, so you must be,
Prepare for death and follow me"

In MEMORY of Capt Daniel Cook who died
on his birth day, August 14th 1809 Aged
49 Years
"Harke my gay friends, that Solemn toll,
Speaks the departure of a Soul;
Tis gon that^s all, we know not where;
Or how th' unbodi^d Soul doth fare"

Consecrated to the memory of Dotha,
daughter of Peter & Lois Farvour &
intended consort of Adoniram French,
who departed this life August 25, 1821,
aged 17 y., 9 m. & 27 d.
"Stay, fond lover, stay thy tears
And weep not o'er my tomb
Thinck not thy DOTHA's fate severe
Since God has calld her home"

Mrs. Salome S., wife of Birdsey Gibbs,
died May 30, 1828 aged 30
"Earths attractions could not chain thee
Earthly prospects could not keep
Love of friends could not detain thee
Nought's left them save to weep"

J. E. Church, South Farms, is inscribed at the base of the Gibbs headstone. Salome was the young wife of the village schoolmaster. The epitaph could be original.

In memory of Mrs. ABIGAIL, wife of Capt.
ELIPHAZ PARSONS, who departed this life
Feb. 22d, 1799, In the 57th year of her age
"In memory of life that's past
In hope of life to come,
The Husband of the deceas'd
Doth consecrate this Tomb"

Early Milton families found in Milton Cemetery include among others: Bassett, Beach, Birge, Clark, Cook, Dickinson, Gibbs, Gilbert, Guild, Hall, Hart, Jennings, Osborn, Page, Parmalee, Perkins, Seelye, Smith, Stewart, Welch, Wetmore and Wright.

Headquarters Cemetery

As with Milton Cemetery, knowledge is lacking as to when the first land was set aside to be used as a burying ground at Headquarters, the area halfway between Milton and Bantam. This cemetery was established sometime around the late eighteenth century. On September 6, 1875, a piece of land was added to the original tract when Michael Flaherty sold a quarter of an acre to the Town for seventy-five dollars. Additional land was acquired to the south in the mid-1900's.

Headquarters Cemetery with stone wall

A definite income was assured for the care of Headquarters Cemetery by Fremont M. Granniss, who died in 1931, and Weston G. Granniss, who died in 1940. Following is a clause in the will of Weston Granniss: "Seventh: I give and bequeath to the Town of Litchfield, Connecticut the sum of One Thousand Dollars ($1000.00) to be kept by it as a separate fund, and the income thereof to be applied to the maintenance of the cemetery in the westerly part of said Town in that section known as Headquarters." Care of this cemetery is now undertaken by the Milton Cemetery Association.

As is common, there are many unmarked graves in Headquarters Cemetery. In the far northwest corner is reported to be the grave of an unnamed hired man, according to Harry T. Haviland, long-time Milton resident and sexton of both Headquarters and Milton Cemeteries for years.

Headstone inscriptions are of importance to those interested in antiquity and to genealogists, and Headquarters has its share. Among such memorials is one very old stone near the roadside which marks the grave of a small child with the following inscription:

In memory of Israel, Son to Capt Israel
& Mrs Mary Potter, died O^{ct} 12th, 1785,
aged 1 year
"The first in this burying ground"

Another of interest is this:
In Memory of Mrs Polly, Wife of M^r
Hezekiah Smith, daugh^{tr} to Capt Israel
Potter, died Oc^t 27th, 1793, in the
23rd year of her age
"Here my dear polly lies
Obscur^d in the dust
Thus all but virtue dies
Whose memory cannot rust"

An example of well-expressed appreciation in Headquarters:
Mrs. Abigail Dudley, wife of William
Dudley, Died Aug. 24, 1827, AEt 65
"If worth departed e'er deserved a tear,
O gentle stranger pay the tribute here"

Worthy of being copied are these:
In Memory of Mr William Granniss, who
departed this life March the 27th, 1792
in the 58th year of his age
"Sleep on, dear friend, till Jesus comes
And Gabriel's trump shall bust the tombs
Then all immortal thou shalt rise,
And may thy death instruct us to be wise"

Our Darling Mamie, daughter of W. B. &
Jennie S. Morgan, died June 28, 1874,
AE 16 Mo's

"Budded on Earth
To bloom in Heaven"

This touching sentiment also appears at the grave of seven year old Asa W. Granniss.

Another poignant verse is this one:
John S., Son of Hiram M. & Harriet B. Griffin, Died Dec. 17, 1856, Aged 10 yr's
"In the cold grave without a stain
We lay thy little form to day
But hope to meet the [sic] once again
When the long night has passed aw^{ay}"

Old Milton family names among those buried at Headquarters are: Benson, Birge, Carter, Catlin, Den(n)ison, Dudley, Frisbie, Goslee, Griffin, Granniss, Moulthrop, Potter, Seelye and Smith.

Crooked Esses South East Cemetery

The Crooked Esses area of Cornwall was associated with Milton in both business and social activities in the early days. From Edward C. Starr's *A History of Cornwall, Connecticut*, comes the following: "This cemetery lies not far North of the proposed crossing of that road [through Cornwall Bridge to Litchfield but never constructed] and the Crooked Esses. It contains few graves and much brush, but one soldier of the Revolution and one of the Civil War are buried in it. It is indifferently cared for by the town, its owner." Starr also states that the South East Cemetery at Crooked Esses was opened sometime in the middle of the nineteenth century.

The run-down condition of the cemetery at the Crooked Esses prompted the copying some years ago of the tombstone inscriptions found there. They are included here for permanent record.

1) Abel Avery died Apr 30, 1846 Age 86
   Revolutionary War Capt Dewey's Co.
2) Elizabeth Avery wife of Abel died Dec. 29, 1851
3) Lyman Avery died April 29, 1838 age 34 yrs 7 days
   "So man lieth down & riseth not till the Heavens be no more, they shall not awake nor be raised out of their sleep"
4) Mary M. wife of John Avery died May 6, 1833 Age 24
5) Abraham Bishop died May 4, 1849 Aged 64 yrs
6) In memory of James Blake who died Nov. 19, 1817 aged 47
7) Dorcas, widow of James Blake, who died Apr 2, 1852 Aged 75 years
8. Stephen Curtiss died Oct 5, 1852 AE 73
   "I have fought the good fight
   I have finished the course
   I have kept the faith"
9) Daughter [no name] of Evits & Minerva Curtiss died Dec 26, 1860
10) Benjamin Doolittle June 30, 1856 87 yrs.
    wife Harriet, July 10, 1855, 80 yrs.
11) In memory of Erastus Doolittle died Oct 12, 1813 In the 4th year of his age Son of Benjamin and Harriet Doolittle
12) George Johnson, son of Wakeman and Harriet Johnson, died Aug 2, 1854, 14 yrs 2 mo 11 days
    "Weep not for him who's now at—
    Where care & pain no more annoy

His spirit smiles from that bright shore
And—whispers weep no more"
13) David Moss died May 13, 1812 Age 43
14) Milo Moss Apr 3, 1869 Age 72
"Blessed are the dead who die in the Lord"
15) Wife Sophia, May 10, 1866 Age 62
"Blessed are the poor in spirit for
they shall see God"
16) Cornelius C. Parmelee Died Dec. 14, 1876 AE 36
17) Amelia S., wife of David Parmelee Died Apr 30, 1877 AE 66
18) David B. Parmelee Died Sept 28, 1878 Aged 70
19) In memory of Sarah Peck, March 1809 AE 21
20) Daniel W., son of Jesse & Polly Peck died
Feb 17, 1816 AE 11 months
21) Ruth Peck, who died Jan 8, 1876 AE 60

Six men, of all those who contributed to the care of the two Milton Cemeteries, should be noted: Harry T. Haviland, G. Herbert Griffin, Edward A. Williamson, Stanley W. Birge, Jason F. Hallock, Jr. and Carroll L. Fischer. These men have given countless hours and effort to make Milton and Headquarters Cemeteries places where people can stop to admire the beauty.

Information comes from "Milton History Papers"; Charles T. Payne, Litchfield & Morris Inscriptions, 1905; gravestones in Milton Cemetery; Marjorie Pikosky, Harriet Clark and Esther Nicholson, Little Old Stories of East Cornwall; Milton Cemetery Association Records; Edward C. Starr, History of Cornwall, second edition, 1982.

Chapter XI

IN DEFENSE OF FREEDOM
— Our Fighting Men and Women

Revolutionary War
War of 1812
Mexican War
Civil War
Spanish-American War
World War I
World War II
Korea
Viet Nam

Those Who Served

Revolutionary War
Francis Barber
Benjamin Birge
Beriah Birge (no stone)
James Birge
John Bissell
Isaac M. Catlin
Sgt. Lot Chase
George Clark
Capt. Daniel Cook
Chauncey Dennison
Oliver Dickinson, Jr.
Gershom Gibbs (died in service)

Moore Gibbs
Lt. John Griswold
John Hall
Burritt Jennings
Ens. Daniel Landon
Daniel Page
John Page
Jehiel Parmele (died in service)
Eliphaz Parsons
Israel Potter
Joel Potter
Stephen Ranney
John Seelye
Jared Stewart (died in service)
Maj. Abram E. Welch (died in service)
Maj. David Welch
1st Lt. Hugh P. Welch
John Welch
Ens. Jonathan Wright

War of 1812
Noah Bishop
Benjamin K. Bissell
Jeremiah Griswold
Julius Griswold
Truman Gilbert
Salmon Hall
Daniel Perkins
Horace Smith
David Welch

Mexican War
Capt. Lyman Bissell

Patriot War
Maj. Gen. John W. Birge

French & Indian War
Benjamin Bissell
Oliver Dickinson, Sr.
William Hart
Justus Seelye (stone missing)
David Welch

Spanish-American War
Clarence Gillette

Civil War
Cornelius G. Birge
Capt. William Bissell
Francis Gilbert
Julius Glover (not located)
Wesley Glover
Capt. John E. Granniss
William J. Hall
Salmon Hall
Charles E. Hart
Reuben Hart
Joseph S. Hubbard
Levi Jacus
Frederick T. Jennings
J. Wesley Jennings
Lewis Jones (buried in Milton)

Henry Morehouse
Andrew Nichols
Willard H. Parmalee (killed; grave not located)
William K. Parmalee
William Snyder
Lebbeus J. Welch
Seth Whiting
Wesley Woodin

World War I
Jacob Benson
Francis L. Doyle
Murray Hatch
Charles E. Hart
Charles I. Page, Jr.
Clarence E. Perkins
Albert Perrett
Edward Snyder

World War II
William P. Ackerman
Archibald Bennett
John S. Buell, Jr. (listed as Milton)
Archibald C. Doty, Jr.
Richard E. Dudley
Emil Fox, Jr.
Severin J. Fox
George H. Griffin, Jr.
Thomas R. Kitchin
Aune Lillian Koski
Francis P. Kubish
John A. Kubish

Martin G. Kubish, Jr.
Edward J. Litwin
Robert Bruce McCaskill (died in service)
Grace Alison Raymond
Edward A. Raymond
Kenneth A. Richard
Oscar G. Richard
Walter A. Richard
James H. Scott
Malcolm E. Smith
Howard R. Taylor
John E. Taylor, Jr.
Richard F. Woodington

Korea
Charles F. Birge
Hugh Brown
Carroll L. Fischer
Ernest Fisher
Alford J. Fretts
Raymond L. Gray
Philip G. Pepper
Edward A. Raymond

Viet Nam
Gregory C. Deering
Donald P. Dennis
Kirby E. Dennis
Noel T. Fisher
Dewey L. Kizzia, Jr.
Craig E. Litwin
Edward A. Raymond

Bruce Thoma
James B. Winn
William W. Winn, Jr.

Post Viet Nam
Richard Todd

They Gave Their Lives

Revolutionary War
Major Abram E. Welch
Gershom Gibbs
Jehiel Parmele
Jared Stewart

Civil War
Willard H. Parmalee

World War II
Robert B. McCaskill

Military

Milton residents have answered the call to arms whenever there was a threat to our Country. They served in all branches of Service, from the Indian Wars to the present.

When the Colonies declared their independence and the Revolutionary War began, each town was given a quota of men needed to join the State Militia. The Town of

Litchfield, at a Town meeting on April 15, 1777, decided the following:

> "Voted to pay on the first day of Jan. Annually out of the Town Treasury, to each and every Non Commissioned Officer and Private Soldier who already hath or hereby shall enlist into either of the Eight Continental Battalions now raising in this State for three years or during the War after the rate of 12 pounds said annually during the time of his continuance in said Service after this day to the number of 92 being the quota of men to complete the quota for the Town, as ascertained by the Governor and the Council of Safety."

Excerpt from Record
J. Strong Town Clerk

The practice of towns offering bonuses to people serving in the military was common. The bonus would be paid either yearly as Litchfield decided or upon discharge. The term of service varied from one battle to the duration of the war. The most common length was for a few months, so that the family responsibilities could also be met. In 1792, the Congress of the United States passed a uniform militia training law. In the course of time it was confirmed and amplified by the legislatures of the various states and made a state law.

After the Revolutionary War, our military system consisted of small military companies being formed in different parts of the Town. Certain days of the year were set aside as "training days" where military maneuvers were carried out. One particular day was called "general training day," when two or more companies met at some designated place and trained together as a unit. This general training day was considered by the community as somewhat of a holiday. Picnics might be held, and enterprising boys or girls might earn a few pennies by offering "goodies" for sale. These might have included popcorn or popcorn balls at 1¢ or a hunk of gingerbread at 3¢. Imagine our modern youth considering such food as delicacies!

Milton and Bantam — then know as Bradleyville — each had a military company. These two companies trained together by alternating locations, which apparently produced some friction among the men. A compromise was reached between the two companies which moved the training half-way between the two villages to the area known as Headquarters.

An example of life as a soldier can be obtained from the records of men applying for pensions after an Act of Congress authorized benefits to Revolutionary War soldiers in 1832. The following is taken from the application of Jonathan Wright of Milton, dated July 23, 1832:

"On this 23^d day of July A.D. 1832, personally appeared in open court — Jonathan Wright, a resident of said Town of Litchfield aforesaid, aged 86 years..." There follows a record of Jonathan Wright's service, beginning in 1776 when he was a Sergeant in Capt. Amos Barnes' Company in Col. Elisha Sheldon's Regiment of the Connecticut Militia.

In mid-August of that year the Company marched to the city of New York. When they retreated from Brooklyn to New York, Wright was on ferry guard. They marched to Horn's Hook, "staid about a week," and retreated to Harlem Heights where they were attacked by the British. In October they were dismissed. Wright acted as Sergeant Major from Horn's Hook until discharge, and "after the regiment was dismissed I staid to deposit our ammunition, etc.," acting as Commandant to the regiment that remained.

In March 1777, Wright received a commission as Ensign of 1st Company 17th Regiment "of the Alarm List," and went in April with the Company to the Danbury Alarm, arriving there after Danbury was burned. During that summer, teams with ammunition and other supplies arrived in Litchfield en route to the army "in the Jersies," and Wright furnished a guard of forty enlisted men which he commanded.

Later that summer, or in the fall, Wright marched as an Ensign to Stoney Ridge in Capt. Joseph Vail's Company; they were there for two months and then were dismissed and went home.

In the spring of 1778 he enlisted in the Connecticut State Troops in Capt. Joel Gillet's Company, Col. Roger Enos' Regiment, commissioned as an Ensign. He was sick when the Regiment marched to White Plains and joined them two weeks later as they marched to West Point. There they erected fortifications.

Late that fall Wright "had a short furlow" and came home, rejoining the Company later in the Horse Neck area where he stayed until the year expired in the spring of 1779, guarding the coasts of Connecticut. He was discharged there or at Old Greenwich. He enclosed affidavits from Truman Marsh, Samuel Seymour, James Birge and Oliver Dickinson. The application was first denied, then later approved.

Among others from Milton who applied for pensions under this Act were John Griswold, Gershom Gibbs, Moore Gibbs, Joel Potter and Francis Gilbert.

By the statute passed in 1792, all physically fit men between youth and middle age were enrolled and took an active part in general training. This established a form of home guard which would be, with training, more effective in battle.

One of the great occasions of rural life was the annual May gathering of the men from the farms to display the result of their training and to inspire the company. In September there was a general muster of the whole regiment. It was "a day of patriotic fervour and delicious excitement, ended late at night when the weary patriots trudged home with a sheet of gingerbread and a headache."

In 1862, President Lincoln called for volunteers to fight to preserve the Union. Governor William Buckingham asked Connecticut to raise at least seven new regiments. Litchfield responded by fielding an entire regiment. The 19th Connecticut Infantry, later known as the 2nd Connecticut Volunteer Heavy Artillery, was composed of men from all over Litchfield County. They marched off to war on September 11, 1862. During the remainder of 1862 and through 1863 while attached to the Army of the Potomac, they served on provost duty in Alexandria, Virginia.

On May 17, 1864, they were summoned to the front. Even though they were a heavy artillery unit, Gen. Grant needed replacements for the infantry, and the 2nd began serving as infantry. They participated in the Shenandoah Campaign of 1864 and were in the battles of Cold Harbor, Cedar Creek, Spotsylvania, Manassas, Petersburg and others during that bloody summer. Of the original 850 enlisted men who marched from Litchfield in 1862, only 183 would march back in 1865.

During the Civil War the Welch family in Milton received a letter from a man who looked after their brother, Abram E. Welch, in a Union Hospital in Tennessee. Following are excerpts from that letter written by H. Haskill, Ward Master:

"Dear Sir — As I was with your brother during his last moment and for the most of the time for the last 48 hours previous to his death, I have thought I would write a few lines. I asked him once or twice if you had not better be sent for. No he said you could not come to do any good. He said nothing to me about writing his friends, but I believe he left messages with Adjutant Smith of the 74th Regt. Jud. who was boarding at the same house as also what to do with his effects, as he Smith probably has already informed you." Haskill was also a member of the 2nd Reg. Minn. Volunteers and knew Major Welch "by reputation as being one that did not run from the battlefield at Bull Run."

Ward Master Haskill visited Major Welch often and brought him things including "some blackberry cordial" from the Sanitary and Christian Commission. Because Maj. Welch's room was chilly, Haskill brought him into the building he was in which was warmer. Maj. Welch then moved into a boardinghouse and hoped to travel to his "Uncle Jay's" in Kalamazoo, Mich, but was unable to make the trip.

Haskill goes on to tell of caring for Maj. Welch and being with him when he died. The letter ends, "Thus has gone a noble patriot and brave soldier. He has yielded his young life on the Altar of his Country. His memory with the thousands of others that are daily falling will be cherished by a grateful Nation..."

Through the years of the Civil War the women of Milton made and accumulated articles for the servicemen which they sent to the Sanitary Commission at Washington, D.C., articles such as towels, shirts, mittens, blankets, socks, bandages, "a can of peach sauce," farina, etc. The women contributed items for both World Wars, rolling miles of bandages, gathering necessities which were sent to the soldiers. Their letters, too, helped bolster morale. The women weren't left behind; they went along with the men in these ways of assisting and caring. During World War I and after, they went along physically, as several Milton women joined in the ranks.

With the first hints of the coming World War I, the people of Litchfield again revived the home guard idea, as their forefathers had after the nation was formed. This guard was called "The Litchfield Military Association." As in the past, it was expected that all able-bodied men would be called upon to defend the country in time of serious need; therefore it was of utmost importance to maintain a system of training by which an efficient soldiery could be established.

In Litchfield it was proposed on November 30, 1915, that a platoon of cavalry and a company of rifles be organized on military lines and drill in accordance with military regulations. This was to afford men living throughout the countryside opportunity for such training which was not otherwise available. The men in Milton were included in this plan.

It was for this reason that on July 17, 1916, at the house of George Guion, a group of men formed a cavalry and an infantry unit. They were known as "The Litchfield Light Horse" and "The Litchfield Rifles." They had one hundred thirty volunteers: one hundred went to the Rifles under the command of Hobart Guion, and thirty went to the Light Horse.

The end of the war was not the end of the Association. It was reorganized in 1937, and helped in the capture of German spies who were relaying information about ship sailings. This resulted in a reduction in the number of ships sunk off New England.

A letter during World War II from a former pupil and neighbor of Ellen Doyle's, Kenneth A. Richard, gives a picture of the daily life of a serviceman. He rose at 6 A.M. and fell out for roll call and exercises until 6:30, then swept and mopped the barracks and had breakfast. After that he fell out again and went to the drill field until 10:30. An hour or so later he fell out again to go to work. He wrote, "Do a lot of falling out, don't I?" He was an air cadet, so work for him was engine changes. At 4 P.M. he marched to the barracks for dismissal until 11 P.M. bed check. Although his days were full and regimented, he wrote that it was a lot of fun. He complained because it was expected of him; and he missed home and family and Milton, and enjoyed receiving the Litchfield newspaper and catching up on news from home. His ideas and viewpoints on many things were changing, he said.

Special mention should be made of a miracle in Milton which occurred during the military action involving United States forces in Lebanon, October 1983. With the first reports of a terrorist suicide bombing at U.S. Marine headquarters in Beirut when nearly 250 United States marines and soldiers were killed, came word that one of Milton's own was stationed there — Richard Todd, son of Hugh and Barbara Todd.

For three days the community held its breath and prayed. Then the good news came: Dick had been away from the barracks when the bomb was set off — he was safe. The village came together at Trinity Church to thank God and rejoice, filling the church full and finally releasing tears — the tears of joy. They wept also for the ones who would never come home.

As a sequel to this story, Richard was also in Saudi Arabia

when United Nations troops were sent to quell Saddam Hussein's attempts to take Kuwait with his Iraqui forces. It was a tough tour of duty for the servicemen, but again Richard made it home safely.

Each service person from Milton has been our son or daughter, and Milton cares deeply about their well-being. Each one lost has been a hurt beyond telling, the latest being Robert Bruce McCaskill during World War II.

From every war or military action to which Milton has sent her men and women have come tales of heroism, tragedy, even humor. Unfortunately they cannot all be recorded here.

Information for this chapter comes from "Milton History Papers"; Honor Roll in Milton Congregational Church; and Monuments in the Center Park on the Green in Litchfield.

Chapter XII

CATASTROPHIES — Our Times of Trouble

❖

As with every other place where people live, Milton has suffered tragedies, near-tragedies and catastrophes which have touched everyone in the community and have united the people in their common sorrow.

Fires

Among such events in Milton are the various fires they have experienced. One of the earliest fires described in the "Milton History Papers" occurred in the 1880's, when a house located close to where the schoolhouse-Todd home now stands caught fire and burned to the ground. Inside the house was Wadham(s) Beach who lost his life in that fire. There is not much information in the records about this fire, but it was a tragedy for the community.

Another fire occurred in January 1894, when the Barnes and Earle store burned down. It was located next to Trinity Episcopal Church where Milton Public Hall stands today. This sad event is described in the chapter on "Social Life."

Three other fires of note within recent memory were those which damaged or destroyed the homes of Stuart (Svante) S. Rydehn and Karolina K. Rydehn, Auguste A. Gray and Karl and Adelaide Thoma.

The fire at the Rydehns' on the night of September 28, 1946, burned down the gracious old house on upper Shear Shop Road. An oil heater in the woodshed, only a few feet from the house, caught fire when the "oil burner overflowed," causing a quickly spreading fire which engulfed the house. Many possessions from the first floor were saved, but everything on the upper floors was destroyed. Lack of water from the shallow well greatly hampered firemen from Goshen, Bantam and Litchfield. With no telephone at the farmhouse, a neighbor who was at the house that evening, Auguste A. Gray, had to drive the two miles or so to the village to telephone for help.

As always, neighbors came together quickly and efficiently to help the Rydehns, their daughter, Lillian O'Neill and her two children, Patricia and John. The family spent that night with H. Ernest and Edith D. Axford. They stayed at the Raymond Cottage on the Green and later at the house owned now by Janet Sibley on Headquarters Road. A new house was built on the site of the old one on Shear Shop Road.

The fire which almost completely gutted the home of Auguste A. Gray on Blue Swamp Road (now #23) took place in the early morning hours in November 1957, and produced such heavy smoke that firemen were prevented at first from entering the house. The fire burned between the ceiling of the first floor and the floor of the second, emerging into the living quarters of the first floor. Eventually firemen from Bantam and Litchfield contained the flames, but Mrs. Gray lost many of her possessions including her piano, grandfather clock, books, papers and furniture, nearly everything in the first floor rooms. One special item destroyed in that fire was a crosstitched yarn rug designed and made by Mrs. Gray, which depicted the Harwinton Congregational Church and stone chapel.

Fortunately, the Marshepaug river runs behind the house, and water from it was brought up to the house by two pumps. Again, Milton people rallied around with help and support. Mrs. Gray stayed for a time at the home of Charles and Dorothy Earle in Milton Center (#552 Milton Road).

Under the heading "Love Thy Neighbor," is an article written for local newspapers by M. Adaline Seymour of Milton regarding the fire at the home of Karl and Adelaide Thoma. It is excerpted here: "The quavering wail of the fire siren keened out through the night of Wednesday, April 14, 1954. Those on the outskirts of the little Connecticut village were startled awake, peered from their windows, saw no glow of fire and went back to bed. But up in the center there was the roar of the blaze, the crackle of flames as they swept through the big white house, the shouted commands to the firemen and men's voices as they dragged the fire hose down to nearby Milton Pond.

"In the Howard Sheldon house across the road from their doomed home, nine barefooted children huddled in their nightclothes, wrapped in blankets. Richard, aged 14, who slept near the head of the stairs, had wakened, choking with smoke, and had called to his parents. Instantly alert, father Karl Thoma commanded, 'Mother, you call the fire department. Richard, get the boys out; each of you grab a blanket. Ilena, get the girls in blankets out on the porch.' Brought up to obey, the children were marshalled outdoors, and within less than a minute, all of them were safely outside. Adelaide, the mother, had called the fire department. Moments later, flames swirling through the hallway, the stairway was impassable.

"Three fire companies in all fought the flames surging up from the cellar through the pipeless furnace opening. Columns of water saved the shell of the house, but by 5:30 a.m. that was all that was left. Even the newly-adopted dog was dead.

"At the big house of the Edward H. Raymond family in the Center, women of the newly-formed Civil Disaster Committee served great stacks of sandwiches and gallons of hot coffee. Over and over one heard, 'What a damned shame! What will Karl and Adelaide and all those kids do now?' Ilena and Margaret went to school that morning, but the others didn't. Wan-faced Ilena said, 'Daddy says he's going to rebuild. But I don't see how he can do it'."

But Karl was a builder and repairman, and he said to his wife, "The house can be repaired."

The strong, indomitable New England spirit prevailed. Truckloads of food, clothing and bedding appeared that next day so the family could settle temporarily in the Charles and Dorothy Earle house next door. A meeting was set up by the Milton Public Hall Association at the Hall for the following evening. It was opened by Dr. Edward Raymond who began by saying to the seventy-five people gathered there, "Let us thank Almighty God that we are meeting not to report a tragedy, but rather to discuss how best to repair a serious damage."

Officers named were: Dr. Raymond, general chairman (later replaced by Edward J. Murphy); Joseph F. Bergmann, treasurer; Ellen M. Doyle, secretary; Archibald C. Doty, Jr., fund raising; J. Russell Ackerman, supplies; Edward J. and Theodore P. Litwin, co-chairmen of rebuilding; Edward J. Murphy, insurance; Mrs. Thomas (Alice) Lindsay, furniture and lunches; Mrs. Malcolm P. (Adaline) Seymour, publicity.

Men experienced in the several facets of the rebuilding took charge of various aspects of the renovation.

The following sub-committees involved almost everyone in Milton: Stairs - Clarence Ackerman; Joists - Oscar Richard; Floors - Charles Birge; Windows - James Lindsey; Deodorizing - C. Hinkle Brown; Partitions and Sheetrock - Frank Fisher; Baseboard and Trim - Arthur Haviland; Painting - Edward Dennis and G. Herbert Griffin; Scraping Paint - Thomas Lindsay; Plumbing - Oscar Anderson; and Roof - Frank Birge.

Work began on Good Friday, two days after the fire, when over forty men arrived at the house at 7:30 in the morning and started clearing away the huge amount of debris. By nightfall, the rubbish was gone, carried to the Town dump, and work had started on patching holes in the floors and scraping plaster from the walls.

The women helped throughout, providing food for the workers and beginning the collection of furniture and household items. A letter from the Thoma family expressing grateful thanks for help and comfort was read at the Easter Sunday service at Milton Congregational Church.

Each weekend the work went on, as well as evenings, with a large squad of workers. Mishaps occurred: one man on a ladder had a nail pounded into his hat from above; another had his shoe nailed to the floor from below. Miraculously, a bottle of "spirits" which Karl Thoma had on hand kept replenishing itself.

Fund-raising and publicity via local radio stations and newspapers brought supplies as they were needed, at cost or free. Money poured in; people all over the area helped the effort. Five weeks after the fire it was reported, "The walls, ceilings and floors are whole, electricity and plumbing have been installed. Everything is paid for. The house is not finished, but the family can live in it." Fifteen hundred hours of donated labor had accomplished the impossible.

In spite of the tragedy to a Milton family, the fire helped the community come together in unison with one purpose, to rebuild a house for a family who was respected and loved here. Pulling together as a cohesive unit, Milton neighbors came to know each other, sharing work, ideas and laughter, as they always have.

The 1989 Tornado

Garage at Donald and Janet Sibley's after July 10, 1989, tornado

One of the most frightening days in the annals of Milton was Monday, July 10, 1989, a muggy day of some sun, some rainshowers and a lot of wind and black clouds — an uneasy day. The forces of nature were gathering to turn that summer day into the worst nightmare imaginable.

From Canada through the Adirondacks a monster storm was moving towards Milton. Local weather bureaus had no way of predicting the storm or warning the people. The stage was set.

Around 4:30 in the afternoon the skies over Milton grew very dark, and the wind went wild. The north sky was black and yellow-green. Rain began to sheet down with huge hailstones. At 4:45 the world seemed to blow apart. In a matter of minutes the village was irrevocably changed — terror and utter confusion, the blackness of night, a constant all-encompassing roar, crashing, smashing. Then it was over, eerily silent except for the streaming rain and wind. Milton had taken one of the worst blows from the multi-tornados spawned up north. Black branches and green leaves blocked doors and windows; trees were strewn like pick-up sticks; the familiar was lost.

In the aftermath of the storm, Glenn Winn from Headquarters Road and Lawrence Voight from Saw Mill Road started out on foot around the square to check on people. Everyone was in shock, but no one was hurt. Roads were choked with trees and debris; routes had to be cut out by hand. Headquarters Road became Main Street for a few days.

The awesome task of cleanup began that night. Power saws growled and whined and would continue to do so until snow time. Electricity was gone as was most telephone service. People pooled food, cooked on gas stoves and shared. The task ahead was staggering. The residents knew they needed help — they had to organize, pool energies and resources. For some reason the outside world, except for the Bantam Fire Department, forgot them in their tragedy. They had to help themselves those first few days.

A community-wide meeting was held at Milton Public Hall on Sunday, along with some invited Town officials and professional people. From a list of eighteen topics and concerns some answers were received. Teams were organized and started working at repairing the damage. The prevailing mood at the meeting was, "How can we help you?" Glenn and Donna Winn were unofficial leaders, competent and tireless.

In the days that followed, brush piles beside the roads

grew to impressive heights. Town crews worked long and hard to chip and haul them away. Logs, too, were stacked high. Armies of volunteers from many nearby towns came from the first day and kept coming into November. No one will ever forget these people.

From a book recording the memories of those who lived through the tornado come the following words: John Winter said, "Through all the fierceness of the storm, the flag still bravely flew." Eileen Litwin wrote, "A sad time and yet such a wonderful community." From Eileen Winn came the words, "Through it all, we *survived*." Thoughts from Ann Winter, "I found it amazing that in such a short time an area I was so familiar with was so unrecognizable." Don Sibley, whose new garage was destroyed by a large pine tree, wrote, "I heard a whoosh!... felt a bump, heard two thuds, and it was quiet." He added, "The only power to equal it was that of the love that flowed from everywhere for the ensuing weeks. It's strange to believe that a tornado could turn out to be remembered as such a positive experience." His wife, Janet, tried just about every road into Milton to get home; all were blocked. She finally found Don at Milton Road and Maple Street, having made his way there, and together they crawled and climbed their way home. She said, "It was a bleak enough winter [referring to the winter of 1989-1990], but the greening of Milton this spring has renewed it into the changed, but lovely community it has always been."

Morton Matthew said, "God bless the volunteers who cleared our driveway in our absence." He added, "We now have more sunlight, less leaf raking, and firewood for life." He included a limerick: "Tornados can catch you off guard/ They hit people's trees very hard/ And when they subside/ And you venture outside/ You are lost in your very own backyard."

Malcolm Forbes also tried his hand at rhyming: "Mother Nature went on a rampage last year/ And tore through Milton in really high gear/ Trees were felled in the wake/ Of this aerial earthquake/ We should really thank God we still are all here!"

Suzanne Litwin found the experience very frightening. She wrote, "Unable to hold back my tears, I turned to my husband and said, 'I love you,' not knowing what was going to happen to us. But through it all there was the love and support of the town and our neighbors. We've met neighbors we never knew we had. We've all become closer, thanks to the tornado." Suzanne's neighbor, Milton native Elizabeth (Betty) Kizzia, had a unique tale to tell of the tornado and why she missed seeing it: "We have a reclining chair that only works electrically, and when the power failed I was stranded in the chair. No one heard my cry for help. I heard the roaring of wind and storm, and that made it seem much worse not being able to see anything." Her husband, Dewey, eventually rescued her.

On Blue Swamp Road Evelyn Williamson had this reaction, "It was quite an exciting day and night. Thank God no one was hurt. We were so glad to see all our neighbors after it was over." In the house just above Evelyn's, Richard and De'Lis'Ka Bates and Tony and Alice Salcito described the sound of the tornado as "a rumble as though many planes were overhead," and they "felt a terrible vacuum closing down." They said, "Milton was isolated," and spoke of the men from the Town Highway Department who worked tirelessly to open roads, and the National Guard with their super equipment helping them to get "us out of our trapped environment." Their final sentence was echoed by many, "God spared lives throughout the area — renewing our Faith for evermore."

Lynn Lovrin spoke of the day as "hazy, humid and hot...It felt strange all day, almost as though the air was charged with electricity." Her husband, Garry, had to abandon the bucket truck of his tree service at the corner of Saw Mill and Headquarters Roads. Both he and Lynn had much trouble getting home to Hubbard Pines, and resorted to walking and crawling through an unfamiliar landscape. They were lost in their own driveway. Lynn concluded with these words, "...the new plants struggling cannot relieve the sense of loss. Even so, Milton is still a very special place."

Mike, Kelly and Kerry Bowden and Luann Urfer later came from Vermont to check on family members here. They said that, "Through it all the comradeship and support within Milton was tremendous (and enviable!). It will take more than this to crush them!"

On Saw Mill Road, Ruth DuPont lost her "beautiful private green world around her pond." She wrote that it wasn't until she "heard the breaking of glass in the front room that I realized I was watching no ordinary storm. 'It's a twister,' I told the dog, who probably knew that already." She added later, "The redeeming aspect was the goodness of people. Volunteers from Bantam, themselves very hard hit, appeared and just pitched in, as did people from Goshen, Winsted, Warren, Morris. The kindness of strangers was never more in evidence, and I will never forget these good generous people."

Up by itself, just off the hard-topped section of Headquarters Road, Barbara Winn's property held her captive for some hours. Fallen trees, downed wires, piled branches made every exit impassable. The most traumatic moment for her was the realization that the Sitka spruce tree she had planted as a nine-year old child was lying on the ground. "It's too much to absorb, too hard," she wrote. She spoke of "the birds, all around the deck with their feathers in complete disarray — the strong smell of pines for weeks, the sound of saws, the poor, confused mother red fox walking up the middle of the dirt road with her babies, the crashing of trees in the woods, still falling days later." She added later on, "It was like a sudden death. For days following the tornado we all needed to be together, to talk and share experiences and aimlessly walk the roads. Then the meeting at the Hall was like a memorial service after which we could go on to put things to rights."

Just down the road from Barbara's, Kathleen Lang was enjoying the afternoon when "the storm grew worse. It was unusually dark. The thunder got louder and the wind was immense." She and her husband Gary went to the cellar, as did many others. After the storm they had only a few trees left standing, and "trees blocking us in all around." She stated, "It was a difficult time just to survive! As with most tragedies, the passing of time heals our wounds."

Col. Edward A. Raymond and his wife Mary lived in the big house in the Center next to Trinity Episcopal Church. They were "rushing so hard to close doors against the rain that we did not realize at first what was happening." Afterwards Ted got his chainsaw and began to cut a path to Milton Road through the Trinity parking lot. Many trees were downed on their property, thirty of them on the house lot itself. But, like almost everyone else, he praised the volunteers. "We shall never cease being grateful for all the help from friends and neighbors," and he expressed his pride in Milton itself.

The following was recorded by Orcelia Winn, who wrote that without any warning, "the whole world seemed to collapse in an instant. It was almost as dark as night, with lightning and torrential rain, and I heard the ferocious rush and push of wind, the worst I ever heard." She went on, "...I cannot find words in our language to describe what happened or what I felt. In the back of my mind I thought the world was coming to an end." About the sharing she said, "It was therapeutic for all of us." After praising the volunteers, she went on: "We coped, tired to the bone," and concluded, "What I recall most vividly about the tornado is great noise, darkness, total helplessness, panic and fear."

Milton was in the direct path of the tornados. No one will ever forget that July day. Everyone suffered, hurt beyond words — but they shared, reached out to one another, coped and survived.

Floods and Hurricanes

Milton Center after 1938 Hurricane

1938 Hurricane

Much damage was done to roads in the area by the autumn hurricane of September, 1938. On September 22, following the storm, the following notice went out to all teachers in the Litchfield school system which included Milton:

NOTICE TO ALL TEACHERS   September 22, 1938

I

Due to collapsed sections of concrete highways, washed out or blocked secondary roads, dangerously leaning trees, and weakened bridges on routes over which heavy buses filled with children must pass, it had been considered safest to close the Litchfield public schools until Monday, September 26.

Electricity failed and has made it impossible to keep electric pumps functioning in connection with water supply for heaters and toilets. This is an additional reason for the closing of school.

II

Since no additional days are provided in the calendar for the time lost, it... (The notice ends abruptly here in the "Milton History Papers." One can assume that these days had to be made up at the end of the school year).

The center of Milton was under water all across the flat from Milton Road to Shear Shop Road, down Headquarters Road past the little bridge. The front lawns of the Peter Ackerman house (formerly Guild Tavern), the Milton Public Hall, Trinity Episcopal Church, the Green and the schoolhouse were all flooded, with water pouring in a waterfall into the river just west of the Ackerman house at 542 Shear Shop Road.

1955 Hurricane and Floods

1955 Flood

Harassed by Hurricane Connie just shortly before, this area was much affected by Hurricane Diane which followed. Rain began in mid-August, and by Friday, August 19, 1955, so much had fallen that it had swollen rivers, overflowed streets and taken out dams all over Connecticut. Damage beyond estimation mounted up — the destruction caused major problems all over the state.

Here in Milton, roads were submerged or washed out by the early morning of that fateful Friday, and the Center was under water. It was difficult to find a way out of Milton. There were gaping holes in Milton Road — Headquarters Road, which had been rebuilt earlier that year, was flooded from the present Janet Sibley house to the Center, waist-deep in water. With the Center flooded, there was no way to go except perilously on foot through the water which was rushing down Shear Shop Road, Milton Hill, Potash Road and Headquarters Road. A torrent of water raced across the yard of the old Guild Tavern (then home of Miss Helen Gage and Mrs. Douglas Whalen). At the foot of Headquarters Cemetery the old interesting arch sluice was ruined, leaving a gully no car could cross. Cellars were filled with water, and while most had electricity and telephones, no one could call outside the local area.

The men went off to help wherever they could in relief

and cleanup work. Some with experience from World War II went to Torrington to help with setting up a Bailey bridge in the center of that city. There was a tremendous amount of work to be done. Nearby cities were under martial law; clinics were set up to give typhoid shots. Life went on, but limpingly. School, supposed to open September 7, was postponed until the 19th, much to the delight of the children. Outlying roads were badly damaged; mailman Joseph Coffill went miles out of his way to deliver the mail. His usual 49-mile route was extended to 94 miles.

Saw Mill bridge and dam at Milton Pond were demolished by the flood and the road was unusable for more than a month. By the Martin Walker farm on Maple Street the road was dangerously narrowed by washed out gutters.

People in Milton sent a carload of food, clothing, blankets, etc. to help Winsted, which was devastated. Later Miltonites were asked to help individual families, which they did.

Blizzards

There were at least two blizzards of note in Milton's history which are covered in the "Milton History Papers." The earliest one took the life of Mary Muggleston Birge and left her husband Elisha injured. It occurred on December 9, 1786. The Birges lived in the old house, long gone, at what is now Fox Crossing off Milton Road. The fury of the storm shook the old house fearfully, and Mary, terrified that the wind would blow the house down, panicked when live coals were blown out of the fireplace onto the floor where they began to blaze. She ran out of the house heading for the safety of a neighbor's house. Her husband followed, caught up with her and urged her back to their house. He lost his way in the swirling snow and finally found some cover beneath a large tree where he sheltered Mary in his arms. By then she had fallen into a deep sleep from which she never wakened. It was some five hours before Elisha was able to get back to his house, and his ears and hands were frozen. He recovered, but he lived from then on with his son, James. According to the obituary of December 12, 1786, in the *Litchfield Monitor*, Mary was mourned by the whole community.

There was also a blizzard in March 1888 — the infamous "Blizzard of '88." From the diary which he kept for that year comes this description in the words of Walter Hall, who lived on Blue Swamp Road where the Harris Hildings live: "Two dozen men and boys with help of oxen opened roads"; all were snowbound. He recorded on March 23, "It is very bad traveling. The road is fenced off between here and Litchfield on account of the water by the schoolhouse near Jay Gilbert's." That was the James Gilbert house at the junction of Maple Street and Brush Hill Road.

James Monroe Birge lived in the old Birge homestead at Headquarters that same year. His account of that awesome storm also comes from a diary, the one he kept for many years. It was cold early in March of that year with a warming around the eighth. Sunday, the eleventh, it "snowed a little." The diary continues:

"Monday: Mar. 12, 1888 — An awful day — I think the worst I ever knew. Snowed and blowed awfully all day — Snow to the top of the windows. Did not get cattle to water. Hard work to get to the barn, 9 p.m. still blowing.

"Tuesday: Still snowing and blowing. Made out to do chores. Carryed some water to cattle.

"Wed: Storm about over. Everything drifted in. Dug a path through the shed and cattle out for first time since Sunday — The worst storm ever known.

"Thurs: Got a road through the lot to Electa's [Electa Goslee who owned farm over east, where the Peter Litwins now live at 67 Litwin Road]."

A week after the storm James Birge wrote, "Went to Milton and dug snow." The same for Tuesday. By the twenty-eighth he could write, "A verry [sic] nice day."

A bad storm in April 1894, was described in yet another diary, that of Newton Tyler of Northfield, father of Mrs. Chester Bissell. Although he wasn't a Milton man, the same conditions doubtless prevailed in Milton:

"April 11, 1894 Terrific blow and snow storm. Commenced to blow on Monday April 9th and continued to blow until noon on Wednesday, Apr. 11, snowing and blowing a gale. Men working for the Telephone Co. snowed in. We kept 3 of them overnight. They put their horses in the neighbor's barn.

"April 12, Thurs. Still snowing and blowing but not so forcibly. Telephone men still here."

These storms are remembered one hundred, even two hundred years later and talked about as exceptionally bad storms, even for this area.

ACKNOWLEDGEMENTS

❖

A special acknowledgement and many thanks are due to Orcelia Birge Winn for her perseverance and dedication to the task of completing this history, which was greatly hampered for many years by the loss of the researched material. Her countless hours of writing, organizing and recruiting volunteers led to the book's final completion. Orcelia never wavered from her dream of recording the history of her beloved Milton.

We would also like to thank the writers who tirelessly researched and authored their particular chapters of the *Chronicles of Milton*. They suffered silently as manuscripts were edited — sometimes severely — to yield a succinct, readable narrative of Milton history that would be factual yet enjoyable for the general public. In addition, we would like to acknowledge the important contributions of the following people, without whom the writing of this history would have been a difficult, if not impossible, undertaking:

Russell and Helen Ackerman - loan of Milton material; memories, interest and encouragement

Edith Dickinson Axford - loan of Dickinson book

* Frances Doyle Barrett - raw material which produced the History; opening paragraph of book, which was her suggestion

William C. Birge - his father's diaries; memories

Harold and Frances Bunnell - loan of photos; memories

Charles and Muriel Castle - loan of family items; memories shared

Harriet L. Clark - use of her published books; interest

Wilbur and Edith Coffill - gift of book *Milton Deaths*; newspaper items

Fletcher Cooper - photos and other material

Blaine, Jr. and Eleanor Cota - constructive help with material

Theresa Dempsey - gift of pamphlet re: Litchfield and Milton

Mary Hurley Derby - social life memories

Archibald C. Doty, Jr. - photos of Milton; line drawing for cover; gift of old Milton nails; offers of help; encouragement

Evelyn Doyle - help with obtaining school photos

Ruth A. DuPont - writer; helpful suggestions throughout

James (Jay) Birge Gilbert and Lena Gilbert - memories, especially humorous ones

Florence A. Gray - pictures; memories; encouragement

Howard Gray - interest; memories

Raymond Gray - interest; memories; pictures

G. Herbert Griffin - memories; confirmation of information and events; interest and encouragement

Reeves W. Hart, Jr. - family items; interest

Robert and Caroline Griffin Jefferies - loan and gift of photos; memorabilia; memories; interest

* Frank and Anne Kerrigon - editing; computer inputting of manuscripts; photography; assistance and encouragement throughout

Peter A. Litwin - offers of help from outset; loan of old Milton shears

Helen Pepper Loomis - use of Dennison-Granniss Bible; memories

Helen Barrett McCarthy - gift of old school photos

Lee James Pantas - line drawings of Milton Center

Shirley Haviland Parrott - numerous photos and other items given; memories

Carrie Peck (Mrs. Allen) - reminiscences and memories

Everett Hall Perkins - use of pamphlet by his uncle, Walter Hall; gift to Milton community of "Friendship Quilt"; interest

Hazel W. Perret - support throughout and strong guiding hand through publication

Andrew M. C. Pikosky - writer; first-hand knowledge; much interest

Col. Edward A. Raymond - use of material from his history of Litchfield; knowledge of Milton history; providing access to Milton History material

Oscar G. and Dorothy Richard - loan of photos; memories shared

Caroline Blake Sanford and Daniel Sanford - writers; encouragement

Ruth C. Schele - gift of material gleaned from old issues of *Litchfield Enquirer*

Fred H. Seelye - material; memories; pictures; encouragement and interest

* Walter C. Sheldon - immeasurable help throughout and final okay on material

Donald and Janet Sibley - gift of drawings of Milton buildings; encouragement

Ernest K. Smith - his father's diaries; memories shared; information from his oral history

Marjorie P. Starr - loan of Edward C. Starr's *History of Cornwall*; memories shared

* Walter E. Vaill - incomparable and countless memories and facts shared by one who lived Milton history

Kirby B. Weik - drawings of old Milton shears and old Milton nails

Edward and Evelyn Williamson - gift of two books of local interest

David R. Wilson - leadership and guidance; organization; copying of material

Barbara B. Winn - proofreading; sorting and catagorizing original material

Virginia Wolven - loan of information re; publishing; encouragement; sharing first-hand knowledge of producing book

Ralph and Helen Bristol Woodward - newspaper items; other information

* Special Mention

Many, many thanks to all others who made this history of Milton possible, including all those who wrote memories of Milton School, etc., and those who wrote chapters for the book, including Eleanor Cota, Ruth DuPont, Hazel Perret, Andrew M. C. Pikosky, Caroline B. Sanford, Daniel Sanford, Janette B. Winn and Orcelia B. Winn.

Special thanks to two anonymous donors whose generosity facilitated publication by providing financial support.

Book Committee
Eleanor Cota, Hazel Perret, Lorraine Skidmore,
Lillian Webster, Janette Winn, Orcelia Winn

APPENDIX

❖

Excerpts from the "Wright Letters"

In 1796, the land on the Western Reserve east of the Cuyohoga and Tiscarawas Rivers was surveyed in townships — in 1798, Township No. 4 in range No. 10 fell to six Goshen men. It is not known whether members of Milton families of Wright, Collins, Roe, Guild, Landon, et al, were affected by this, but it is established that they went out to western New York, Ohio and Illinois to make their homes.

Information on Milton families taking part in America's westward expansion in the nineteenth century is based on family letters found in a chest belonging to Ensign Jonathan Wright (Ackerman-Kizzia house at 115 Saw Mill Road): John Wright, son of Jonathan and Leah Bissell Wright, born Milton January 4, 1776, went to Shoreham, Ohio — was there August 19, 1808; Alice, youngest daughter of Jonathan and his third wife Thankful Landon Wright, married Daniel Roe — in Wolcott, New York, September 19, 1808. Both wrote letters included in "Wright Letters," as well as Daniel Roe, Sr., father-in-law of Alice. In his letter to Jonathan Wright from Wolcott, February 19, 1814, writes of death of Mrs. A. Collins; also: —"please to inform Mr. Joseph Birge that Elias [Joseph's son?] was at our house about three weeks past who had been to Oswego on business—"; also, Daniel and son Daniel and families had moved into new houses. In another letter Daniel speaks of his nephew J. B. Roe, school master, and gives news of Mary Ann, granddaughter of

Daniel and Jonathan; asks for news of Isaac Baldwin.

Names mentioned: John Wright, Alice Wright Roe & Daniel Roe, Jr. and Sr., J. B. Roe, Calvin Collins (three Collins brothers in Illinois), 'rastus Landon, Benjamin and David Gibbs, twins, sons of Benjamin and Thankful Landon Gibbs — Benjamin married Rhoda Woodruff and David married Ruth, Rhoda's twin, daughters of Andrew and Miranda Norton Woodruff; Calvin Collins married Clarissa Guild in Milton.

Letter from Emily Guild, granddaughter of Jeremiah Guild, cousin of Everett H. Wright, to Everett: "...Well what do you suppose I did after breaking the seal [of letter from Everett] why I laughed and *laughed* until I cried and you meant I should grieve...Oh! I suppose you really think you have pulled the wool over my eyes...yet, I'm sure it's Miss — Somebody if not Miss Birge — The Colonel's lady is very handsome but my choice is in Milton."

Katherine Landon, daughter of Heman and Pheby Beach, married Chauncey Isbel; wrote to parents from Brimfield, Ohio.

Ebenezer Landon, brother of Thankful, son of David and Thankful Dickinson Landon, to Jonathan Wright: "...therefore to request you to assist me if you can in obtaining proof of my services [Army], I wish you to procure James Birge's affidavit of my service and your own...served six months under command of Col. Bradley...served six weeks on militia duty under Capt. John Osborn, six weeks under Capt. Zebulon Taylor...six weeks under Capt. Catlin..."

Letter from Mary Ann Roe to cousin Alice Wright, Milton, after Mary Ann's visit east — Alice daughter of Samuel and Desdemona Guild Wright: "...in the stage there was but one passenger aboard that was Mr. Marsh went to

Milton and then took six more passengers they were Mr Collins people bound for New York." She goes on to describe a long and arduous trip home to Wolcott, New York. Stage is Litchfield/Albany stage.

In another letter from Mary Ann to another cousin, Mary Ann Wright Perkins, also daughter of Samuel and Desdemona Wright, she writes, "I often think when I sit down in the evening I should be extremely happy to be in Milton..."

Susan Wright, daughter of Jonathan and second wife Tryphena Tracy Wright, married Sylvester Cone; wrote from East Haddam of the loss of a daughter, Eliza, in a ship accident.

Everett H. Wright taught school in New Milford; corresponded with friend Orlando Frisbie in Milton. Letter included in "Wright Letters" from Everett Wright speaks of home, Milton: "...With me, time nor distance could never diminish the regard I have for the snowy hills and warm hearts of my native village...Most truly can I say as did the bard 'Milton with all thy faults I love thee still';" spoke also of girls, "not quite up to 'old Milton' yet..."

Reply from Orlando with news of people in Milton:— lots of snow, roads "much blocked up...weather extreamly cold"; worked for Mr. Dudley some that winter..."he keeps our school...school averages about 14 and they love him." Mr. Dudley was teacher for Everett & Orlando. Schools that winter, Orlando says, were very good. Singing school: "Mr. Beach came down untill new years two or three times a week" (referring to Almon J. Beach); he "improved the choir very much. Mr. E. Norton has been down once in two weeks all winter until now the two choirs joined Christmas eve and sang they say first rate. The county temperance meeting met here last Tuesday owing to the state of the roads, we did not expect many present but we were hapily disapointed there was ten or fifteen delagates present and reported favorable for temperance..."; "...Welch & Kilborn will not sell it [liquor] to a temperance man but a toper can have all he wants...Mr. D. Beach is at our head as president and your honor one of the V presidents Leander Jennings secretary." Meetings were held in the Gilbert District schoolhouse at the corner of Maple Street and Forge Hollow Road.

Also from Orlando's letter: "...Charles Chase attends up to Emma Gilbert regular — George Bradley attends to Louise, I suppose, as usual. Give my love to all the pretty girls..."

Last letter is from Alice Ferriss, daughter of Samuel and Desdemona Wright, sister of Everett, to parents. Speaks of Aunt Sophronia, Louise and her baby; Huldah going to Milton, etc.

Jonathan Wright, founder of the family in Milton, was married three times and was father of fourteen children.

There is record that Augustus Ward and family received assistance from this community to remove to Ohio. "An arrangement has been made with Mr. Henry Gilbert to carry Mr. Ward to Albany"; and "Albany, 7 Sept. 1838 — I do hereby agree to take A. Ward to Buffalo for fifteen dolers and do also agree to send them to Cleaveland from Buffalo for six dollars. by the hand of W. H. Gilbert [William Henry] — Rec'd payment — Capt. N. B. Phelp."

Friendship Quilt

A Friendship Quilt, given to the Milton community by Everett Hall Perkins and stored at the home of Orcelia Birge Winn, was made by women in Milton in the mid-1800's. It contained the following names of those who worked on the quilt:

Martha Hall (Mrs. Henry), Emily Hall, Mrs. Stephens, Eliza Hall, Aunt Martha Hall, Mrs. Harrison, Mrs. Bennett, Great-grandma Swift, Mrs. David Parmalee, Sally Dains, Jennie Stone, Grandma Merriman, Aunt Mary, Addie Malery, Aunt Hannah, Mrs. Vail, Gussie Griswold, Electa Hall, Clorinda Tuttle, Josie Plum, Electa Spenser, Mrs. P. Smith, Mrs. S. Griswold, Mary Page, Mrs. Northrop, Lillie Northrop, Abbie Smith, Mrs. Smith, Mollie Page, Annie Harrison, Emma Dains, Libbie Duggan, Jennie Seelye, Carrie Parmalee, Hattie Merriman, Ada Parmalee.

1860's Milton Quilt

Miss Maria Addis, Miss Hattie Ames, Mr. Charles Beach, Eliza Beach, Miss Samantha Beach, Mr. Vergil Beach, Mr. Wesley Beach, Mrs. H. Birge (on back, "1869"), Miss Kate Birge, Mrs. Clara Bishop, Mr. Hiram Bishop, Mrs. Hiram Bishop, Miss Carrie Bissell, Mrs. Charles Bissell, Miss Cornelia Bissell, Mr. Frank Bissell, Miss Henrietta Bissell, Jerome Bissell, Mr. Philip Bissell, Mr. Warren Bissell, Mrs. William Bissell, Miss Delia Buell, Miss Laura Collins, Mr. Abner Collins, Miss Dellie Gilbert, Mrs. Roxana Gilbert, Mr. Horatio Griswold, Mary Griswold, Miss Addie Guild, Mr. Gould Guild, Mrs. Gould Guild, Grandfather Guild,

Grandmother Guild, Mrs. Sarah Guild, Miss Annie Harrison, Rev. Mr. Harrison, Rev. Mrs. Harrison, Mr. Ike H. Hutchinson, Miss Melissa Jennings, Miss Gussie Johnson, Charley D. Kilbourn, Mrs. James Lyons, Mrs. Henry Morehouse, Mr. Jacob Morse, Mrs. Jane Morse, Mr. Stephen Odell, Mrs. Hannah Peck, Rev. Wm. L. Peck, Mr. John Peterson, Miss Ellen Plant, Mrs. Josephine Pope, Mr. Julius Pope, Mr. Dwight Seelye, Mr. George A. Smith, Mr. Mark Smith, Miss Thank(ful) Smith, Miss Gertrude Welch, Miss Jennie Welch, Mr. Charles Wheeler, Mrs. Charles Wheeler, Mr. Christopher Wheeler, Mrs. Christopher Wheeler, Rev. Mrs. Williams, Mr. John Williamson, Mrs. John Williamson, Miss Harriet Willy

Committees for the 1931 Fourth of July Picnic

Soliciting Money

Chairman: Mr. Wm. Birge; Herbert Griffin, Walton Morehead, Gordon Pepper, Frank Birge, David Gray, Stewart Rydehn, Jr.

Setting Up Tables

Chairman: Dr. Raymond; Jacob Ackerman, Clarence Ackerman, Stewart Rydehn, Sr., Wilbur Haviland, John Perret, Ted and Bob Raymond

Setting Tables and Placing Food

Chairman: Miss Nellie Doyle; Mrs. Alice Ackerman, Mrs. Walton Morehead, Mrs. Mary Derby, Mrs. Clarence Ackerman, Mrs. J. Gilbert, Mrs. Stewart Rydehn, Mrs. Zelim Richard, Mrs. Walter Vail (sic), The Misses Thompson, Mrs. White, Mrs. Ernest Smith, Mrs. James Scott

Clearing Tables, Washing Silver
Chairman: Mrs. Wm. Birge; Mrs. Wilbur Haviland, Mrs. Vaill, Miss Louise Lamb, Miss Walkley

Serving Ice Cream
Chairman: Ernest Smith; Fredk. Bunnell, Ernest Axford, J. Gilbert, David Gray

Soliciting Food
Chairman: Mrs. Alice Ackerman; Mrs. Elwood Dudley, Mrs. Herbert Griffin, Mrs. Harry Haviland, Mrs. Mary Derby, Mrs. Wilbur Haviland, Mrs. Harry Kilburn (sic)

Making Punch
Chairman: Clarence Goslee; Harry Haviland, Stewart Rydehn, Walter Richard, Clarence Ackerman

Waiting on Tables
Chairman: Mrs. David Gray; Miss Alice Phillips, Mrs. Edward Raymond, Mrs. Lena Haviland, Mrs. Ernest Axford, Mrs. Frank Birge, Mrs. Gordon Pepper, Mrs. Clarence Goslee, Miss Virginia Perret, Miss Nettie Sheldon, Miss Mildred Morehead, Miss Alison Raymond, Miss Margaret Kilburn, Miss Lois Kilburn, Miss Stiles

Clearing Grounds
Chairman: Mr. Walter Vaill; Neal Doyle, Oscar Richard, The Boys

Returning Tables and Chairs
Chairman: Albert Fox; Walton Morehead, Frank Birge, Clifford Haviland, Walter Perret, Tom Kitchin

Milton Hall Association

List of Original Subscribers
April 27, 1901 (from Litchfield Land Records, Vol. 78, pp. 72-73)

E.P. Dickinson E.B. Bissell, J. H. Hurley, Geo. A. Smith, W.E. Seelye, T.B. Doyle, I.T. Dickinson, P. Ackerman, Austin Page, T.H. Doyle, Thos. Hinchliffe, H.T. Register, Sr., H.T. Register, Jr., J.L. Guild, W.O.[?] Page, Elias N. Page, Fred. J. Brahen, P.W. Driscoll, Wm. J. Hall

The Milton Woman's Club

Original (Charter) Members
Mrs. Ernest (Mary) Smith, Mrs. DeLos (Mary) Gilbert, Mrs. James (Lena) Gilbert, Mrs. John Walker, Mrs. Fred Goslee, Mrs. William (Mercy) Birge, Mrs. Elwood (Sarah) Dudley, Mrs. Jacob (Alice) Ackerman, Mrs. Henry (Edith) Axford, Mrs. Walton (Abby) Morehead, Mrs. Jesse (Mary) Derby, Mrs. Zelim (Burga) Richard, Miss Ellen (Nellie) Doyle, Miss Alice Phillips, Miss Beatrice McKechnie, Miss Frances Walkley

Officers
President: Mrs. Ernest Smith; Vice President: Mrs. James Gilbert; Secretary/Treasurer: Mrs. Henry Axford

Gifts to Milton Congregational Church

1856 - Silver Communion Set - Miss Lucretia Deming

1873/4 - One Dozen Ives Patent Bracket Side Lamps - Orville L. Adams (most were in parsonage and have disappeared; present lamps in church are not original; globes are original) Orville L. Adams also contributed to purchase of new stove

1882 - Chandelier - Mrs. Orlando (Sarah) Perkins
- Second Chandelier for gallery - Ira Page (given to Trinity Episcopal Church); - Communion Table at front of church - Rev. George J. Harrison, by brother, Francis Harrison

1901/2 - $500 - Orlando Perkins

1925 - Large Pulpit Bible (still used) - Fremont M. Granniss

1926 - $200 - Julia Northrop estate

1930 - $500 - Hattie T. Benedict estate

1932 - Norway Maple Tree - Milton Woman's Club, commemorating the bicentennial of George Washington's birth
- $1000 - Fremont M. Granniss

1937 - $1070 to Sunday School - Jacob Benson

1938 - $1000 in memory of Mrs. Charles (Elizabeth) Blake, by daughter Marian Blake
- $800 - in memory of Judge Hugh Welch and Helen M. Welch, by daughter Gertrude Welch

1939 - $1000 - in memory of Samuel D. Page, by Rev. Wesley E. Page

1940 - $1000 - Weston G. Granniss estate

1944 - $ 500 - Peter Ackerman

1954 - Electrification of Church - time and labor donated by Edward N. Richard

1955 - Christian Flag - Mr. and Mrs. Willis Perkins, in memory of their mothers, Mrs. Eva Perkins and Mrs. Eliza Hall
- Hymnal Board - Mrs. and Mrs. Willis Perkins
1956 - $100 - in memory of Trena Ackerman Seaton, by husband Frank Seaton
1957 - Brass Cross and two Brass Vases - in memory of Marie E. Wilcox, by her daughter, Hazel W. Perret
1957/8 - Two Brass Collection Plates - in memory of Mrs. Irving J. Enslin, by husband and son, Rev. Irving J. and Francis I. Enslin
1961 - $500 - Willis Perkins estate
- $100 - Clarence E. Perkins
- 48-Star Flag
- Drop-leaf Table at back of Church - Everett H. Perkins and Doris P. Webster
1962 - Book of Remembrance and Case - in memory of Mr. and Mrs. Willis Perkins, by Mr. and Mrs. Clifford Perkins
1963 - Material and Labor for Parking Lot - Reeves W. Hart, Roland Campbell, Clyde Tibbetts, Richard Wilcox
1966 - Front Plantings and Landscaping - in memory of Zelim Richard and Waldburga Ackerman Richard, by Richard family
1967 - Railings at Front Steps - in memory of Miss Beatrice M. McKechnie, by Walter C. Sheldon;
- Railings on Stairways - Walter C. Sheldon
- Outside Front Light - in memory of Miss Frances S. Walkley, by Walter C. Sheldon
- Floodlights outside Church - Walter Snyder
1975 - School Bell, in belfry - Donald K. and Ruth R. Peck
1986 - Bequest - Irene C. Richard estate

1992 - Gifts of Money for Purchase of Old Side Lamps, taken from Trinity Episcopal Church, purchased from Thomas McBride

Pastors of the East Cornwall Baptist Church:

1787-1793 - Elder Isaac Root
    twenty-four years without pastor or records
1817-1828 - Rev. Ananais Derthick
1828 - Rev. Silas Ambler (one year)
1836-1841 - no records; Rev. Daniel Baldwin came from New Milford once a month to preach
1845 - Rev. Thomas Benedict
1846 - Rev. Daniel Baldwin
1847-1850 - no pastor
1849 - Rev. James D. Avery visited; helped raise $1000
1850 - 1853 (April) - Rev. Luther B. Hart
1853 (April) - Rev. J. F. Jones
1856 (March) - Rev. Richard Thompson
1857-1861 - Rev. Jackson Ganun
1862 - Rev. Thomas Benedict
  - Rev. C. W. Potter sometimes supply minister until 1866
1867-1871 (May) - Rev. J. Fairman
1871 (July) - Rev. D. F. Chapman
1876-1878 - Rev. Edwin Bowers
1878 (June) - Rev. H. G. Smith (had three churches: East Cornwall, Bantam Falls and Cornwall Hollow)
1883-1884 - Rev. Walter B. Vasser
1884 to end of year - Rev. Jackson Ganun
1885-1894 - Rev. Elbridge B. Elmer

1895-1897 - Rev. S. T. Smith
1897-1898 - Rev. Cornelius Malley and Rev. C. W. Potter, sometimes assistant
Summer 1898 - Rev. Charles L. Owens (student)
1899-1902 - Rev. Fred S. Leathers
1903 (Jan.) - Rev. Alfred H. Stock
1905-1908 - Rev. Peter Stubbs Collins
1909 - Rev. Elmer, supply minister
1909 - Rev. B. F. Nye, for a time
1911 - Rev. Virgil Blackman
1913-1915 - no pastor
1915-1917 - Rev. Eugene L. Richards
1919-1920 - no records

Roster of Second School District of Milton Society, Connecticut

Teacher Leonard C. Bissell, November 23, 1840

Names	Age	Parent or Guardian
Girls		
Desire Grannis	15	A. Griswold adopted
Emmer Gilbert	13	TrumanGilbert, Grandfather
Almira Frisbie	12	S. Frisbie
Lois Page	13	R. Page
Ruth Kilbourn	7	Ethan Kilbourn
Eliza C. Baldwin	8	N. Baldwin
Lucelia S. Dudley	5	Samuel Dudley

Boys

Orson Buel	11	C. Buel
Joel Potter	15	N. Baldwin
Joseph Grannis	13	A. Griswold
Ozias Frisbie	9	S. Frisbie
Olander Frisbie	16	S. Frisbie
John Page	15	R. Page
Charles Page	8	R. Page
Alanson Merriman	16	George Merriman
Elmore Merriman	9	George Merriman
Leanord Dickinson	16	O. Dickinson
Charles Chase	15	Philo Chase
John Chase	5	Philo Chase
Samuel R. Terril	12	Samuel Dudley
Sidney Moore b. in 1828	12	Samuel Dudley

Newspaper hand-written by Milton School children around 1903

MILTON CHRONICLE
EDITORIAL
Editor — William C. Birge

Milton is west of the village of Litchfield. And is near the north-western part of the town of Litchfield. And is on the Marshapaug river which furnishes excellent water-power. Milton has grown very fast within a few years. It was settled about one hundred and fifty years ago. The inhabitants in Milton number about one hundred and fifty. There are twelve public buildings. There are two churches, two stores, three black smith shops, one school house, one shear shop, one grist and saw mill, one hall, and one post office. The shear shop is owned by Mr. Hinchliff who sends off many pairs of shears in a year but there is not as much going on there as there was a few years ago. The hall was built in the winter of (1900) by Mr. Derby. The woods south of Milton center were bought about a year ago by a Frenchman named Mr. Peltzer who moved a steam saw mill on the job from Waterbury and is now carrying on quite a business.

INDUSTRY
Ed. Allan H. Page

(Feb. 10, 1903) The only industry of Milton is the manufacture of shears conducted by Mr. Hinchliff. The shop is situated north of the center of Milton. They make nothing but steel lined shears and scissors. There is forging room where the blades are forged on to the handles. And then they go into another room where they are ground. And than they go into another room where they are polished and last of all they come out in the office. They than are sent to Waterville, New York and Philadelphia. There is a good water power. Mr. Hinchliff has been in business for thirty six years. Six in Hoadleyville and thirty years in Milton. He has employed as many as thirty seven men but now he only employs seven now. His shears have always ranked high and are as good as any made in the country.

GENERAL NEWS
Ed. Ernest T. [K.?] Smith

Motorman Madden who ran into the presidential party last September near Pittsfield pleaded guilty and was sentenced to six months in prison.

Some 4,000 dollars in gold and bills was burned which was drawn from the bank for safekeeping after a bank robbery.

Maine railroad show an increase of 833,066 dollars in gross earnings for 1902 over the previous year.

Allen Swisher of Kan for two years has published a written news paper there are four pages 7x11 and are often illustrated with crayon.

A recent invention has been tested and have complete success by the Glouscester fisherman. It was perfected by Prof. Gray it is a simple device by which sound is transmitted under water by means of a submerged bell. They can warn ships at a distant of rocks and dangerous coasts.

A carnation league has been organized to keep the birthday of McKinley. As the carnation was McKinley favorite flower the members will wear them.

Senator Scott of West Virginia is urging upon Congress to give a pension of twelve dollars a month to every man who served 90 days in the Civil War.

A distinct earthquake was felt at various places in Southern Illinois, Missouri and Kentucky Feb. 9.

The Eskimos now have their own translation of the Bible, which was begun 1752 by Hans Egede and finished by a Bible Society of Denmark.

Engineers are working on plans to utilize the Grand Canon of the Colorado to make electric power. The plan is to gain the power by diverting the water into tunneles.

LOCAL NEWS
Charles. H. Birge. Editor

Mr. Charles Earle has been confined to the house for several days.

Fred Stoddard has been sawing wood with his gaselene engine for Free Granniss.

Mr. Fred Goslee's son is just getting around from the measles.

Next Friday night there will be a dance at Milton Hall.

Mr. Arthur Somerse's hors had the colic Sunday night and is very weak.

Mr. George Tompkins of Milton was coming from Cornwall Plains when he went off a bank and he had to cut down four trees to get his horse out.

Mr. J. Derby of Milton has taken the job of re building the Island House at Bantam Lake.

Mr. Walter Seeley and Mr. Alfred Giles of Milton are agoing to build a shop for the manufacture of hubs for wheels.

Mr. Walter Seeley's horse got down in the stable and they had to kill it.

Jerome Bennett of Milton had a horse get down in front of Mr. Cole's shop and they had to kill it.

Mr. & Mrs. James Hurley entertained Mr. & Mrs. Ozias Benedict at their house Saturday night.

SCHOOL NEWS
Editor. Oscar A. Tompkins

There was a public school built on the Milton Green about eight years ago and about a year ago it was found necessary to build another room on; it will seat about sixty pupils, and it is finely decorated inside.

Miss. J. M. Peacocke is teacher of the first Dept. and Miss C. Smith is teacher for Second Dept.

Ernest Smith who had the measles was present Monday.

The boys have great sport coasting on Potash and Toll-gate hills.

There are several double rippers as well as single sleds, belonging to the scholars.

The school has a fine library of between seventy and eighty books. They were obtained by the scholars giving Entertainments.

Arthur Beach who was coming to school the fore part of the winter was transferred to the Litchfield High school

Frank Doyle who was present yesterday was absent today.

The Examination has been going on for the last week for Sixth, Seventh, and Eighth Grades.

HOUSEHOLD DEPARTMENT
Editor, Irene Snyder

Baked Indian Pudding
Boil 1/2 pt of milk, stir in four tablespoons of cornmeal. Cook 10m cool and add 1 pt of cold milk, 1/2 cup of molasses, 2 egg, 1/2 cup of sugar, 1/2 teaspoon of salt, 1/2 teaspoon of cinnamon. Bake 2 hors. When baked 1/2 hour add 1 cup of milk, eat with cream or butter.

Poor Man's Pie
Peel and slice large greening apples in deep buttered pie dish. Sprinkle with sugar and cinnamon. For batter. 1 pt of buttermilk, two well beaten eggs, 1/2 cup of sugar, a little salt, 1 pt of flour, two teaspoons of soda. Spread over apples; eat with cream sweetened, and spiced with cinnamon.

Washington Pie Filling
1/2 pt of milk. When hot, 1 egg add, 1/2 cup of sugar, two teaspoons of corn starch. Add flavor when cold.

Johnny Cake
2 cup of sour milk, 1 egg, 1/2 cup of sugar, 1/2 cup of molasses, 1 teaspoon of soda and salt. It will be very thin, but leave it as it is.

Cold Slaw
Slice cabbage fine. Mash with potato masher, and mix with salt and pepper — not very much. Throw over this 1/2 cup of cream.

Useful Hints

If turnips are bitter or meat of any kind is tough add a teaspoon of vinegar to the salt you boil them in.

When ironing rub hot iron of a green piece of ceder to prevent sticking. It answers the place of beeswax and costs nothing.

When lamp wicks smoke the chimney wash in vinegar and dry.

Carpets may be cleaned and freshened by going over them once a week with a broom moistened in hot water to which a little turpentine.

Do not put salt in soup till done shimming. As salt will prevent rising of skum.

When you want to clean willow ware or matting wash in water to wich salt has been added.

Excerpts from the Milton Academy Catalog published in 1856

Location — The Second Session of this Academy will open Monday, October 19th, 1857. It is pleasantly located in the village of Milton, Litchfield County, Conn., four and one half miles from Litchfield the county seat. It is easy of access being nine miles from the Housatonic and Naugatuck Railroads, with daily stage connections at Kent and Litchfield Station. Fronting the Academy is a beautiful playground. The buildings will be wholly completed before the commencement of next term, and is admirably planned and well adapted to the comfort and convenience of Pupils.

Government — The discipline of the Institution is moral and parental. Disgraceful punishments are not inflicted. The moral sense will be appealed to, yet no one exerting a bad influence, or neglecting his studies, will be allowed to remain.

To Parents — Parents may rest assured that no pains will be spared in giving a thorough education... Special attention paid to those preparing to teach or for college.

Apparatus — To the Chemical Apparatus purchased the first session, will be added next term, a Philosophical apparatus among which may be found Surveying and Leveling Instruments, Terrestrial Globes, Planetarium, Tellurion, a set of mechanical Powers, Working Models of Steam Engines, Double-barrel Air-Pump Plate Electrical Machine, working Telegraph Model, Grove's Battery, Pyrometer, Compound and Solar Microscopes, etc, etc... Students will have access to the Principal's Cabinet, containing nearly two thousand Geological and Mineralogical specimens, seven hundred of which have recently been imported from Germany.

General Course — In addition to the English, Mathematical and Classical Departments already established, which include all English Studies, Sciences, higher branches of Mathematics, Latin, Greek and Modern Languages, there will be added commencing with the Fall Term, Commercial and Primary Departments; the latter under the charge of a Lady Teacher. The superior skills of the teacher of Music, Painting, Drawing and Ornamentals, enables us to offer great advantages in these branches.

Commercial Department — The Student is familiarized with every department of business, including Single and Double Entry Book Keeping, Science and forms of

Merchants' Commission, Manufacturers' Banking, Publishing, Foreign and Domestic Shipping, Hotel, Steamboat and Railroad Books...

Terms and Vacations — The year is divided into two terms of twenty and twenty-two weeks, each followed by a vacation of four weeks. There is also a vacation of one week in the middle of each term.

Tuition for Quarter

Primary Department	$2.50
Common English	4.50
Higher English	5.50
Ancient Languages	6.50
Incidental Expenses	.50
Commercial Course with English branches	15.00
Extras. Piano Music, with use of Instrument	$10.00
Melodeon, with use of instrument	6.00
Water Colors, Oriental and Grecian Painting, each	3.00
Monochromatic, Pastel and Pelliswork, each	3.00
French and German each	3.00
Oil Painting	10.00

Board — Board at public or private houses, $2.00 per week. Those residing in the vicinity who return home on Friday, $1.25. Rooms may be rented in the village by those wishing to board themselves.

Miscellaneous — No making use of either Tobacco, Intoxicating Liquors, or Profane Language will be tolerated.

Gentlemen's Catalogue for the first Session lists these students:

Aljemon Beach	Milton
Thomas Beach	"
Warren W. Bissell	"
Frank L. Bissell	"
John L. Brown	"
Alden Chamberlain	Warren
Leman A. Clark	Cornwall
Benjamin Griswold, Jun.	Litchfield
William J. Hall	Milton
George J. Harrison, Jun.	"
Mark Hazen	"
Wesley Jennings	College Street
Henry Newton	Cornwall
Hiram Northrop	Milton
Charles I. Page	"
Frances D. Perkins	"
G. Wilson Potter	Woodville
George Seelye	Goshen
Andrew Seelye	"
Dwight H. Seelye	"
George Smith	Milton
Ralph P. Smith	"

Ladies Catalogue

L. Eliza Beach	Milton
Harriet M. Beach	Goshen
L. Caroline Bissell	Milton
Cornelia L. Bissell	"
Almira G. Boothe	Litchfield
Lily Bogert	Brooklyn, N.Y.
Catherine Bogert	"
Esther L. Brown	Milton
Elvira J. Clemens	Woodville
Mary A. Downs	Seymour
Florine A. Dudley	Milton
Anna S. Harrison	"
Mary C. Hart	Goshen
Harriet E. Merriman	Milton
Clarissa O. Potter	"
Mary J. Nichols	Goshen
Frances G. Potter	Woodville
Adah A. Richards	Goshen
Virginia M. Seelye	"
Elizabeth M. Smith	Milton
Rosa P. Vaill	"

The *Litchfield Enquirer* of October 1, 1857, carried this advertisement:

Piano Wanted Oct. 8, 1857 at Milton Academy a good second hand PIANO. A LIBERAL rent will be paid for a good instrument from October 19, 1857 until March 26, 1858.

A. S. Morse
Milton, Conn.

The Milton Historic Distric

The Milton Historic District was formed in 1975 to preserve the area of Milton Center including a portion of Headquarters Road, Milton Road halfway up Milton Hill, sections of Saw Mill, Blue Swamp, Shear Shop and Potash Roads and Maple Street. Properties in the Center are also on the National Register of Historic Places, and the David Welch house was listed in 1978 as an Historic American Building.

INDEX

❖

A.T. & T. - 14, 106, 189, 203, 205
Ackerman, Clarence & Edna - 172, 249, 331
Ackerman, Jacob & Alice - 14, 24, 58, 92, 169, 200, 203, 235, 241, 257, 258
Ackerman, J. Russell & Helen - 173, 234, 235, 237, 330
Ackerman, Peter - 200, 201, 339
Ackerman, William P. - 241, 316
Addis, Sam - 263
Aetna Shear Shop - 12, 19, 20, 52, 53, 83, 92, 181, 185, 187-190, 203, 230, 287
Ambler, Mrs. - 80, 175
Anderson, Oscar - 331
Antique Horribles - 110-112
Avery, Abel, Elizabeth, John, Lyman, Mary - 310
Avery, Rev. James - 271
Axford, Henry Ernest & Edith Dickinson - 16, 84, 264, 303, 328
Bailey, Benjamin & Ethel - 82
Baker, Roy - 119
Baldwin, Rev. Ashbel - 263
Baldwin, Horace & Rachel - 79
Baldwin, Isaac - 10, 39, 79, 201
Baldwin, Isaac, Jr. - 160, 268
Baldwin, John - 163, 178
Barber, Francis - 313
Barnes, Clarence, Frank - 14, 105, 106
Barnes, Daniel - 8, 61
Barnes & Earle Store - 14, 105, 117, 327
Barnes, Moses - 73, 163

Barrett, Frances Doyle - 3, 36, 237, 240
Barton, Frank, John, Mary - 104, 106, 112, 122, 203
Bassett, Squire Nathan & Mehitable Buell - 79, 150, 162, 192
Bassett, Samuel F. - 19, 79, 192, 206
Bassett, William & Lydia Fisher - 79
Bates, Richard & De'Lis'Ka - 172, 183, 335
Bauer, Dr. Thorpe - 260
Beach, Almon James & Antoinette Birge - 23-25, 27, 104, 114-117, 169, 171
Beach, Anson Bradley & Elizabeth Perkins - 23, 25, 26, 53, 171, 192, 193
Beach, Anson & Pamelia Abernathy - 23, 25
Beach, Daniel - 254
Beach, Capt. Heman - 80, 302
Beach, Virgil - 167, 172, 198
Beach, Wadham(s) - 80, 175, 327
Beard, Samuel - 254
Beeman, Anna, Rachel, Truman - 270
Beeman, Charles & Delia - 58
Beers, Seth - 168, 210, 264
Bennett, Archibald - 316
Bennett, Samuel - 26, 193, 302
Benson, Jacob - 316
Benson, Morton - 86, 176
Bergmann, Joseph F. - 330
Bird, Joseph - 7, 280
Birge, Albert - 168
Birge, Rev. Benjamin - 80, 313
Birge, Beriah - 313
Birge, Charles F., Sr. - 241, 247, 317, 331
Birge, Charles F., Jr. & Kelli - 176
Birge, Charles H. -230, 233

Birge, Cornelius G. - 176, 315
Birge, Elisha & Mary Mugleston - 26, 27, 341, 342
Birge, Frank S. & Priscilla Kitchin - 176, 331
Birge, Harvey & Thankful Griswold - 92, 176
Birge, James & Sarah Palmer - 26, 27, 77, 86, 87, 160, 163, 313, 321, 342
Birge, James M. - 175, 176, 207, 342, 343
Birge, Maj. John - 315
Birge, Joseph & Elizabeth Kilbourn - 26, 160
Birge, Joseph & Marcella Ward - 80, 91
Birge, Joseph, Jr. - 159, 263
Birge, Stanley W. - 311
Birge, William C. & Mercy Stock - 16, 37, 124, 174, 230, 257, 258
Bishop, Abraham - 310
Bishop, Amos & Almira - 36, 80, 81, 84, 178
Bishop, Anna - 254
Bishop, Noah - 85, 92, 314
Bissell, Benjamin - 61, 81, 151, 314, 315
Bissell, Mrs. Chester - 343
Bissell, Erwin & Susan Birge - 168, 265
Bissell, Hiram & Beata Wetmore - 27, 81, 82, 107, 263
Bissell, Isaac - 153
Bissell, Joel, Mercy Bishop, Hulda Chapel - 81
Bissell, John & Mary Dickinson - 27, 28, 81, 153, 175, 313
Bissell, Capt. Lyman - 315
Bissell, Warren - 27, 81, 117, 188, 202
Bissell, Capt. William & Amanda - 9, 23, 27, 28, 81, 112, 153, 181, 187, 263, 265, 302, 315
Blake, Albert & Harriet Morey - 82
Blake, Bessie (Mrs Clarence) - 234
Blake, Caroline Stock - 45

Blake, Charles S. - 24, 117, 193, 257
Blake, James & Jane Seelye - 82, 272
Blake, James & Dorcas - 310
Blake, Marian - 303, 304
Boardman, Benjamin - 159
Bogert, Kate - 221, 222
Bolles, Asahel H. - 199
Bouteiller, George - 204
Bowden, Mike, Kelly, Kerry & Luann Urfer - 336
Bradley, Joseph & Lucy Stoddard - 82
Bradley, Leaming & Anna - 82
Bradley, Sybbill - 254
Brewster, Bishop William J. - 265
Bristol, Harry James & Elizabeth Haviland - 89, 90
Brown, Bertha - 257
Brown, C. Hinkle - 331
Brown, Hugh - 317
Brownell, The Right Rev. Thomas C. - 62, 262
Buell, Ira & Prudence Deming - 79, 83, 150, 254
Buell, John & Mary Loomis - 83, 164
Buell, John S., Jr. - 316
Buell, Peter & Avis - 164, 165
Buell, Capt. Solomon & Eunice Griswold - 83, 133, 150, 156, 163, 165
Bunker, Eli & Fanny Watson - 19, 28, 29
Bunker, Rufus & Rexa - 28
Bunnell, Fred G. & Louise C. - 18, 232
Bunnell, Harold F. & Frances M. - 74, 98, 194, 235
Campbell, Rev. Thomas - 260
Carberry, Elizabeth - 274, 275
Carriage & Sleigh Shop - 12, 20, 83, 84, 93, 98, 182-186, 207
Carroon, Very Rev. Dr. Girard - 265, 266

Carter, John & Lucius - 24, 263
Carter, Tim - 117
Catholicism - 276
Catlin, Ashbel -200, 292
Catlin, David - 255
Catlin(g), Eli & Theodore - 155
Catlin, Isaac M. - 36, 148, 313
Catlin(g), Isaac, Jr. - 186
Catlin(g), John - 148, 155, 156
Chase, Sgt. Lot - 313
Childs, Dr. Albert - 35, 238
Christensen, Lans - 173
Clark, Mrs. Andrew - 28
Clark, Charles & Emma - 35, 83, 182, 185
Clark, George O. - 197, 313
Clark, Harriet L. - 204
Clark, Henry - 300
Clark, Jaleel & Susan - 301
Clark, "Little Caroline" - 301
Clark, Lydia - 300
Clarke, Charlotte Page, 265
Clark's Dam - 181, 196, 197
Clark, Sheldon - 28, 196, 207
Clothing & Carding Mill - 198, 199
Coe, Jennie - 229
Coffill, Joseph D. - 122, 123, 341
Cogswell, Jemima - 270
Collins, Ambrose - 181, 194, 298
Collins/Collens, John - 154, 155
Collins/Collens, Rev. Timothy - 60, 160
Conklin, Lavinia - 175
Cook, Capt. Daniel - 305, 313
Cook, Phineas - 263

Cota, Blaine A., Jr. & Eleanor H. - 95
Cotton, John - 154
Crichton, Rev. Arthur B. - 258
Crooked Esses Cemetery - 17, 297, 309-311
Cropsey, Joyce M. - 35
Curtiss, Mary Walker - 250
Curtiss, Evits, Minerva, Stephen - 310
Datun, Eli - 270
Dautrich, Dr. Albert W. - 35
Dearborn, Mona Leithiser - 32, 33
DeCosa, Alice Walker - 244, 250
Deering, Gregory C. - 317
Deering, Otto & Mary - 201
Deering, Paul & Patricia O'Neill - 14, 24, 53, 106, 169, 203, 328
Deming, Julius - 83, 150
Deming, Mehitable - 254
Dennis, Donald P. - 317
Dennis, Edward - 331
Dennis, Kirby E. - 317
Dennison, Chauncey - 213, 313
Dennison, John - 34
Derby, Jesse & Mary Hurley - 14, 53, 54, 116, 118, 189, 235
Derthick, Rev. Ananias - 271
Dickinson, Amos & Sarah Perry - 30, 83
Dickinson, Anson & Sarah - 20, 27, 29-33, 150, 173
Dickinson, Edwin P. & Harriet Gilbert - 54, 83, 118, 159, 219, 302
Dickinson, Ebenezer - 30, 31, 149, 150
Dickinson, Ithamer & Celia A. Pratt - 83, 84, 119
Dickinson, Oliver, Sr. & Mary - 30, 31, 88, 315

Dickinson, Oliver, Jr. & Anna Landon - 9, 30, 46, 81, 150, 262, 265, 313, 321
Dickinson, Reuben - 20, 30, 31, 89, 149, 150, 196, 290
Dodge, Clark - 116
Doolittle, Benjamin, Erastus, Harriet - 310
Doty, Archibald C., Jr. - 316, 330
Dougherty, Minnie - 70
Doyle, Edward - 36, 119
Doyle, Ellen M. - 3, 10, 16, 24, 30, 33, 36-39, 48, 84, 110, 111, 113, 119, 120, 224, 231-235, 237, 241-244, 246-250, 257, 325, 330
Doyle, Francis - 36, 316
Doyle, Neil - 36
Doyle, Terrence & Mary Harris - 36, 81, 84, 224, 228
Doyle, Thomas - 84, 116, 119
Doyle, William H. - 36, 189, 193, 194
Driscoll, Mrs. Michael - 119
Dudley, George C. - 293
Dudley, Richard E. - 316
Dudley, Dea. Samuel - 9, 84, 224
Dudley, Sarah Kitchin - 124
Dudley, William & Abigail - 9, 308
Duggan, Amy Archer Gilligan - 40, 41
Duggan, James & Family - 39-41, 58, 112, 173, 228
Duggins, The Rev. Gordon - 264, 265
Dunning, Benning, Isaac, Mercy - 270
Dupont, Ruth A. - 336
Earle, Charles & Dorothy L. - 23, 124, 170, 329, 330
Earle, Frank & Mary Beach - 14, 23, 24, 110, 117, 122, 169, 170, 259
East Cornwall Baptist Church - 4, 9, 44, 45, 257, 269-273
East Cornwall School - 11, 213, 215, 228, 271

Enslin, Rev. Irving J., Elizabeth, Francis I. - 42, 43, 259, 260
Farvour/Ferver, Dotha, Peter - 198, 303
Fennell, Rev. William G. - 43-46, 271, 272
Ferris, Charles & Mehetible Parsons - 84
Ferris, Ezra - 199, 216
Ferris, Gerardus, Ithamer, Robert, Stephen - 199
Ferriss, William G. & Almira Monroe - 84, 172, 302
Fischer, Carroll L. - 18, 34, 285, 311, 317
Fisher, Ernest, Jr. - 317
Fisher, Frank - 247, 331
Fisher, Noel T. - 317
Flaherty, Michael - 307
Forbes, Malcolm - 28, 79, 84, 97, 335
Foster, Esty, Jr. - 83
Fourth of July Picnics - 15, 103, 110-112, 248
Fox, Emil, Jr. - 316
Fox, Severin J. - 316
Fretts, Alford J. - 235, 241, 317
Frisbie, Friend H., Betsey, Lucy - 47, 85
Frisbie, Henry - 187
Frisbie, Jonathan - 181, 194, 201
Frisbie, Levi - 195
Frisbie, Noah - 85
Gage, Helen & Mrs. Douglas Whalen - 201, 340
Gardner, John - 85
Gauger, Elizabeth Taylor - 40
Gibbs, Benjamin & Abigail Marshall - 60, 85, 158
Gibbs, Birdsey & Salome - 10, 199, 215, 306
Gibbs, Gershom & Tabitha Moore - 85, 158, 254, 313, 318, 321
Gibbs, Moore & Patience Skeel(s) - 85, 86, 158, 191, 215, 254, 256, 314, 321

Gibbs, Oliver - 198
Gibbs, Zebulon - 90
Gilbert, Abner & Roxanna Guild - 86, 302
Gilbert, Francis - 315, 321
Gilbert, Hobart DeLos & Mary Pepper - 86, 176
Gilbert, James (Jay) B. & Lena Merriman - 33, 86, 108, 111, 257, 342
Gilbert School - 11, 215, 223, 224, 226, 228, 342
Gilbert, Truman & Selima Birge - 87, 223, 314
Gilbert, William H. & Ellen Gibson - 86, 87
Gill, Barbara Gray - 38, 246, 250
Gillette, Clarence - 315
Gillette, Joseph - 46
Glover, Julius - 315
Glover, Wesley - 315
Goslee, Chester, Electa, Fred, Hiram - 126, 343
Goss, Paul - 91, 274
Granniss, Asa L. - 177
Granniss, Asa W. - 309
Granniss & Elmore Store - 104, 189, 203
Granniss, Fremont M. & Martha E. Millen - 177, 257, 307
Granniss, Capt. John E. - 315
Granniss, Thomas - 213, 288
Granniss, Weston G. - 203, 307
Granniss, William - 34, 308
Gray, Auguste A. - 172, 327-329
Gray, Florence - 172
Gray, Howard - 172, 235, 245
Gray, Raymond - 172, 241, 249, 317
Gray, Bishop Walter H. - 264
Great Hill Iron Ore Mfg. Co. - 204, 205
Grendahl, Bernard - 31

Griffin, G. Herbert & Ethel Bunnell - 15, 168, 241, 243, 246, 264, 311, 331
Griffin, George H., Jr. & Mildred Helding - 168, 177, 316
Griffin, Hiram, Harriet Birge, John S. - 309
Griffin, Dr. Orwin B. - 243
Griswold, Asahel - 46, 162, 177, 178, 194
Griswold, Benjamin & Elizabeth Smith - 112, 168
Griswold, Benjamin, Sally Wright, Benjamin, Jr.- 34, 162, 178, 197, 263
Griswold, Frederick, Sr. & Jr. - 263
Griswold, Henrietta - 175, 218
Griswold, Homer - 175
Griswold, Horatio P. & Augusta Johnson - 18, 49, 87, 106, 110, 112, 125, 161, 185, 200, 201, 302
Griswold, Howell & Thankful Smith - 87
Griswold, Jacob - 83, 150, 153
Griswold, Jarvis & Susan Page - 87, 263
Griswold, Jeremiah & Hannah Gibbs - 4, 8, 39, 46, 47, 60, 61, 65, 66, 72, 73, 87, 146, 149, 150, 154, 156, 162, 165, 181, 194, 314
Griswold, John & Mabel Boardman - 46
Griswold, John & Rhoda Wetmore - 8, 39, 46, 87, 88, 97, 156, 157, 173, 315, 321
Griswold, Julius & Asenath Hall - 88
Griswold, Julius & Betsey Stewart/Stuart - 88, 173, 174, 314
Griswold, Lucius & Desire Granniss - 168, 178, 197, 265
Griswold, Dr. Stanley & Sarah Leverage - 34
Griswold, Sylvester - 162, 302
Gross, Capt. - 74, 151, 171
Grove, Thomas & Truman - 198
Guild, Alban & Roxanna Dickinson - 18, 47-49, 86, 87, 94, 161, 181, 199-201, 265, 291

Guild, Alfred T. - 193, 302
Guild-Blake Grist Mill - 93, 181, 182, 186, 190-192, 196, 198, 230
Guild, David D. & Sarah Strong - 49, 181, 185, 198
Guild, Frederick F. - 192, 193, 207
Guild, Gad & Henry - 192, 193
Guild, Jeremiah & Elinor/Eleanor Evarts - 47, 161, 191, 193
Guild, Jeremiah & Hannah Hale/Hall - 47, 48
Guild, Jeremiah & Laura Clark - 193
Guild, Jeremiah & Lucinda Fenton - 47, 88
Guild Tavern - 18, 49, 87, 94, 161, 200, 339, 340
Guild, Truman & Lamira Catlin - 9, 88, 222, 265, 302
Guion, George & Hobart - 324
Guitteau, Judson - 155
Hall, Byron - 176
Hall, Daniel & Desire Dickinson - 88, 192
Hall, John - 314
Hall, John & Damaris Everett - 88, 153, 155, 173
Hall, Norman - 192
Hall, Salmon C. - 88, 314, 315
Hall, Walter - 342
Hall, William & Anne Hinchliffe - 52
Hall, William J. & Mary Smedley - 89, 116, 149, 201, 205, 207, 228, 302, 315
Hall, William & Mercy Barnes - 89
Hallock, Jason F. & Family - 172, 311
Harmon, Rev. Bradford - 260, 261
Harrison, Rev. George J. & Elizabeth Jewett - 11, 24, 49-51, 63, 115, 220, 256, 302
Harrison, Sara - 24, 49, 50
Hart, Charles E. - 315, 316
Hart, Rev. Luther B. - 271

Hart, Reeves W., Sr. & Jr. - 66, 72, 216
Hart, Reuben - 315
Hart, Seelye - 24, 117
Hart, William - 315
Hatch, Murray - 316
Haviland, H. Arthur B. - 331
Haviland, Harry T. & Lena Birge - 59, 89-91, 154, 194, 249, 307, 311
Haviland, Wilbur A. & Amy Ogden - 30, 39, 40, 89, 90, 258
Headquarters Cemetery - 17, 18, 27, 85, 86, 88, 90, 124, 289, 290, 297, 299, 303, 304, 306-309, 311, 340
Headquarters School - 11, 215, 222-224, 227-229, 233
Helding, John & Augusta - 177
Hilding, Harris - 177, 207, 286, 342
Hilpert, Lukas - 177
Hinchliffe, Thomas & Anne Morris - 12, 19, 52, 53, 57, 92, 112, 119, 181, 185, 188-190, 203
"History of Cornwall, Connecticut, A" (Rev. Edward C. Starr) - 28, 217, 309
Hubbard, John T. - 173, 193, 194
Hubbard, Joseph S. - 315
Hubbell, Hubert - 91, 179
Huften, Nettie (Sheldon) Rydehn - 58, 241
Hurley, James H. & Theresa Maher - 53, 54
Hurricane of 1938 - 338, 339
Hurricane Diane of 1955 - 4, 8, 14, 18, 123, 194, 284, 290, 340, 341
Hutchinson, James - 26, 193
Hutchinson, Lewis - 26, 171, 192, 193, 217
Isaac, George - 61
Jacquemin, Cecile Richard - 250
Jacus, Levi - 315

Janssen, Webster & Arlene - 49
Jefferies, Robert & Caroline Griffin - 168, 245, 264
Jennings, Burritt - 314
Jennings, Frederick & Clarissa - 90, 175, 315
Jennings, J. Wesley - 315
Jennings, Truman Leander & Jane Page - 90, 168, 227, 302
Johnson, David - 87
Johnson, George, Harriet, Wakeman - 310
Johnson, Seymour - 107, 203
Jones, Rev. Isaac, Jr. - 48, 263
Jones, Lewis - 315
Judd, Rev. Benjamin - 255
Kenney, Joseph - 93
Kenney, Leon & Louise - 82
Kerrigon, Frank & Anne - 173
Kilbourn, Carl - 172
Kilbourn, Dwight - 226-228
Kilbourn, Ethan - 302
Kilbourn, Harold - 202, 206
Kilbourn, Roswell - 89, 156
Kilbourn, Samuel - 263
Kilgus, Dr. John - 35
Kirby, Roger - 300
Kitchin, Thomas R. - 316
Kizzia, Dewey L. & Elizabeth Ackerman - 74, 171, 172, 235, 335
Kizzia, Dewey L., Jr. - 317
Knapp, Shepherd & Mrs. (Fresh Air Camp) - 19, 120, 121, 162, 178, 228
Koski, Aune L. - 316
Kubish, Francis P. - 316
Kubish, John A. - 316
Kubish, Joseph - 268

Kubish, Martin, Sr. - 8, 201
Kubish, Martin G., Jr. - 241, 316
Ladies Aid Society - 16, 43, 258-260
Lamb, Adella & Kate Louise Lamb) Osborn - 175, 241
Landon, Abner, Eunice Gibbs, Martha Youngs - 90, 186, 191
Landon, Daniel & John - 90, 191, 314
Landon, Dr. - 34, 35
Lang, Gary & Kathleen M. - 337
Leatherman - 54, 109
Lee, Thomas - 200
Leonard, Lucius D. - 201, 231
Lewis, Algernon S. - 263
Lindsay, Thomas & Alice - 201, 330, 331
Lindsey, James - 331
"Litchfield Enquirer" - 30, 111, 114, 119, 121, 122, 187, 193, 198, 206, 275, 283, 292, 300
"Litchfield Monitor" - 80, 196, 342
"Litchfield & Morris Inscriptions" (Charles T. Payne) - 46, 295, 297-299
"Litchfield Sentinel" - 185, 188, 193, 206
Litke, Grace Fisher - 244
Litwin, Craig & Suzanne - 10, 49, 267, 317, 335
Litwin, Edward J. - 244, 317, 330
Litwin, Peter A. & Eileen - 156, 334, 343
Litwin, Theodore P. - 237, 330
Lockwood, Henry & Enid Richards - 58
Loomis, Helen Pepper - 176
Lorber, Charles - 302
Lorber, Harriet - 304
Lord, John - 270
Loveland, Theron - 116
Lovrin, Garry & Lynn - 336

Lyman, Dr. & Mrs. Elijah - 254
Malbone, Edward - 31
Manley, Rev. H. Waldo - 59, 264
Marcy, Dr. - 35
Marsh, Ebenezer - 186, 187
Marshepaug/Shepaug River - 3, 4, 8, 12, 14, 30, 46, 169, 181, 182, 186, 187, 191-194, 197, 198, 200, 253, 255, 284, 287, 290, 291, 300, 329
Marsh-Simmons Forge - 182, 186, 187
Marsh, Isaac - 154
Marsh, John - 61, 89, 147, 154, 202
Marsh, Mary Fox - 243
Marsh School - 222, 228, 229
Marsh, Rev. Truman & Clarissa Seymour - 55, 56, 80, 96, 118, 263, 321
Marsh, Capt. William - 72
Matthew, Morton - 334
Mattson, Ruby - 293
McCaskill, Robert Bruce - 317, 318, 326
McGavran, Rev. Donald - 258
McKechnie, Beatrice M. - 53, 56-59, 190
McKinney, James & Anne - 30, 39, 40
McMahon, Audrey Raymond - 242
Merriman, Sarah - 270
Methodist Church, Milton - 4, 10, 20, 266-269
Milton Academy - 2, 11, 24, 50, 51, 66, 94, 170, 197, 220-222, 224, 225, 240, 256
Milton Cemetery - 17, 24, 25, 27, 30, 34, 35, 47, 49, 50, 52-54, 60, 61, 65, 67, 73, 75, 79-94, 96-98, 124, 244, 274, 297, 298-306, 311
Milton Congregational Church - 2, 3, 9, 10, 15, 24, 42, 43, 50, 51, 58, 64, 68, 70, 73, 75, 76, 78, 80, 81, 85, 86, 89, 91, 96, 106, 115, 120, 124, 158, 168, 169, 213, 215, 220,

246, 248, 253-261, 264, 266-268, 271, 272, 289, 331
Milton Flower Farm - 207
Milton Library - 15, 70, 120, 158, 246, 259, 260
Milton Pond - 4, 8, 13, 14, 46, 61, 87, 91, 154, 182, 184, 194, 249, 290, 329, 341
Milton Post Office - 96, 105, 121, 122, 170, 230
Milton Public Hall - 1, 2, 14, 15, 38, 43, 52-54, 94, 104, 118, 119, 121, 124, 170, 189, 197, 202, 230, 263, 327, 330, 333, 339
Milton School - 10, 11, 18, 36-40, 120, 167, 168, 212-216, 222, 224-243, 245-248, 250, 263, 267, 327, 339, 341
Milton Stores - 14, 24, 73, 92, 96, 97, 104-107, 117, 121, 122, 147, 169, 170, 189, 201-205, 216, 235, 237, 325
Milton Wheel Club - 116, 117, 119
Milton Woman's Club - 3, 16, 17, 38, 123-125, 249, 302
Morehead, Walton, Abigail, Mildred - 238
Morehouse, Henry - 316
Morey, Augustus & Harriet Birge - 91, 162, 263, 285
Morgan, W. B., Jennie, Mamie - 308
Morozov, Vladimir - 274, 275
Morris, Asa - 9, 214, 255
Moseley, Dorothy (Wagstaff) Ripley - 82, 206, 248
Moss, David, Milo, Sophia - 311
Mt. Tom School - 11, 215, 224, 226-228
Munson, John & Avis - 254
Munson, William - 181, 195
Murphy, Edward J. - 330
Napolitano, Gerald & Nadine - 90
Nesbitt, Ingrid & Family - 53, 75, 96, 171
Nettleton, Rev. Asahel - 75, 76, 255
Newcomb, James - 298
Newcomb School - 11, 215, 222, 228
Newton, James I. - 197

Nichols, Andrew - 314
Nichols, Horace - 302
Nichols School - 216, 228
North, William & Zelah - 198
Norton, Abraham & Lyman - 191, 198
O'Brien, Daniel - 173
O'Brien, William - 174
O'Neill, Lillian, Patricia Deering, John - 328
Osborn, Lewis & Lillian - 116, 119
Page, Austin & Kate Hinchliffe - 52, 91, 116, 179, 206
Page, Charles & Mary - 35, 302
Page, Dr. Charles I. - 34, 35, 126, 302, 316
Page, Gilbert & Mary Dean - 91
Page, Ira & Elizabeth - 91, 179
Page, Ithamer & Janette Birge - 90, 168, 265
Page, John - 314
Page, Roswell - 34
Page, Dea. Samuel D. & Susan - 76, 256
Page, Rev. Wesley E. & Mary - 76, 254, 256, 257
Palmer, Daniel & Elizabeth Hillyer - 77
Palmer, Rev. Solomon & Abigail Foote - 26, 77, 80
Parmalee, Cornelius, Amelia, David - 311
Parmalee, David - 91
Parmalee, George B. - 302
Parmalee/Parmele, Lt. Jehiel & Mary - 8, 46, 59, 60, 66, 72, 149, 300, 314, 318
Parmalee, Joshua - 59
Parmalee, Willard H. - 91, 174, 316, 318
Parmalee, William K. - 91, 217, 316
Parsons, Capt. Eliphaz & Abigail - 84, 91, 92, 306, 314
Parsons, Eliphaz & Lois Bishop - 84, 91, 92
Parson(s), Sarah - 254
Peacock, Julia - 119, 120, 229, 230

Peatt, Dr. Harry L. - 260, 261
Peck, Carrie (Mrs. Allen G.) - 124, 264
Peck, Daniel, Jesse, Polly, Ruth, Sarah - 311
Peck, Donald K. & Ruth (Richard) Gray - 234, 241, 260
Pepper, Gordon & Irene Benjamin - 86, 176
Pepper, Philip G. - 176, 317
Perambulations - 9, 88
Perkins, Beecher - 26
Perkins, Clarence E. - 168, 316
Perkins, Daniel - 25, 314
Perkins, Everett H. - 17
Perkins, Gladys - 234
Perkins, Orlando - 257
Perkins, Willis 0. & Florence Hall - 119, 201, 203
Perret, Herman - 80
Perrett, Albert - 317
Phillips, Alice - 124, 207
Pickett, Rufus - 191, 199
Pikosky, Andrew M.C. - 204
Plumb, Fred - 119
Plum(b), Henry - 163
Potter, Capt. Israel & Mary - 254, 308, 314
Potter, Israel, Jr. - 17, 308
Potter, Joel - 314, 321
Potter, Thankful - 254
Pratt, Abigail - 270
Prigmore, Rev. Joseph D., Amy Davis, Edith, William - 78, 257
Prospect Mt. School - 215, 222, 224, 226, 228
Ranney, Stephen - 196, 314
Ravenscroft, John - 90
Ravenscroft, William & Lulu Dickinson - 84, 119

Raymond, Col. Edward A. & Mary - 28, 61, 72, 104, 202, 317, 337
Raymond, Dr. Edward H. & G. Isabel - 92, 168, 250, 264, 330
Raymond, G. Alison (Mrs. Albert Lanier) - 317
Raynold, Hannah - 270
Register, Herbert T., Sr. & Jr. - 14, 92, 169, 189, 203, 205
Richard, Kenneth A. - 241, 317, 325
Richard, Oscar G. - 239, 240, 317, 331
Richard, Walter A. - 317
Richard, Zelim & Waldburga - 98, 121, 178
Richards, Elbert & Lyman - 197, 298
Richards, Rev. Eugene L. & Elizabeth Stock - 257, 258, 272
Richardson, Bradford & Lauren - 168
Rodenbach, Barbara O'Shea - 292
Root, Rev. Isaac - 270
Russell, Belle G. - 304
Russian Orthodox Greek Chapel - 91, 274, 275, 276
Rydehn, Svante (Stuart) & Karolina Koski - 59, 85, 327, 328
Salcito, Tony & Alice - 335
Saw Mill, Marshepaug - 8, 19, 61, 90, 181, 194, 195, 198, 207, 230, 290
Scott, James H. & Mrs. - 298, 317
Seabury, Bishop Samuel - 263
Seelye, Fred H. - 51, 52, 183, 188, 196, 207, 304
Seelye, Fred M. - 23-26, 169
Seelye, George & Jennie - 173
Seelye, Aunt Hannah - 152, 210
Seelye, Harmon, Horace - 196, 263
Seelye & Holmes Edged Tools & Andrew H. Seelye - 182, 196

Seelye, John - 314
Seelye, John & Martha - 60
Seelye, Julia F. Guild - 304
Seelye, Justus & Elizabeth Gibbs - 4, 8, 17, 19, 46, 60, 61, 72, 73, 93, 94, 146, 147, 151, 153, 154, 156, 157, 163, 181, 190, 191, 298, 315
Seelye, Norris - 52
Seelye, Walter E. & Florence Hinchliffe - 52, 57, 119, 189, 203, 230
Sepples, Michael - 106, 107
Seymour, Malcolm P. & M. Adaline Stock - 45, 88, 173, 174, 272, 329, 330
Seymour, Maj. Moses - 56
Shanley, Anna - 241
Sharp, Alva & Lucy - 175, 263
Shear Shop Dam & Pond - 4, 12-14, 19, 53, 57, 58, 181, 189, 190, 196, 249, 287
Sheehan, Mary - 234
Sheldon, Howard & Edna Birge - 59, 172, 173, 229, 329
Sheldon, Walter C. - 10, 59, 64, 81, 172, 185, 210, 232
Sibley, Donald & Janet - 174, 175, 328, 334, 340
Simmons, John, Solomon - 186, 187
Smith, Andrew P. - 183
Smith, Anson C. & Clarinda Birge - 87, 92, 93, 112, 113, 126, 178
Smith, Benajah - 254
Smith, Chester F. & Helen Griswold - 93, 183, 184, 204
Smith, Chester F. & Gertrude - 183
Smith, Eli - 163
Smith, Ernest K., Mary Benjamin & Family - 16, 82, 92, 93, 123, 124, 126, 178, 179, 231
Smith, Rev. George A. - 260
Smith, George A. & Josephine Kenney - 93, 113, 302

Smith, Gregory - 179
Smith, Hezekiah & Polly Potter - 308
Smith, Horace & Sarah - 92, 314
Smith, Rev. Levi - 255
Smith, Malcolm E. - 317
Smith, Moses - 263
Smith, Palmer - 93, 98
Smith, Rev. Ralph - 255, 256
Snyder, Edward - 316
Snyder, Irene - 231
Snyder, William - 316
Spencer, Mary - 254
Spooner, Abigail - 270
Sprats, William & Elizabeth Seelye - 60, 93, 94, 156, 157, 163
Stanton, Henry & Mary - 97
Starr, Marjorie Woodington - 235, 241
Stevens, Edward Seward & Virginia - 18
Stevens/Stephens, Seymour & Emeline Guild - 94, 117, 197, 203, 291
Stewart/Stuart, Jared/Jirad - 94, 154, 314, 318
Stewart/Stuart, Nathan & Martha - 94, 154
Stock, Rev. Alfred H. & M. Augusta Teall - 45, 122, 174, 257, 272
Stone, Beriah - 156
Stone, Elihu, Thomas - 254
Stone, Rev. Hiram - 62, 63, 227, 256, 263, 265
Stone, Willis - 287, 288
Strong, Supply, Jedediah - 47, 94, 95, 161
Sturdivant, Abner, Samuel, Sr. & Jr., Sarah - 270
Sutton, Stephen & Virginia - 37
"Tater John" - 110
Taylor, Daniel - 175, 240

Taylor, Howard R. - 317
Taylor, John E., Jr. - 317
Thatcher, Dr. & Mrs. Partridge - 254
Third Society of Litchfield - 3, 8, 9, 28, 47, 73, 183, 191,
    192, 194, 209, 212, 213, 253, 255-257, 269, 298, 299
Thoma, Bruce - 318
Thoma, Karl, Adelaide & Family - 17, 171, 327, 329-332
Thompson, Guion, Léonie - 95, 233
Thompson, Marie-Louise - 95
Thompson, William W. & Mary Louise Guion - 95, 290
Thomson, Jerusha - 270
Todd, Hugh, Barbara & Family - 80, 167, 231, 250,
    325, 327
Todd, Richard - 318, 325, 326
Tompkins, Oscar - 231
Tornado, 1989 - 2, 5, 15, 175, 234, 269, 304, 332-338
Trinity Episcopal Church - 2, 5, 9, 24, 30, 33, 48, 55, 56,
    59, 62, 63, 92, 97, 105, 117, 118, 150, 202, 213, 235,
    247, 250, 255, 256, 258, 260, 262-266, 325, 327, 337,
    339
Tuttle, William - 191
Tyler, Newton - 343
Urban, Venerable Joseph T. - 265
Vaill, Benjamin & Sylvia Landon - 64
Vaill, Charles H. & Rose Welch - 65, 66, 79, 300
Vaill, Rev. Harmon L. & Flora Gold - 64-66, 256
Vaill, Joseph - 65, 321
Vaill, Walter E. & Sarah Murray - 5, 23, 27, 28, 34, 39,
    47-49, 51, 52, 54, 62, 65-67, 79, 81-83, 90, 91, 93, 95,
    97, 98, 106, 110, 117, 125, 172, 173, 183, 192, 193, 197,
    198, 200, 202, 216, 217, 301
Vaill, Willard - 240, 245, 247
Vose, Charles R. - 274, 275

Voight, Lawrence - 333
Vought, Rev. Gordon - 261
Wadhams, Abraham - 10, 181, 194, 268
Wadhams, Wallace - 298
Wadhams, Walstein/Walliston C. - 93, 104, 178, 202
Walker, John S. & Mrs. - 178
Walker, Martin & Catherine - 178, 341
Walker, William & Mary Ann - 32
Walkley, Frances S. - 15, 16, 42, 68-71, 120, 158, 248, 258, 259
Ward, William & Anna Palmer - 77
Warner, Dr. Charles N., Sr. & Jr. - 35
"Waterbury Republican" - 122
Wedge, Asahel, Hannah, Ira, Salmon - 270
Weir, Mary - 233
Welch, Maj. Abram Edwards - 96, 314, 318, 322, 323
Welch, Maj. David & Irene Marsh - 4, 8, 10, 12, 14, 46, 52, 60, 65, 66, 72, 73, 79, 82, 92, 96-98, 104, 108, 109, 131, 147-149, 151, 153, 156, 170, 190, 191, 196, 201, 202, 254, 262, 298, 301, 314, 315
Welch, David T. - 96, 202
Welch, Garret/Gerritt P. & Clarissa Marsh - 28, 34, 72, 82, 93, 96, 104, 121, 183, 202, 216, 263, 296, 300
Welch, Hugh P. & Helen Williams - 24, 25, 53, 96, 97, 170, 202, 216, 263, 314
Welch's Iron & Puddling Works - 8, 12, 19, 27, 52, 73, 81, 82, 148, 153, 181, 186, 188, 194, 196, 287
Welch, Judge John & Rosanna Peebles - 9, 34, 72, 96, 97, 106, 109, 117, 147-149, 169, 202, 213, 314
Welch, John & Deborah Ferris - 72
Welch, Lebbeus J. - 316
Welch, Warren & Annabelle - 273
Welch, William H. & Henrietta Edwards - 96

West Goshen Cemetery - 17, 28, 297, 298
West, Hubbel - 198, 199
West, Dr. John M. & Sophie - 34, 35, 93, 197, 305
Westover, Noah - 156
Wetmore, Daniel & Dorothy Hall/Hale - 97
Wetmore, David & Sarah Stanton - 87, 97
Wetmore, Elihu - 163
Wetmore, Noble - 179
Wheeler, Charles D. & Elizabeth - 97, 265
Wheeler, Christopher, David - 97, 181, 298
Wheeler, Lorenzo - 9
Wheeler, William - 187
Whiting, Seth & Abbie Smith - 98, 316
Williams, Bishop - 62
Williams, Rev. Thomas A. & Bertha Register - 257
Williamson, Edward A. & Evelyn - 172, 311, 335
Wilson, David R. & Rosanne - 23, 170, 260, 261
Winn, Barbara Birge - 174, 234, 336, 337
Winn, Donna K. - 333
Winn, Glenn E. - 333
Winn, James B. - 318
Winn, Janette Birge - 249
Winn, Orcelia Birge - 242, 247, 304, 337
Winn, William W., Jr. & Eileen - 318, 334
"Winsted Herald" - 64, 65
Winter, John & Ann - 169, 334
Women's Guild, Trinity Episcopal Church - 16, 264
Woodin, Wesley - 316
Woodin, William, Mrs. Woodin & Wolsey - 98, 172
Woodington, Richard F. - 317
Woodington, William & Laura - 91, 179
Woodward, B. M. - 302
Worthington, the Misses - 18, 34, 162

Wright, Everett H. - 98, 174, 222, 223, 265, 302
Wright, James & Elizabeth - 156
Wright, Jonathan & Leah Bissell - 73-75, 151, 156, 159, 162, 171, 196, 212, 254, 305, 314, 320, 321
Wright, Samuel & Desdemona Guild - 98, 300
Wright, Samuel & Martha Knowles - 73
"Yankee Magazine" - 40
Young, Dan - 116

MI

TOWN OF
Scale 30

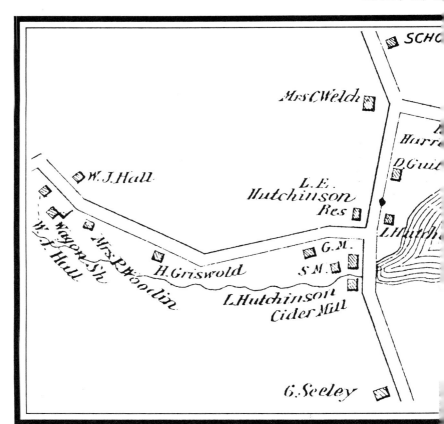